Essays on Physical Education and Sport

ESSAYS ON
PHYSICAL EDUCATION AND SPORT

John Andrews B.A. M.Ed.
Senior Lecturer
St Paul's College, Cheltenham

Stanley Thornes (Publishers) Ltd
Cheltenham

First published in 1979 by
Stanley Thornes (Publishers) Ltd
EDUCA House
Malmesbury Road
Kingsditch
CHELTENHAM GL51 9PL
England

ISBN 0 85950 460 3

Text set in 11/12 pt Photon Baskerville, printed by photolithography, and bound in Great Britain at The Pitman Press, Bath

CONTENTS

Section Four TEACHER EDUCATION AND PROFESSIONAL TRAINING

Section Five OUTDOOR PURSUITS AND OUTDOOR EDUCATION

Foreword

by Dr. Pierre Seurin, F.I.E.P. President

It is always difficult to write a foreword for a friend's book, particularly when it expresses ideas akin to those which one has held for a long time! In such cases, there is a risk of not being objective and of appearing too kind to the author. However, it is with true sportmanship – that is with sincerity and frankness – that I write these few lines to emphasise the great interest of this work.

I have been at the centre of the Fédération Internationale d'Education Physique for 30 years and for nearly 50 years embedded theoretically and practically in the problems of physical education and sport, so from long experience I know the human and social importance of these matters. Also I well understand the thinking of the author of this work since he has been my immediate and very efficient colleague as British Delegate, Journal Editor and Secretary General of F.I.E.P. since 1970.

John Andrews is one of those educationists who has, despite being highly academic, nevertheless recognised the need 'to keep his feet on the ground'. He does not revel in philosophies of physical education which border on 'grand theories', far removed from the daily realities of teaching. He studies problems pragmatically, with constructive determination – in fact, sportingly.

Although it is perhaps invidious to select just one from amongst the wealth of ideas contained in this work, there is one theme of great importance which has often appeared in various publications. This concerns the dangerous evolution in modern sport, which in the forms of harshly selective competitions and spectator sports, is tending to separate sport more and more from the fundamental aims of education.

It is of paramount importance that all teachers combat, both energetically and methodically, such evolution. Teachers and all those people with social consciences must be aware of this danger and must make themselves heard. Putting aside differences of opinion about techniques and teaching methods, which are of secondary importance in this struggle, they must join together to defend fundamental ideals in such a way that sport remains as far as possible 'in the service of man'. Such principles are clearly in evidence in the work of my colleague, John Andrews, and in this book he makes a precious contribution to our common cause. There is no doubt that this work will gain the great success that it merits.

Arreau, France. Jan. 1978

Introduction

The five sections of this book reflect my own special spheres of interest and experience. Despite their diversity I hope that all the essays included show a blend of theory and practice, a combination of study, experience and common sense, which should appeal to a wide readership.

The essays included have been published in many different countries and one of the reasons I have been encouraged to bring them together under one cover is that too few students have easy access to journals and congress reports from India, Australia, Poland, Israel and Belgium – just some of the countries in which these papers have appeared. My thanks are due to the various journal editors and congress organisers for their permission to include papers in this book.

Experience in visiting, advising and lecturing in some twenty-one different countries has convinced me of the tremendous progress which is being made in physical education and sport in many parts of the world. British physical educationists are sometimes accused of being too insular but this work should demonstrate the influence of international contacts whilst at the same time it may make known to a wider readership some of the basic ideas about physical education and sport which have been generally accepted in Britain for a number of years.

I was particularly pleased to include the translation of the F.I.E.P (Fédération Internationale d'Education Physique) World Manifesto and work done in conjunction with Michel Favre of Switzerland and Ted Ravenhill, my colleague at St. Paul's College. In both cases my colleagues were the principal authors and were kind enough to publish jointly in acknowledgement of my additional work on their papers.

The work of every author is the product, to some extent, of the many influences and experiences in his life. I gratefully acknowledge the great help and influence of: my parents, wife and family, the staff of the University of Birimingham – particularly, David Munrow, Peter McIntosh, Barbara Knapp, Bill Slater, James Oliver and Philip Taylor; St. Paul's

College, Cheltenham staff and students; and my friends in many countries around the world, especially Dr. Pierre Seurin, the dynamic President of F.I.E.P., who has so kindly written the Foreword to this book. Finally for typing and other help with assembling and producing this book I must thank Mrs. Dorothy Ravenhill, Mrs. Maureen Smith, Stanley Thornes and Roy Kendall.

The book is dedicated to all students of physical education and sport – past, present and future.

Cheltenham John Andrews.
1978

SECTION 1

The Nature, Purpose and Process of Physical Education*

* A revised edition of a paper first published in the B.A.A.L.P.E. *Bulletin of physical education*, vol. 8, no. 3, pp. 21–27. July, 1970.

1

Physical Education and Education

Once again a number of physical educationists are turning their attention to a consideration of the total picture of physical education. Among a group of people of whom most are practically involved in teaching their subject, it is understandable that questions of "What?", "Where?", and "How?", should have received considerable attention at a practical level, whilst the more difficult ones of "Why?" and "In what total context?" should have been relatively neglected. This neglect reflects the greater difficulty of the questions and the fact that often the final justification and evaluation of what has been done must come later and may be in the hands of others than those closely involved, sometimes people working outside physical education and not committed to it in any way. Another reason for the neglect is that a total picture of physical education must be related to a full picture of education and ultimately to some concept of the meaning and purpose of life itself. This obviously demands considerable thought and study because both of these concepts are difficult to define. Is it surprising that physical education is a complex concept and that even physical educationists find it so?

At the descriptive level it is easy to point to the apparent confusion. How to dispel it is the real problem. For example, if one wished to try to elucidate the concept of 'house', one might describe differences in appearance, materials, contents, etc., and then look at uses of the word such as in 'public house', 'dog house' or 'house match' and finally turn away despairingly and say, "This is so confused, let's not talk about houses any more but talk about 'tents' instead. Of course, because I am a trained employee in the Ministry of Housing I will explore the housing potential of tents"! Interesting and valuable as this new departure might be, this is hardly a way to put 'a house' in order.

If one accepts that the concept of physical education is complex and bound up with a personal concept of life as a whole, then it is no longer surprising that people working in the field have some difficulty in explaining their concept and that different people have different concepts. This also means that what follows can only be a personal contribution put forward for discussion, in this case with only a few references to the experiences, empirical evidence and study on which it is based. It is an attempt to answer, "What is physical education?". Furthermore it attempts to point to a way in which more meaningful questions can be asked about the nature of P.E. and to pick out a few of the pressing problems which need to be solved.

What is Physical Education?

Physical Education is essentially a process, one of the family of processes which make up Education.

Peters [6] says, "Education is a concept like reform; it picks out no particular process but rather it encapsulates criteria to which a family of processes must conform". Therefore if one accepts Peters' criteria for education, then these are the criteria to which physical education must also conform. However, whatever criteria are established, the point remains that the processes of education and physical education must be related.

It follows that the ultimate aim of physical education is the same as that conceived for education as a whole. One needs, therefore, to look carefully at the many statements of the ultimate aim of education. One might follow Peters [7] and look ultimately for 'the educated man' or perhaps Dearden [3] who seeks "an ideal of personal autonomy based on reason", or again look for "an education which grips a child by his moral coat collars and lifts him up to see over the crowd to the task of taking personal responsibility for being human", Morris [5] – an existentialist point of view.

Physical educationists need to be aware of current thinking about both the ultimate and the general aims of education and should also make their contribution to the discussion. Possibly one of the major factors in the declining recognition of the importance of physical education in education – a fact reported by many colleagues and visible in many administrative decisions being made – is the failure of physical education to keep contact with and contribute to developments in the philosophy of education.

One cannot go far with a discussion of "What is P.E.?" before employing the terms *aims* and *objectives*. These words are in common use but are employed differently by different writers. The following usage appears to be fairly generally accepted in education (though many exceptions can be found). **Aims** are directional statements of a a general nature. Boyle [2] enlarging on this view writes: "An educational aim is much more like the inspiration for a voyage of discovery than it is like drawing a bead on a bulls-eye, or routinely catching the eight-forty for town. It did not matter in the end that where Columbus got to was not India but America. It was the inspiration taking him overseas that counted". **Objectives** may be most meaningfully ranged along a continuum from general objectives to specific teaching objectives. Kerr [4] says of objectives, "Teachers have in mind certain cognitive skills, attitudes and interests which they encourage pupils to acquire by the provision of appropriate learning experiences. It is in this sense that we speak of curriculum objectives as the intended outcomes of learning". He continues, "there are operational criteria associated with an objective: that is, the pupil must have been or will be involved in a particular kind of behaviour if the objective has been achieved". Stones [8] would regard as an unsatisfactory teaching objective any statement which did not specify "exactly what he (the teacher) expects them (the pupils) to be able to do at the end of the instruction". It is debatable whether all aims can be achieved with quite this degree of precision and immediacy but the present discontinuity between aims and specific objectives in P.E. is too marked. Archambault [1] sums this up when he writes "the major difficulty is the fact that we have failed to understand that educational aims, if they are to have any meaning and vital force, if they are to serve as genuine criteria and standards for crucial procedure, must be translated into specific teaching objectives . . .". This is true of P.E. although he was referring to education as a whole. It does show that physical education is not alone in falling short on this crucial point.

Accepting these definitions, an attempt is made in Figure 1.1 to relate the terms to working situations in P.E. and to suggest where written expressions of them might be found.

Two other words are in common use to describe aims – 'intrinsic' and 'extrinsic'. An intrinsic aim is defined as the pursuit of something inherent in the activity; 'doing something for its own sake'. Conversely an extrinsic aim is towards something external and not essential to the activity itself. These can be useful distinctions for analysis but unfortunately values appear to be added to the words so that intrinsic equals 'good, worthwhile and genuine' whilst anything extrinsic is assumed to be in-

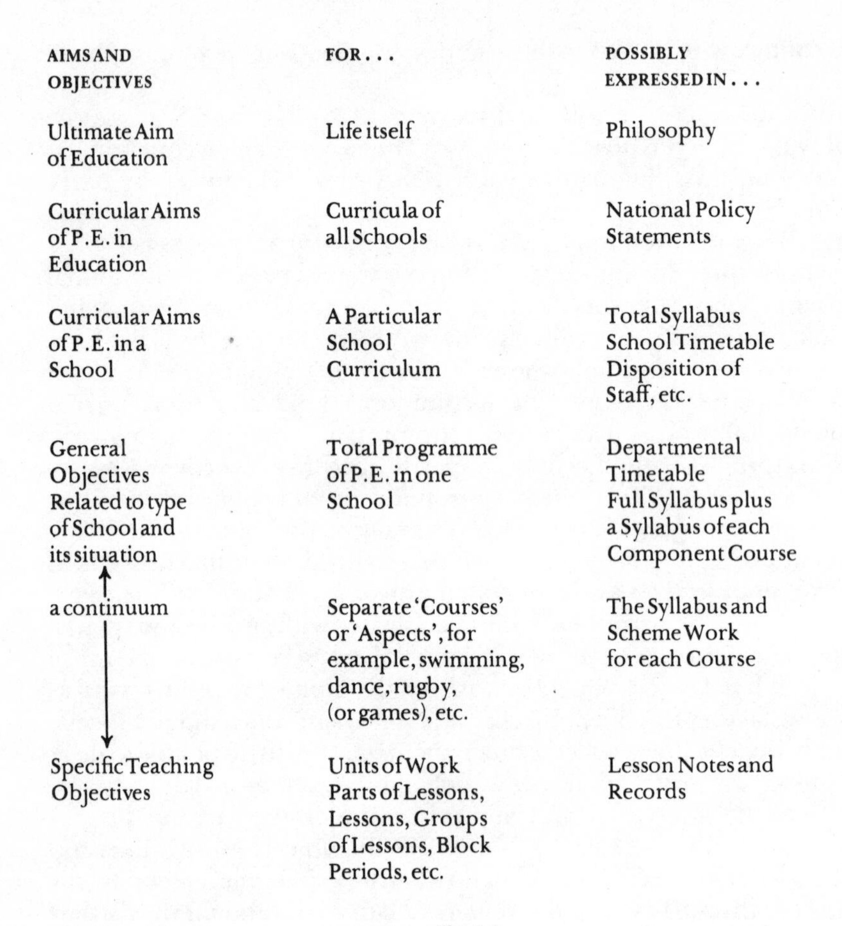

AIMS AND OBJECTIVES	FOR . . .	POSSIBLY EXPRESSED IN . . .
Ultimate Aim of Education	Life itself	Philosophy
Curricular Aims of P.E. in Education	Curricula of all Schools	National Policy Statements
Curricular Aims of P.E. in a School	A Particular School Curriculum	Total Syllabus School Timetable Disposition of Staff, etc.
General Objectives Related to type of School and its situation ↑	Total Programme of P.E. in one School	Departmental Timetable Full Syllabus plus a Syllabus of each Component Course
a continuum	Separate 'Courses' or 'Aspects', for example, swimming, dance, rugby, (or games), etc.	The Syllabus and Scheme Work for each Course
↓ Specific Teaching Objectives	Units of Work Parts of Lessons, Lessons, Groups of Lessons, Block Periods, etc.	Lesson Notes and Records

Fig. 1.1

essential and of less worth. In fact most human activities are pursued for a vast mixture of intrinsic and extrinsic reasons; psychologists are only scratching at the surface in their struggle to understand human motivation. Certainly the evaluation of the worth of stated aims should be a separate matter from a description of whether these aims are intrinsic or extrinsic. Anyone unconvinced might care to consider the activities of a sadist in these terms.

At this stage in the exploration of 'physical education', it might help to draw a 'map'. This is fraught with difficulties because of the absence of agreed boundaries. Despite this it will serve to illustrate one total view of physical education.

The main stream of physical education is seen as one of the family of processes which make up the education of an individual throughout his

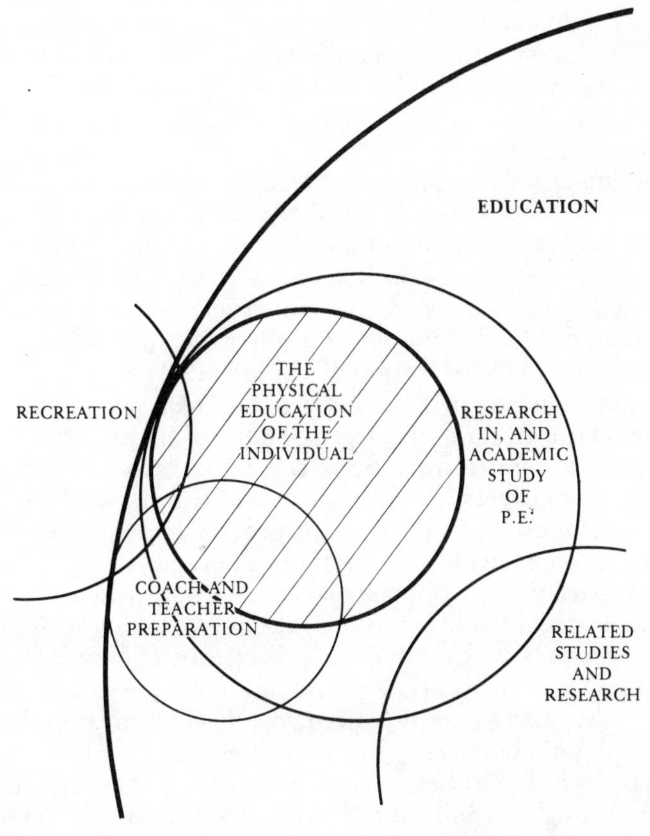

Fig. 1.2

or her life. The amount of participation in P.E. will vary for each individual. Some will continue physical education at the tertiary stage, some will not participate in any organised learning situations in adult life, others may not continue their P.E. for a period and then return with renewed interest. Whatever the pattern of individual P.E., it is the sum of this participation that constitutes the main stream of physical education.

Physical recreation is shown as accompanying physical education through life but not as part of P.E. Recreation is defined here, as essentially self-chosen activity, for intrinsic rather than extrinsic ends although not solely so, not concerned with the everyday routine of earning one's living, primarily concerned with personal satisfaction. At times aspects of education could be recreative by these criteria. Certainly all recreation need not be physical recreation. In as much as P.E. provides the skills, attitudes and knowledge that are used in physical recreation, so they are linked. Furthermore, an interest aroused in a recreative context may lead an individual to seek further education so that he can participate more satisfactorily in his chosen recreation. The amount to which individuals seek and value physical activities as forms of recreation could be viewed as a partial measure of the influence of physical education on life as a whole.

On the 'map' the preparation of teachers, coaches, etc., is shown as serving the main stream of physical education. Courses for intending teachers should be constantly looking for applications in the main stream of P.E. whilst seeking new insights from the academic study of P.E., research findings and knowledge in related fields of study. What progress is made in the personal physical education of the student is seen as part of the tertiary stage of the education of an individual.

The academic study of P.E. is shown as encompassing the study of both the main stream of physical education and the teaching, coaching and administrative aspects. It can also examine, with the aid of knowledge from other related fields of study, some of the underlying problems in, for example, the learning process, human physiology, biomechanics or even the philosophical problems of relating P.E. to life in general. As part of this probing it may involve empirical research. In this sense P.E. is an academic discipline. It is not 'a discipline' in the purist sense in that it does not have its own discreet 'form of knowledge' but this is in common with many academic disciplines in the general use of this term. It might more correctly be termed a 'field of study'. It draws from other disciplines – not necessarily 'pure' themselves – often taking from them aspects which may be considered of peripheral interest in that discipline, but which are judged to be of more central importance to the study of physical education. It is the unique focus of interest and information which divides the study of P.E. from other studies. This may worry some physical educationists who seek a discrete body of knowledge but others will look at the world around them and observe that most important problems involving people are solved by an inter-disciplinary approach. At the level of academic study the scope of possible areas of investigation is very wide. This alone makes selection inevitable and with limited time and resources available it is obvious that large variations in the selected content can and will occur. In as much as these studies help to elucidate the main stream of physical education so this variation involves a spreading of attention which is to be encouraged and may be valuable.

So much for comments on the way the 'map' has been drawn. If these areas are subjected to a secondary analysis by questioning on four fronts – *Aims and Objectives, Content, Methods,* and *Evaluation Techniques* – then one can begin to ask many more meaningful questions about the nature of different areas of P.E. One can make some sense of some of the confusion which appears to exist.

Taking for example, **objectives,** even at a fairly general level, one would expect to find considerable differences between those of P.E. in a primary school and those of an academic study of P.E. at a university. The content of an adult evening class might be expected to be different from that of a lecture in a college of education or a primary school indoor lesson. Certainly teaching methods differ greatly between a secondary school games lesson and a university lecture or seminar period. Finally one would not be surprised to find different methods of evaluating progress in use in, for example, a college of further education, a primary school and a research project. If one cares to quote **content** in one area, **aims** in another and refer to **methods** used in a third, it is all too easy to create great confusion. In discussion it could prove useful to use this 'map' and secondary analysis to ensure that one is at least attempting to talk about roughly the same area of P.E.

What binds the main stream of P.E. together? Some attempts have been made recently to put forward a singular unifying concept for P.E. This is unnecessary; it could lead to over-simplification and, possibly, eventual misrepresentation and distortion of the main stream of P.E. In this view, P.E. is characterised by its constant place in the family of processes which make up education, by its continual reference to the ultimate aim of education as a whole, and by its consistent aims at curricular level. Furthermore, its methods are continually subject to evaluation against those criteria which decide 'what is an educational process'. It becomes increasingly defined in practice as its aims are translated into specific teaching objectives.

Its content need not be constant. Activities should be selected (a) in the light of curricular aims and (b) for those which are feasible, taking into account at this stage, for instance, historical, cultural, economic and geographical factors. The content of the resulting P.E. programme will consist of a series of activities – learning experiences – which show only certain family resemblances. For example, if all physical activities were analysed and certain ones selected for their contribution to the curricular aims of P.E., then it is possible that three or four of these aims would be achievable in all the activities but not necessarily the same aims or the same number of aims in each. Hence the notion of a family resemblance amongst the activities – common features being present throughout but no one feature being necessarily present in all, and certainly not prominent throughout.

Without including the evidence on which the opinion is based or further amplification, in this view of physical education it is maintained that there are six major aims at curricular level (see Figure 1.1) that are applicable at all stages in the main stream of physical education. There will be a variation in emphasis given to the promotion of these aims at the different stages of the physical education of the individual but they are all present, or should be, throughout the duration of the process. They are:

1. The promotion of cognitive development.
2. The promotion of aesthetic education.
3. The promotion of moral education.
4. The promotion of social education.
5. The promotion of education for leisure – a recreative element.
6. The promotion of fitness for 'positive living'.

It will be seen at once that these aims overlap considerably with those of education. Indeed, it is only by the achievement of aims in a variety of 'subject areas' that the aims of education as a whole are achieved. One could ask, "To what extent can physical education promote all these aims?" It is not claimed that physical education can promote all these aims equally or that every activity in physical education can contribute to all six aims. What is contended, is that where there is overlap with the educational aims of other 'subject areas', physical education either offers a substantially different perspective, as in cognitive development, or perhaps a very fertile situation – as in moral and social education. It could be that other aims, such as in areas 5 and 6, although perhaps accorded less importance in education generally, make the contribution of physical education particularly valuable because they are present only to a minor degree or not at all in the aims of other subject areas. Could it be that the **fitness** aim, not overstated and seen in relation to all other aims of physical education, is, in fact, one unique contribution of physical education to education?

Finally, one might select four tasks which appear vital at this stage in the exploration and development of physical education:

1. A close examination of statements of tenable aims and their justification.

2. An evaluation of all activities at present included, or which could possibly be included in the P.E. programme in the light of their possible contribution to the aims of physical education. (Speculating wildly, this might result in the grouping of series of 'recommended activities' from which a selection could be made according to traditions, facilities, staff expertise, etc., available. Providing a certain selection of activities was made, taught with expertise and, particularly, an understanding of the aims of P.E.,

then these aims might be achieved irrespective of differences in actual content from place to place.)

3. The involvement of each teacher in the process of translating general aims into specific teaching objectives. Although this is a difficult task it is essential and it is at this point that the L.E.A. advisory staff could instigate widescale checks on schemes-of-work in schools such as that being conducted in Gloucestershire at the time of writing. Problems so exposed could be remedied by group discussion and further in-service education.

4. The development of evaluative techniques which are relevant and integrated with work at all levels – evaluation must become a more accepted feature of P.E. Much of the confusion which exists in the practice of physical education is due to the considerable changes of method and content which have been promoted largely on the basis of what can only be inspired guesswork, by teachers who would be excellent whatever they taught. All too often there has been no real attempt to evaluate what is good in the current situation, no attempt to preserve anything of proven value, and all has been swept away in the enthusiasm for innovation. Those who have failed to make an objective appraisal of the past are even less likely to consider this as a necessary procedure following automatically on the introduction of new methods or material with which they are themselves concerned. Evaluation procedures must become part of the system if P.E. is to avoid wild 'swings of fashion'.

References

1. Archambault, R. 'Manner in education', *Philosophy of education,* p. 32. Philosophy of Education Society, U.S.A. 1968.
2. Boyle, G. C. 'The question of aims in education', *Education for teaching,* p. 28. A.T.C.D.E., Summer 1969.
3. Dearden, R. F. *The philosophy of primary education,* Routledge & Kegan Paul, 1968.
4. Kerr, J. F. *Changing the curriculum,* p. 21. U.L.P., 1968.
5. Morris, V. C. *Existentialism in education,* p. 116. Harper & Row, 1966.
6. Peters, R. S. 'The philosophy of education', in Tibble, J. W. (ed.), *The study of education,* p. 71. Routledge & Kegan Paul, 1966.
7. Peters, R. S. 'What is an educational process?' in R. S. Peters (ed.), *The concept of education,* p. 9. Routledge & Kegan Paul, 1967.
8. Stones, E. *Learning and teaching,* p. 97. Wiley, 1968.

2

The Curricular Aims of Physical Education*

Philosophy and Physical Education

Mason and Ventre [32] attempt "a classification of philosophies of physical education on accepted philosophical attitudes or positions". They list these as, "Naturalism, Realism, Idealism and Pragmatism (Experimentalism)". This approach is valid and interesting but the modern philsopher of education is more often concerned with conceptual analysis. The modern approach to the philosophy of P.E. is also to look very closely at the concepts which we employ rather than to trace historically the roots from which these concepts have evolved.

The main benefits of language, whether written or spoken, are to facilitate thought and to communicate ideas. In a situation where two people are struggling to understand each other, "What do you mean?" is often the basic question. Because concepts, particularly abstract ones, are built partly through experience, it is virtually impossible that two people's concepts will ever be exactly the same. A concept is a generalisation and so *must* be less clearly defined than a description of one specific thing. This means that in seeking to establish common concepts and working definitions – which are the basis of living and

*A revised version of a paper first presented at the Association of Teachers in Colleges and Departments of Education (Physical Education Section) Conference in September, 1970 and published in the Conference Proceedings.

working together, we are seeking only a certain level of precision. You may ask, "Why bother – we all know what P.E. is don't we?" To me the answer is simple. The exercise focuses our attention, allows us to pinpoint the judgements needed and make decisions, and permits the more precise communication of ideas between us.

Needs

Perhaps I can give an example of how conceptual analysis can be helpful and I am indebted to R. F. Dearden [15] for his work on this. We often speak of the needs of children when we discuss P.E. We may answer questions of "Why?" we do certain things, by answering that "the children need this treatment". This would appear, particularly if supported by statistics giving norms and performance levels, to be an objective and scientific approach to making curricula decisions in P.E.

But this is not so. For in order to be termed 'in need' the child must fall below a certain standard and as soon as one sets standards which are somewhere above a simple living or dead dividing line, to talk in terms of need is really only to make a disguised value judgement as to what one considers should be or should happen. In seeming to be scientific (by relating one's work to the needs of children) ultimately one is doing no more than prescribing in the light of one's own, or other people's, subjective judgments. If some of these 'needs' were 'discovered' in times past, when conditions were very different, or in countries where the cultural background is quite different, it is possible that basing one's work on such statements will be quite useless or even harmful.

What is Physical Education?

It should be apparent by now that I believe that in philosophy one cannot avoid being subjective and that one's own concepts are bound up with personal experience and related to a personal concept of the nature and purpose of life itself. This means that this is essentially a personal viewpoint. Despite this, it is possible to arrive at common concepts and working definitions and this task is most important for physical education today. There is a F.I.E.P. *World Manifesto on Physical Education* showing that international agreement may be reached although, because we are attempting to fuse so many personal views, progress is bound to be slow and surrounded by controversy.

I would like to consider for a moment the nature of physical education. Is it football? – or gymnastics? – or is it the result of participations in these activities? – or is it preparation for participation in these activities? If it is the result, is it the automatic result? – is it a certain body of knowledge?

I would suggest that P.E. is none of these things. To me P.E. is essentially a process, one of a family of processes that make up education.

This definition draws heavily on Peters' [37] concept of education as a family of processes. He often likens *education* to *reform* which is a process in which one does not follow a pattern of operations precisely but rather a process in which one proceeds with certain criteria in mind. It is the criteria which determine the nature of the activities selected and the direction in which they proceed.

Because physical education is an integral part of education its activities must be selected and directed by the same criteria as education. It follows also that as one of the family of processes which make up education, P.E. must both make its unique contribution and share many of the aims of education as a whole.

Aims and Objectives

As one turns to a discussion of the purpose of P.E. it is impossible to avoid talking about aims and objectives although some writers do use different words such as 'targets' or 'goals'. There is no generally accepted terminology so I have tried to keep in line with that receiving wide usage in educational writings. To me the essential differences between aims and objectives are in terms of degrees of generality.

Aims, in my view, are directional statements of a general nature – broad guide lines if you like. Boyle [8] gives a picture of aims with which I agree: "An educational aim is much more like the inspiration for a voyage of discovery than it is like drawing a bead on a bullseye or routinely catching the eight-forty to town. It did not matter in the end that where Columbus got to was America and not India, it was the inspiration taking him overseas that counted".

At the level of aims I can accept the possibility of an ultimate aim for the whole of education. This is unlikely to be universally agreed. Peters [38] would state his as "the educated man"; Dearden [16] seeks "an ideal of personal autonomy based on reason". In Eastern Socialist Societies the State is usually put before the individual. Below this, but still at a highly general level, Physical Education has its general aims of physical education, which are applicable at all stages in the educative process although the emphasis given to them will vary with the age of the person being educated.

Below the 'aims' level comes a continuum of **objectives**. Some are general, but are related to the type of school and its situation. Changes of emphasis according to age, mentioned in relation to aims, start to become apparent here. Objectives become increasingly specific as they relate to parts of the school P.E. programme and eventually to the objectives for particular lessons or parts of lessons.

They are no longer just general guide lines. Kerr [27] says of objectives: "Teachers have in mind certain skills, attitudes, and interests which they encourage pupils to acquire by the provision of appropriate learning experiences. It is in this sense that we speak of curriculum objectives as the intended outcomes of learning . . . there are operational criteria concerned with objectives, that is, a pupil must be, or will be, involved in a particular kind of behaviour if the objective has been achieved".

Teaching objectives should be highly specific wherever possible and some would go as far as to say that they should specify what the teacher expects the pupil to know or be able to do at the end of instruction. Obviously, all aims and general objectives cannot be reduced to this highly specific form but more links must be forged between what the teacher sets as day-to-day objectives and the underlying general aims of physical education. This is the problem which needs urgent attention once aims and general objectives have been established.

Intrinsic and Extrinsic Aims in Education

"What is an aim?" and "What could be meant by 'aims of education'" are crucial questions, according to Peters [37]. He maintains that the "Failure to realise that 'ends' or standards are built into the notion of 'being educated' as an achievement has led people to search mistakenly for 'aims of education' which are extrinsive to it". His view supposes that one cannot logically educate for anything beyond 'becoming educated'. However, as Boyle [8] points out: "On this view, it is self-contradictory to speak of 'bad education', since anything which is bad is not education". Thus, Peters' claim "that education has no aims beyond itself, proves to be a disguised tautology (circular argument) from which nothing of consequence for the practice of education could be inferred".

Fortunately, Peters' intrinsic view of education is not universally accepted. Boyle comments, "Despite the limitations of talk about aims in education, it has this virtue of connecting what we do in schools with what is of concern outside; of reminding us that education is one and only one, of the manifold processes of society". Extrinsic aims are accepted by Adams [1] as "Normative latent objectives". In reply to Peters' criticism that games cease to be games if played to develop morality, etc., she argues that whilst one cannot play these games "looking to these virtues as objectives . . . this does not prevent them being serious reasons for including the activities in the curriculum, and even favourably known by the participant to be so included . . .".

Neither would it be accepted that no activity in physical education has value in its own right. Sing-nan, Fen [43], an American philosopher, examines Peters' argument of the worthwhileness of education activities, including aspects of physical education, on the grounds of 'intrinsic value' and 'seriousness'. He concludes that Peters' argument "tends to be circular and materially it cannot be conclusive". He says of Peters, "his emphasis is what characterizes philosophy. Since we cannot have all the good things, we have to choose, to emphasize, and to arrange a priority". Later he writes "Practically, there is no telling whether in education we should always emphasize *cognition*. There are times and places whereby *action*, for instance, is more worthwhile and at another time and place, perhaps *feelings* and *sensitivity* are more worthwhile". Whilst not being against intellectuals he points out that to try to make the cognitive emphasis "overridingly worthwhile is the professional prejudice of intellectuals . . .".

Dearden [16], also uses the Peters argument in discussing play and games but, as Wilson [47] points out in a critical review of his book *The Philosophy of Primary Education* "one *cannot* treat these as non-serious and intrinsically unimportant, even a child must regard his play objects as being intrinsically important, or he would not bother to play with them properly". This notion of 'playing properly' is a feature of much adult participation in 'games'. Wilson continues, "anything which someone is 'serious' about, even when he is a child, is ethically important *to him* and therefore to any respecter of his autonomy". As already stated, Dearden's aim for education is "an ideal of personal autonomy based on reason", so this is a powerful criticism indeed.

I believe there can be considerable intrinsic value in taking part in physical activities. Furthermore, the *manner* in which things are done is also very important in physical education. I have written elsewhere [3] that I believe most human activities are pursued for a vast mixture of intrinsic and extrinsic reasons and I would want any evaluation of the aims of P.E. to be independent of an analysis under these headings.

The Bases of Curricular Aims in Physical Education

Turning from these general considerations, I propose to examine briefly some of the areas where physical education could claim to have a supportable 'aim'. The problem of classifying these areas is by no means easy. One could use that adopted by Bloom [7, 29] and his associates who list objectives in three 'domains': the *Cognitive, Affective* and *Psycho-motor*. Alternatively, one could follow Hirst [23] who is concerned with different basic forms of knowledge and the "development of a rational mind". He says that "all forms of development with which education is concerned are related to the pupil's progress in rational understanding. This means that physical education, for instance, is pursued in accordance with a rational appraisal of the place and value of physical activities in human life which we wish the pupil to acquire, that the activities themselves are viewed as those of a developing rational being, not merely an animal, and that they therefore constitute part of the life of a rational person".

Neither of these approaches commends itself completely in this examination although it is hoped cross reference would not be difficult. The broad subdivisions, used here, examine aims in six areas: cognitive development, aesthetic education, moral education, the development of social relationships, education for leisure, and finally, physical fitness and general health. It is stressed that these divisions are somewhat arbitrary and that new divisions could be suggested without destroying the underlying value of the points made.

The Development of Cognitive Skills and Knowledge

The essential unity of man is generally accepted today. Old divisions between 'body' and 'mind' have largely died with (amongst other advances) the increasing knowledge of neuro-physiology. Oliver [35] says, "Because of the intimate relationship of the functioning of all aspects of growth, an individual cannot be divided into two parts, therefore we do not believe that one type of experience trains the body and that another type of experience educates the mind". There is considerable evidence at the basic level, of the role of physical activity in the development of intellect.

Physical education activities can contribute in a number of ways to the cognitive skills and knowledge of the individual.

Physical skills, particularly those at the 'open' end of a perceptual-motor skills continuum such as that outlined by Knapp [28] (in other words those demanding very much the relating of one's own performance to that of a changing environment), require the acquisition of broad concepts and their use in problem solving and decision making. This is often followed quickly by practical feedback as to the rightness of the decision made. For example, this is true of tactical decisions made in team games, and in many decisions made in racing a sailing boat at sea, or leading a party on a mountain expedition. Alles [2] places intellectual and physical skills on a single continuum and would appear to support this contention.

Knowledge is also closely allied with physical activities. This is not only 'know how' which is important in its own right, but also knowledge of the 'know that' type. For example, Carlisle [12] points out that pursuits such as orienteering, mountaineering and sailing all require a knowledge of aspects of cartography and physical geography. Dance composition is allied to knowledge of the structure of music. The competing pole vaulter will usually be able to discourse most intelligently on the mechanics of his vault and the physical properties of the glass fibre pole. Ryle [42] makes the point that modern sporting activities are so organised and managed as to be only possible within an educated society. For this reason the knowledge involved in them is an extension of the civilised understanding and knowledge of the society at large

Finally there appears to be an important contribution that physical activities can make to build up 'self-knowledge'. Cratty [14] tells us, "It is enough to place emphasis on basic motor activities for no other reason than to improve a child's self-image as he engages in games. A large proportion of a boy's self-concept between the ages of five and fifteen hinges on whether he can perform well in socially approved games". Arnold [5], in an article 'Physical Education, Creativity and the Self Concept', outlines the contributions of these aspects of physical education: Games, Outdoor Pursuits and Dance. He describes how "the personality maps out a log of self-identifying experiences". Jourad [26] gives further evidence of the importance of the self-concept and Owen [36] asks if the way the subject might best serve the pupil is "by extending his knowledge and perception of what it means, in the fullest human sense, to have a physical existence?"

In examining the cognitive contribution it is accepted that the cognitive skills may have a relatively small transfer to non-physical education situations. In general the problem solving approach of, for instance, modern educational gymnastics, is only likely to carry over to other similar situations but the broader problems met, for example, in outdoor pursuits, inasmuch as these activities are more fully integrated into everyday life, are more likely to have a considerable carry-over effect. Moreover, physical activities can provide a central point of interest and application for knowledge and understanding and may, therefore, be of great value as a focus for interdisciplinary studies.

Aesthetic Education

In talking of education in general, Dearden [16] mentions "activities which contribute in distinctive ways to the development of aesthetic understanding". In his list he includes 'dance' which the majority of physical educationists would accept as part of their sphere of interest.

Most accounts of aesthetic education acknowledge the place of dance but quite often they are difficult to evaluate because writers mix up appreciative/observer considerations with expressive/performer factors. The terms 'self-expression' and 'creativity' also obscure a picture in which at other times dance may be seen mainly as an 'interpretive' art.

More unusual are attempts to trace aesthetic value in games and sports generally. Anthony [4] discussed 'Sport and Physical Education as a means of Aesthetic Education', in 1968, and Carlisle [12] went further in his examination of the 'Concept of Physical Education' to suggest that "Physical Education might therefore be defined as that part of general and aesthetic education in which knowledge, understanding and the exercise and appreciation of skill is focused on a range of pleasurable activities which depend on the body as an essential part of the medium and object of action."

Weaknesses in Carlisle's argument are pointed out by Adams [1] in an accompanying paper and the usefulness of a unifying concept of physical education which appears to rely partly on aesthetic appreciation in the eyes of the observer is certainly open to question. What is not so doubtful is that here is an aspect of education to which physical education can make a positive contribution. However, Anthony [4] concluded "a sense of aesthetic awareness *must be deliberately awakened* – it is not a natural concomitant of physical activities. The physical education teacher has the unenviable but challenging task of first creating aesthetic awareness in the exciting but challenging areas of sports and physical education and then attempting to encourage the transfer of any understanding which has evolved to what Goblewicz [20] calls the 'aesthetics of daily life'".

Moral Education

Moral Education as a whole is again an area of rather involved concepts. Peters [37] has set out to reinstate the concepts and principles of moral education as *the core* of education; embodied in both the process and the content. One has to search for a meaning of moral education. Dwyer [18] takes a broad application of the term and talks about "any deliberate moves by educators to influence the ethical beliefs of students". Wilson, Williams and Sugarman [46] reporting for the

Research Unit on Moral Education set up by the Farmington Trust says, "The concept of moral education demands more than just a set of overt (perhaps conditioned) movements. It demands more than intentional behaviour, since we are interested in a person having the right sort of intentions, reasons and motives. It demands more even than this, since we are interested in a person's disposition or state of mind, from which his reasons and motives – and hence ultimately his behaviour – will flow".

Physical education has probably been guilty of overstating its possible contributions to moral education. Often, however, this overstatement may have been the work of interested observers but despite this, physical educationists have been pleased to accept their support. Typical of one type of statement is that attributed to Dame Enid Russell-Smith [41], "All games and sports have rules designed to enforce fair play, which is fundamentally a moral principle and essential to modern society". There may well be a grain of truth in this statement but most physical educationists today would be more cautious. Randall and Waine [39] in 1955 discuss at length and critically the 'development of social and sporting attitudes' and Brailsford [9] in 1959 examines in particular two assertions:

"1. That games develop qualities such as a sense of fair play, good sportsmanship, courage and endurance (how to give and take).

2. That some forms of physical education (especially boxing, mountaineering and outdoor pursuits generally) develop initiative and/or train leaders".

Their examinations sound, quite rightly, a note of warning about attempts to generalise experience in physical education to the complex patterns of life at large. Brailsford [9] found the area to be "so cloudy and speculative that this section cannot provide anything that is really useful as a specific subject aim".

One might have been content to let the matter rest there if not for new evidence to support the subjective ideas of physical educationists who feel that they can *and do* contribute to education in this area. For example Heaton [22] found that moral education was placed as first priority by various groups defining the role of the teacher of physical education. Elvin [19] points out, "there is no real division" between moral and general education and he suggests that the "classic embodiment" of the concept of fairness "is the games field" and in spite of all the fatuities we have heard on that subject at Prize Days (by non physical educationists?) our tradition here is basically right and still potentially most valuable.

The workers for the Farmington Trust Research Unit have done something to clarify the situation. In offering tentative suggestions for practical work in schools they subdivide their considerations into those of 'content' and 'context'. It is not possible here to list their practical suggestions but it is encouraging to see that situations within physical education figure quite noticeably in both lists. It would seem, therefore, that physical education can make a contribution to the moral education of the child. However, the situation is far more complex than the advocates of character training on the games field or in outdoor pursuits would have us believe. Some would see moral education completely integrated within the next section of my examination.

The Development of Social Relationships

"Man as we know him can only exist in society"; certainly it is a powerful factor. Stones [44] also states that, "The school is a microcosm of society and the nature of the school will influence the nature of the children in it". Within the school, physical education can make a considerable contribution to development of social relationships. Bell [6] writes, "the provision of the basic needs of human beings – emotional security, acceptance by a group, the experience of success. How important for us this is we all know – family affection, comradeship with colleagues, success in work, how much we depend on them and how maimed we would be without them".

Brailsford [9] maintained that physical education offers "opportunities for co-operative activity" and a chance to "gain the prestige which attaches to physical skills in children's choices of companions". He continued, "on both the stated grounds physical education stands in a unique position among the school disciplines and the teacher of physical education has more than usual opportunities to observe ... the pattern of social relationships within his classes".

From another side of this picture Oliver [35] examined evidence of the effects of physical handicaps on the process of social interaction and later he showed that, even with handicapped children, physical education can assist in social adjustment.

Professor E. Hoyle [24] is even more certain that physical education has social functions and writes, "it can be argued that where physical activities are engaged in for their own sake, an important social function is being met". He asks that the social functions of the physical education teacher should not be interpreted narrowly or necessarily as a by-product of their teaching activities. Hoyle would claim, "It is the social aspect of physical education which the teacher must not fail to take into account as he comes to reject the broad and optimistic claims for his subject in favour of the more systematic appraisal of objectives and the possibilities of achieving them".

Certainly it would seem that an aim *is* reasonable within this area although I can see considerable problems in specifying a range of specific learning objectives.

Education for Leisure

In certain sectors of physical education a great emphasis is put on the aim of preparing young people for participation in active leisure time pursuits. An essential factor is that the leisure activity should be recreative. This implies that the activity is essentially self-chosen, for intrinsic rewards, not concerned with everyday routine and the earning of one's living and primarily concerned with personal enjoyment. Recreation in this sense is closely aligned with 'play' as outlined by Caillois [11] in *Man, Play and Games.*

A doubt as to the effectiveness of the time spent on this aspect of education is raised by Musgrove [34] who states, "Actual leisure-time behaviour appears to be related to other structural factors – the length of the working day is particularly relevant. Particular forms of education are *only marginally relevant, a residual category* in explanation".

Carlisle [12] points out that in this area the aims of physical education are at greatest conflict with the Peters view of education. Some of the counter arguments possible have already been put forward in the discussion of intrinsic and extrinsic aims and serious and non-serious activities. On balance it *is* possible to affirm with Carlisle that, "while physical educationists do supply children and adults with requisite knowledge to have fun in informal ways, they try to develop the knowledge and understanding required to participate in and appreciate the activities when played to the highest personal and public standards".

Groombridge [21] takes an even wider view of the development of leisure. He says, "we need to be thinking about it in very large and comprehensive terms. We need leisure to rest, we need it for recreation but we also need it for development". In this latter sense physical education may contribute considerably. For part of school life we may educate in preparation for leisure and during post-school life we may further educate during leisure.

Physical Fitness and General Health

When physical education first gained acceptance to the school curriculum it was largely on medical grounds that it made its case. There followed a swing away from a medical to an educational justification which has since led to protests such as that by McDonald [31] in 1957 in which he says, "It seems to me, however, that somewhere along this road of progress we have forgotten that our principal concern is with the physical". This situation is becoming clearer as more research evidence becomes available and it is certainly possible to find evidence to support an aim in this area.

Unfortunately the concepts of **fitness** and **health** and the relationship between *physical* and *mental* health require considerable clarification. Brailsford [9] looks to various degrees of specificity whilst defining fitness. This really resolves into a discussion of 'general fitness' as compared with 'fitness for specific purposes'. When Brailsford was writing in 1959 there was no generally agreed measure of fitness but it appears that by 1969 an adequate measuring method had been developed. Brooke [10] reports "it is clear that fitness can now be satisfactorily measured in the defined sample. This now allows most relevant statements to be made about the condition of other members of the population from which the sample was drawn . . .". McCloy [30] defines the notion of general fitness in terms of "people simply having strength and endurance enough (a) to feel good (b) to be able to do the work of the day without undue fatigue and to reach the end of the day sleepy but not tired and, (c) to be able to meet emergencies adequately".

Oliver [35] has made a case for the beneficial effects of physical activity whilst a child is attending school, and Murray and Hunter [33] show that there is mounting medical evidence to prove that the continuation of physical activity into and throughout adult life, can have a positive protective function in warding off the degenerative illnesses of the cardiovascular, alimentary, respiratory and muscular systems which are prevalent in modern society.

Perhaps at this stage one should also examine the concept of **health.** A common definition is one in terms of absence of illness, but this is an insufficient picture. To diagnose ill health, objective evidence of disordered function, social disability and characteristics of disease, is required. Mental illness may be seen similarly in terms of these criteria, and some doctors would term as a 'personality disorder', a case which had evidence of long-standing deviant behaviour but without the characteristics of disordered neural function and the presence of disease.

Even within this seemingly objective method of determining whether someone is healthy or not, it must be remembered that the evidence is eventually weighed against the value judgements present in the acceptable norms. The sociologist Durkheim [17] for example, "concluded that the existence of some degree of abnormality was socially normal in every society".

Looking to establish a link between P.E. and health, Troup [45] finds that "to a limited extent some relationship between health and physical fitness exists". This is typical of many opinions and there is increasing empirical evidence to support them. The confidence with which the claim is made appears to depend on the date of its supporting evidence and on the particular standpoint and intentions of the writer.

In summary, six areas of advantage may be claimed for physical benefits from participation in physical activities and the acquisition of fitness. They are:

1. To cope with the physiological demands of daily work without undue fatigue.
2. To allow a person to undertake chosen leisure activities with the maximum enjoyment (this may or may not include sporting activities).
3. To cope with physical emergencies and the excess strains which may be encountered from time to time in life at large.
4. To play a contributory part in preventing malfunction of the various systems of the body.
5. To help in the control of obesity where it is a problem, and to help to resist adverse changes due to ageing.
6. To play a part where there are malfunctions which are remediable and to assist where exercise will contribute to and perhaps speed rehabilitation.

In the sphere of *mental health* the evidence is less plentiful. The work of Jahouda [25] in 1958 led to the establishment of empirical indicators as to the presence or otherwise of mental health. One of these factors, 'environmental mastery', would seem to be an aspect which is particularly capable of influence during physical education. Comer [13] assembled a considerable amount of evidence to support a wider relationship between sport and mental health.

In looking for evidence of a link between physical activity and effects on mental health it could be helpful to consider evidence of the use of physical activities in the treatment of mental illness. Treatment can be categorised at four levels, curative, rehabilitative, palliative, and custodial. Although there is no evidence as yet of curative effects from the use of physical activities – remembering that mental disease and/or dysfunction is involved – physical activities are used quite successfully in all other aspects of treatment.

On the evidence presented so far it is possible to claim that physical education may make a positive contribution to personal fitness and may contribute to the general health of the individual. Arnold [5] and Cratty [14] relate the effects of physical activities on the development of the self-concept to the health of the society and the total development of the individual. Arnold suggests that "the health of the society may be measured by the degree to which a person can distinguish himself from others".

Therefore, there would appear to be a case for a concept of mental fitness as well, or better still, a concept of **total fitness** with both mental and physical elements combined. This to me links with an idea put forward by Randall, Waine and Hickling [40] who express this in the notion of *fitness for 'positive living'*.

The Curricular Aims of Physical Education

From this brief analysis, aims which would appear to be tenable are:

1. The promotion of cognitive development.
2. The promotion of aesthetic education.
3. The promotion of moral education.
4. The promotion of social education.
5. The promotion of education for leisure.
6. The promotion of fitness for 'positive living'.

Conclusions

It is not suggested that *all* activities in physical education promote *all* these aims or that the contributions of physical education as a whole will be equally valuable in each area. The contributions will also vary with relation to the emphasis placed on them in certain situations. Factors which will affect this are the type of school, the content of the total curriculum and the selected content of the P.E. programme: others are such practical considerations as costs, time and facilities. The role of the teacher in all these situations must never be overlooked.

In specifying programme and teaching objectives from these aims it is valuable to make an analysis, however subjective, of the possible contributions of different activities. For example 'dance' would contribute in promoting aim (2) whilst 'circuit training' would score more highly in (6). Development of this analysis could lead to a new classification of activities in physical education and it would certainly help in programme construction. It might provide clearer answers to situations where choices have to be made, or prove that decisions are not as crucial as they might appear.

References

1. Adams, M., 'The concept of physical education II', *Proceedings of the annual conference*, pp. 25–35. Philosophy of Education Soc. of Great Britain. January, 1969.
2. Alles, J., 'An outline analysis of psycho-motor aspects of behaviour', *Theoretical constructs in curriculum development and evaluation*, pp. 18–23. Ceylon Ministry of Education, 1967.
3. Andrews, J. C., 'Physical education and education', *Bulletin of physical education*, vol. 8, no. 3. p. 22. B.A.O.L.P.E., July, 1970.
4. Anthony, D. W. J., *Physical education*, vol. 60, no. 179. P.E. Association of G.B. and N. Ireland, March, 1968.
5. Arnold, P. J., 'Physical education, creativity and the self-concept', *Bulletin of physical education*, vol. 8, no. 1, p. 16. B.A.O.L.P.E., January, 1970.
6. Bell, W. O., 'Changing objectives in education', *Physical education*, vol. 54, no. 161, p. 7. P.E. Association of G.B. and N. Ireland, March, 1962.
7. Bloom, B. (ed.), in 'The cognitive domain'. *Taxonomy of educational objectives*, Handbook I, Longmans, 1956.
8. Boyle, G. C., 'The question of aims in education', *Education for teaching*, p. 28. A.T.C.D.E., Summer, 1969.
9. Brailsford, D., 'The aims of physical education', *Research and studies*, no. 19. University of Leeds, January, 1959.
10. Brooke, J. D., 'Human biology, physical education and ergonomics', *Bulletin of physical education*, vol. 7, no. 8, p. 60. B.A.O.L.P.E., October, 1969.
11. Caillois, R., *Man, play and games*, Thames and Hudson, 1962.
12. Carlisle, R., 'The concept of physical education', *Proceedings of annual conference*, January, 1969, pp. 5–22. Philosophy of Education Society of G.B.
13. Comer, G., 'Relationships between sport and mental health', *Physical education*, vol. 60, no. 181. P.E. Association G.B. and N. Ireland, November, 1968.
14. Cratty, B. J., *Perceptual-motor behavior and educational processes*, p. 83. Thomas (U.S.A.), 1969.
15. Dearden, R. F., 'Needs in education', *British journal of educational studies*, vol. 14, no. 3, pp. 5–17. 1966.
16. Dearden, R. F., *The philosophy of primary education*, Routledge and Kegan Paul, 1968.
17. Durkheim, E., 'Man, health and society', quoted in Firth, R., *Education for teaching*, A.T.C.D.E., Summer, 1968.
18. Dwyer, C. E., 'Moral instruction, free choice and rational inquiry', *Philosophy of education*, 1968, p. 148. U.S.A. Philosophy of Education Society.
19. Elvin, H. L., *Education and contemporary society*, Watts, 1965.
20. Goblewicz, E., 'Aesthetic problems in physical education and sport', *FIEP, Bulletin*, no. 3, 1965.
21. Groombridge, B., 'Leisure for all'. *Physical education*, vol. 58, no. 175, p. 63. P.E. Association of G.B. and N. Ireland, November, 1966.

22. Heaton, J., 'The role of the P.E. teacher', *Bulletin of physical education,* vol. 8, no. 2. B.A.O.L.P.E., April, 1970.
23. Hirst, P. H., 'The logic of the curriculum', *Journal of curriculum studies*, vol. 1, no. 2, p. 147. May, 1969.
24. Hoyle, E., 'The role of the physical educationist in contemporary society', *Bulletin of physical education,* vol. 7, no. 6, pp. 9–10. B.A.O.L.P.E., April, 1969.
25. Jahouda, M., *Current concepts in mental health*, 1958.
26. Jourad, S. M., *The transparent self*, Van Nostrand, 1964.
27. Kerr, J. F. (ed.), in *Changing the curriculum*, U.L.P., 1968.
28. Knapp, B., *Skill in sport.* Routledge & Kegan Paul, 1963.
29. Krathwohl, D., 'The affective domain', *Taxonomy of educational objectives*, Handbook II. McKay, 1964.
30. McCloy, C. H., 'Fitness for what?' *Physical education*, vol. 50, no. 151, p. 73. P.E. Association of G.B. and N. Ireland, November, 1958.
31. McDonald, A., 'Some reflections on the physical in physical education', *Physical education*, vol. 49, no. 147. P.E. Association of G.B. and N. Ireland, July, 1957.
32. Mason, M. G. and Ventre, A. G. L., 'Philosophical aspects', *Elements of physical education.* Thistle, 1965.
33. Murray, G. and Hunter, T. A. A., *Physical education and health.* Heineman, 1966.
34. Musgrove, F., 'The contribution of sociology to the study of the curriculum', in Kerr, J. (ed.). *Changing the curriculum,* U.L.P., 1968.
35. Oliver, J. N., 'Physical activity and the psychological development of the handicapped', in Kane, J. (ed.). *Psychological aspects of physical education and sport*, pp. 187–208. Routledge & Kegan Paul, 1972.
36. Owen, J., 'Physical education and needs of the secondary school child', *Bulletin of physical education*, p. 45. Published by B.A.O.L.P.E., Conference Supplement, December, 1968.
37. Peters, R. S., 'The philosophy of education', in Tibble, J. W. (ed.), *The study of education*, p. 71. Routledge & Kegan Paul, 1966.
38. Peters, R. S., 'What is an educational process?' *The concept of education*, p. 9. Routledge & Kegan Paul, 1967.
39. Randall, M. W. and Waine, W. K., *Objectives of the physical education lesson.* Bell, 1955.
40. Randall, Waine and Hickling, M. J., *Objectives in physical education*, Bell, 1966.
41. Russell-Smith, Dame, E., 'The influence of physical education on the mental and moral attitudes of young people', *Bulletin of physical education*, p. 50. B.A.O.L.P.E., Conference Supplement, December, 1968.
42. Ryle, G., *The concept of mind*, Chapter 9, Section 6. Hutchinson, 1949.
43. Sing-nan, Fen, 'On Peters' transcendental argument of justification for worthwhile activities in education', *Philosophy of education*, pp. 134–141. U.S.A. Philosophy of Education Society, 1968.
44. Stones, E., *An introduction to educational psychology*, p. 358. Methuen, 1966.
45. Troup, J. D. F., 'Health, physical fitness and posture', *Physical education,* vol. 54, no. 163, p. 79. Physical Education Association of G.B. and N. Ireland, November, 1962.
46. Wilson, J., Williams, N. and Sugarman, B., *Introduction to moral education*, Penguin, 1967.
47. Wilson, P. S., Book Review of Ref. 16 in *Education for teaching.* A.T.C.D.E., Autumn, 1968.

For a more recent treatment and development of the subject of this essay see:

Munrow, A. D., *Physical education – a discussion of principles*, Bell, 1972.

3

Enjoyment and Satisfaction in Physical Education*

Introduction

"The pursuit of happiness is an inalienable and self-evident right of man", so said Thomas Jefferson [7], at the Declaration of Independance Congress of the United States in 1776. Perhaps in tacit recognition of this right, we have seen an increasing emphasis on pupils' enjoyment and satisfaction in education and physical education.

In a survey, published in 1974, of 468 schools – presenting approximately a one in ten random sample of secondary schools in England and Wales, Kane [8] reported that a number of physical education teachers "suggest enjoyment and satisfaction as important objectives of physical education" and this was supported by: 'enjoyment of participation in physical activity' being ranked first; and 'satisfaction from success in physical activity' being ranked second in the list of *effects on pupils*, as observed and reported by their teachers. Kane describes this result as "somewhat unexpected", but notes that the teachers "were in strong agreement and felt very certain of their view".

Frith and Lobley [5] in 1971, opened their book on *Playground Games and Skills* with this statement, "Within the framework of the broad aims

* A revised edition of a paper first presented at the International Congress of Physical Education, Liege, Belgium in April, 1977 and published in the Congress Proceedings, pp. 385–391.

of education, the general aims of games in the primary school can be summarized as follows: enjoyment, exercise, the opportunity to acquire skill".

Perhaps, like me, you are uneasy about these frequent uses of 'enjoyment' as an educational objective? Too often one hears ill-prepared physical education lessons justified by the words, "but the children are enjoying it". In my view the use of this justification shows a great misunderstanding about the important role of **enjoyment** and **satisfaction** in the teaching-learning process which, if allowed to pass unchecked, could threaten the place of physical education in the school curriculum.

Of course, it is possible to claim that pleasure is the ultimate aim of *all* human activity. Neo-Hedonists like Dr. H. J. Campbell [3] tell us that, "all behaviour in animals, including man, springs from electrical activation of regions of the brain which have come to be called the pleasure areas".

If you believe this, you must consider his advice that, "We must recognise the sub-human and social futility of sensory pleasure-seeking activities (such as sport), and therefore cease to be involved with them to any significant degree, and cease to teach children that prowess in them has any human worth." He also says that, "Winning a sporting contest does not make a person a better man, only a more joyful animal". It seems that those who look to Hedonists for support for enjoyment and satisfaction as ultimate aims for physical education, may not be too happy with some of their views.

Some Definitions

Whether or not one agrees with Campbell's [3] findings on the location and functions of the pleasure areas of the brain, there should be little disagreement with the notion that enjoyment is an emotional response or state.

May I make it clear that I am thinking of 'enjoyment' as 'an *accompanying* pleasure response', whilst the term *satisfaction* is reserved for feelings of pleasure connected with the successful completion of an activity and, perhaps, the attainment of something which was particularly desired.

William Lillie [10] has outlined various conditions under which such 'pleasantness' seems to occur:

"1. As a normal quality of certain sensations and perceptions, such as the sensation of sweetness and the perception of beautiful objects.

2. As an accompaniment of any activity either bodily or mental; provided that the activity is not imposed on its agent from outside, or frustrated by the inability to perform it, or impeded by fatigue or some other impeding factor . . ..
3. As an accompaniment of the successful completion of an activity.
4. As an accompaniment of the attainment of a desire which is, of course, a special case of the successful completion of an activity, but which is such an important source of pleasantness that it is worth mentioning specially".

Using the terminology adopted in this essay, I would describe (1) and (2) as conditions of 'enjoyment', and (3) and (4) as conditions of 'satisfaction'.

Two other considerations: Dearden [4] warns that **satisfaction** can be false response and need not be present, even where it might be expected when something generally considered worthwhile has been achieved. Talking of **discovery,** for example, he writes: "such a connection between making a discovery and glows of satisfaction is purely contingent, since one could have all these feelings in the false belief that one had discovered something, and on the other hand one could really have discovered something, yet without feeling anything in particular about it". Later he adds, "The achievement implied by discovery is getting at the truth in some sought-for respect, and this is a matter independent of our pleasure or our pains".

From this we could conclude that the feeling of satisfaction does not give the achievement value: rather it is the value of the achievement, justified on other grounds, which decides how worthwhile is the satisfaction!

Skinner [19] also adds food for thought. In 1953 he noted, "When a man reports an event is pleasant, he may be merely reporting that it is the sort of event which reinforces him . . .. In any case the subject himself is *not* at an especially good point of vantage for making such observations. 'Subjective judgements' of the pleasantness or satisfaction provided by stimuli are usually unreliable and inconsistent". The whole doctrine of sub-conscious motivation would seem to support this latter point.

So far then we have a picture of enjoyment and satisfaction as emotional states or responses, linked – but not necessarily so – with activities and achievements: not giving automatic value to those activities and achievements: essentially transient states and responses, difficult to recognise even by those people most closely involved. We may ask again, "Can enjoyment and satisfaction serve as objectives for physical education?"

Educational Objectives

A great deal has been written elsewhere on aims and objectives in physical education, so I will confine myself to one or two key issues.

The first is to note that there can be many different types of objectives. Here I need only make a simple distinction between:

1. *Educational objectives*, which are seen as pupil-learning orientated, fairly immediate, well defined 'stepping stones' towards longer term, more general *educational aims*.
2. A broad group of *practical objectives* concerned, for example, with organisation, control, discipline, safety, etc., which teacher may establish and attain. These practical objectives may well be essential, but their attainment does not mean that anything of educational value has necessarily been acquired by the pupils.

Many of us have witnessed reasonably well organised, disciplined school periods during which children have participated in games with apparent enjoyment and the teacher has thus been content that he has taught a lesson of educational value to the children.

But has he? In my view 'an educational contribution' means that some progress has been made, however small, towards the general aims of physical education. It is not sufficient that such progress happens by chance, if at all. There are widely accepted and well substantiated aims of physical education in the domains of social, moral, aesthetic and cognitive education; in progress towards fitness and health, and the active use of recreative leisure time [1]. Lessons leading towards these aims entail knowledge, skills and attitudes to be attained by the pupil.

Other requirements of objectives are that they should be possible to attain and clearly stated. Clear statements of realisable objectives are recognised as essential for evaluation.

Some educationists have pushed these requirements to extremes. Advocates of the 'behavioural objectives approach' say that, "an objective is an intent communicated by a statement describing a proposed change in a learner – a statement of what the learner is to be like when he has successfully completed a learning experience". Mager [11].

Others, whilst acknowledging the clarity of intent which can be achieved in some domains of objectives – and striving for it as far as possible – also recognise that in some areas it may not be possible to be so clear cut. Also the links between immediate objectives and long term aims may be hard to establish and maintain.

Kenneth Richmond [17] has written, "Objectives are like targets.

The nearer they are the easier they are to hit. By taking thought, higher-order objectives are hittable, too, though not so reliably".

In light of these considerations, let us examine the possibility of using **enjoyment** as an educational objective.

We have already noted that enjoyment (and satisfaction) do not automatically confer 'worthwhileness' onto an activity (if you are still unconvinced you might consider the 'enjoyment' of the sadist). The validity of an educational objective must therefore be judged primarily on its contribution to educational aims.

Looking at problems of clarity, and progress evaluation, I would now go further and claim that no teacher can structure a lesson, let alone a full programme, to *make* all pupils in a class enjoy themselves. Enjoyment is too individual and too transient. Even in working towards pupil satisfaction – which is perhaps a more predictable response, we have seen that the response may not be evoked, and even where it is evoked on one occasion, the same event may not evoke the same 'satisfied' response on succeeding occasions.

Perhaps a small practical example may help to sum up some of my reservations about enjoyment as an objective. Imagine it is a coldish morning in early English June, a small boy has been told he is already to attempt his first full-length swim of a typical rural, unheated, outdoor swimming pool. He stands at the poolside, apprehensively; he enters the water and cold water shock catches his breath, a moment of fear?; he starts his swim, growing in confidence; "Well done, Jimmy, keep it up", calls the teacher, a moment of pride; he starts to tire and takes a mouthful of water, unease returns; more tired and the end of the pool still looks far away, in near panic he strikes out more desperately; finally, success, he reaches the end, his teacher praises and his classmates applaud, his emotions register relief and satisfaction.

I am not pretending these *are* the emotional responses which accompany a first one-length swim; indeed my point is how many such possibilities exist. The example only shows the variety of emotional response possible, in just one child, in a relatively short period of time and during a single activity within just one lesson.

Of all the possible emotions, possibly the satisfaction following the achievement is the most predictable, especially (as Lillie [10] remarked earlier) where the success is really desired by the child.

Krathwohl [9, 6] in talking of objectives in the affective domain has made 'satisfaction in response' the third and highest level of the 'responding' category in his 'Taxonomy of Educational Objectives'. He writes: "The category is arbitrarily placed at this point . . ." and "serves the pragmatic purpose of reminding us of the presence of the emotional component and its value in building affective behaviours".

Note that even in this work, satisfaction is not accepted as a true 'end' in its own right.

Perhaps by now enough has been said to make clear why there must be such large question marks against both the value and the practical possibilities of using enjoyment and satisfaction as educational objectives.

The Importance of Enjoyment and Satisfaction

Having exposed a widespread misconception, I must go on and stress the important role that 'enjoyment' and 'satisfaction' can have in the process of physical education.

Firstly, however, we must accept that learning can go on under conditions of pain, punishment, threat of failure in examinations, etc. Although the use of corporal punishment is reducing, teachers still control children and attempt to promote learning by threatening punishment. Skinner [20] remarks: "Education has not wholly abandoned the birch rod. In everyday contact we control through censure, snubbing, disapproval, or banishment". He goes on to say, "the suspicion has also arisen that punishment does not in fact do what it is supposed to do".

On the other hand there is abundant evidence that learning under conditions where enjoyment and satisfaction are the accompanying emotional states, is equally, if not more, effective. Such conditions are clearly more ethically defensible.

Achievement motivation [12] and level of aspiration theories [14, 18] or simply educational clichés like "Success breeds success", all acknowledge the great part that *achievement, linked* (though not solely so) *with satisfaction* can play in stimulating pupils to greater efforts of learning and performance.

Of course children can and do become involved in school activities without any great emotional response. Peters [15] points out that, "children do not have to be interested in something to learn it; it is often sufficient that they attend to it, for whatever reason. If they attend long enough, and if the teacher is skilled and imaginative, they become interested. The ability to *stimulate* interest is one of the greatest gifts of a teacher". Peel [13] has written of two levels of pupil involvement, firstly **task involvement**; and secondly, **ego-involvement**, in which the activity becomes self-relevant. He tells us that, "The feeling of success (satisfaction) can only be experienced by those who are involved. Moreover, ego-involvement is likely to permit greater feelings of satisfaction, and in turn greater feelings of satisfaction are likely to maintain and strengthen ego-involvement.

Peters [15] mentioned the teacher stimulating interest and raising motivational levels; this stimulation is partly *extrinsic* to the activity, at least in its initial stages. Randall and Waine [16] have stated that, "Physical activity involving skill progress produces its own (*intrinsic*) reward in a reinforcement of interest and an increasing satisfaction".

The teacher, extrinsically, both directly through praise, and indirectly through stimulating interest, can raise levels of potential enjoyment and satisfaction. These levels may also be raised, or added to, by enjoyable sensations (for example, muscular sensuousness) and intrinsic satisfactions (such as increased mastery) resulting from learning and performance of the physical activity itself. To sum up, enjoyment and satisfaction are ethically superior and virtually essential components of an *effective* teaching-learning atmosphere.

Other factors in establishing this 'atmosphere' will be *teacher variables* (such as knowledge, enthusiasm, instructional techniques, etc.); *pupil variables* (such as physical health, development, peer group attitudes, etc.); *task factors* (such as difficulty, physical demand, danger, etc.); and *situational factors* (such as facilities, equipment, weather, etc.).

Conclusion

In conclusion, therefore, may I repeat that to seek to justify physical education simply in terms of pupil enjoyment is to avoid the real question of what educational objectives should be pursued. In any case, it is probably impossible to teach for, and evaluate enjoyment as an objective, even where this is claimed to be only one of a list of educational objectives.

Pupil satisfaction is a more useable *teaching* objective provided that the achievements with which it is linked are valuable educationally.

The most important role of these accompanying emotional states is as part of *teaching method*, where they arise, are sought, and serve to stimulate learning and create an ethically sound and effective atmosphere in which pupils may learn.

References

1. Andrews, J. C., 'The curricular aims of physical education', *Philosophy of physical education conference report*, A.T.C.D.E. Physical Education Section, 1970.
2. Atkinson, J. W., *Motives in fantasy, action and society*. Van Nostrand, New York, 1958.

3. Campbell, H. J., 'Science and the pleasure-seekers', *The Sunday Telegraph*, p. 8. February 11, 1973.
4. Dearden, R. F., 'Instruction and learning by discovery', in Peters R. S. (ed.), *The concept of education*, pp. 141–2. Routledge & Kegan Paul, London, 1967.
5. Frith, J. R. and Lobley, R., *Playground games and skills*, p. 1. A. C. Black Ltd., London, 1971.
6. Hooper, R. (ed.) in *The curriculum: context, design and development*, p. 292. Open University Press, 1971.
7. Jefferson, T., Original draft for the American Declaration of Independence, 1776, in Cohen, J. M. and M. J. (eds.), *Penguin dictionary of quotations*, p. 204. London, 1960.
8. Kane, J. E., *Physical education in secondary schools*, p. 57. Macmillan, London, 1974.
9. Krathwohl, D. R., 'The taxonomy of educational objectives – its use in curriculum building' in Lindvall, C. M. (ed.), *Defining educational objectives*, p. 28. University of Pittsburgh Press, U.S.A., 1964.
10. Lillie, W., *An introduction to ethics* (3rd ed.), pp. 60–1. Methuen, University Paperback, London, 1971.
11. Mager, R. P., *Preparing instructional objectives*, p. 3. Fearon, California, U.S.A., 1962.
12. McClelland, D. C., Atkinson, J. W., Clark, R. A. and Lowell, E. L., *The achievement motive*, Appleton-Century-Crofts, New York, 1953.
13. Peel, E. A., *The psychological basis of education*, p. 74. Oliver and Boyd, Edinburgh, 1956.
14. *ibid.*, pp. 77–81.
15. Peters, R. S., *The concept of education*, p. 11. Routledge & Kegan Paul, London, 1967.
16. Randall, M. W. and Waine, W. K., *Objectives of the physical education lesson*, p. 84. G. Bell and Sons, London, 1955.
17. Richmond, W. K., *The school curriculum*, p. 185. Methuen, London, 1971.
18. Singer, R. N., *Motor learning and human performance* (2nd ed.), pp. 420–4. Macmillan, New York, 1975.
19. Skinner, B. F., *Science and human behaviour*, p. 82. Collier–Macmillan, London, 1953.
20. *ibid.*, p. 182.

4

Aspects of the Curricular Process in Primary School Physical Education*

Introduction

Brief general accounts of physical education in England are always difficult to give because education is not centrally directed. One finds variations from region to region, from school to school, and even from class to class within one school.

These variations are caused by differences in teachers' interests, by differences in teachers' initial training, and by the varied effects of a multitude of other constraints which influence the implementation of ideals and of theoretically planned physical education programmes. These constraints include, for example, time allocation to the subject, facilities available – both indoor and outdoor spaces plus swimming pools, etc. – the provision of specialised equipment, and finally, the attitudes and directives of Head Teachers who have a powerful voice in deciding what goes on in their schools.

This potential variety is both a strength and a weakness of our

* A revised version of a paper first presented at the International Congress on 'Physical education of children before puberty,' Gdansk, Poland, in May, 1974 and published in the Congress Proceedings, pp. 106–111.

educational system. In primary schools it has presented the chance for teachers with new ideas to develop them, but also the possibility of unchecked neglect of physical education in some cases.

It is necessary to establish this national background so that it is realised that what follows can only be a series of very broad generalisations which in some cases reflect personal opinion rather than accepted national policy or practice.

Elements in the Curricular Process

The process of physical education is seen as one of the major processes of education: an ongoing process throughout a person's life, not one which stops and restarts as children change from one institution to another (usually done on the basis of chronological age), or as they pass into a certain stage of development such as puberty. However, emphases within the different element of the curricular process do change at different stages and, as here we are concerned mainly with the pre-pubescent primary school child, any particular changes in emphasis for these children will be mentioned.

The curricular process is shown in Figure 4.1, as the interplay between the following elements:

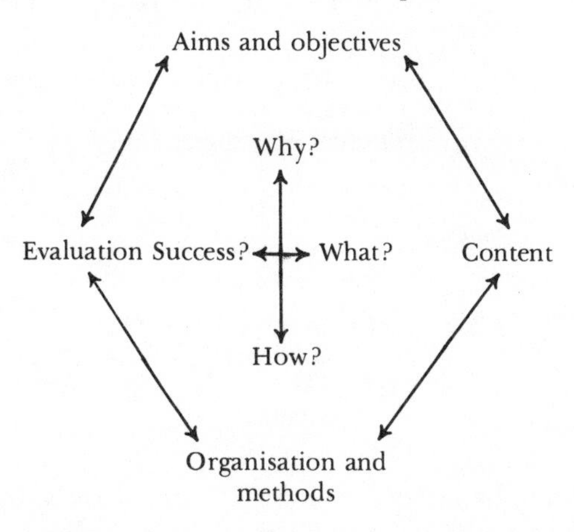

Fig. 4.1

For the remainder of this short essay it is intended to take each of these elements and expand it slightly, making brief comments where appropriate.

Aims and Objectives

In one of my previously published works [2], evidence of various kinds was examined to sort out the areas of educational value towards which physical education could have a tenable aim. The following six groups of aims were identified, each capable of useful sub-analysis in terms of knowledge, skills, attitudes and values. For example, having established a social aim one might then to advantage begin to enquire, "What social skills are necessary?" "What skills promote social acceptance?", or "What knowledge?" or "What attitudes and values must be promoted in order to work towards these social aims?"

SIX AREAS OF CURRICULAR AIM IN PHYSICAL EDUCATION

(a) COGNITIVE AIMS	the promotion of the 'know that' and 'know how' types. Early motor contributions to concept development. The promotion of 'self-knowledge' and the growth of 'self-identity'.
(b) SOCIAL AIMS	the development of social relationships: the 'self' in relation to others; socialisation and the social effects of participation in physical activities.
(c) MORAL AIMS	the development of moral behaviour in the contexts of physical education and from the content of physical education activities.
(d) AESTHETIC AIMS	the growth of aesthetic awareness, both as performer and spectator in physical education situations.
(e) FITNESS AIMS	the promotion of positive well-being beyond the level of absence of illness; concerned with total psycho-physical health.
(f) RECREATIONAL AIMS	preparation for the use of leisure time for active recreation.

Fig. 4.2

There appears to be fairly general (perhaps world wide?), acceptance of these underlying aims, although they are not always stated in these terms. In England, their pursuit is embodied in the content and in the teaching methods adopted. At primary school level there is little emphasis on regular programmed fitness training, and the teaching and coaching of specific recreative sporting skills has not yet really started although important attitudes and the bases of many of the necessary skills are laid down in this period. In some activities, for example – in swimming, considerable demands are made on young, talented performers, although this is not widespread and many teachers question the total effect of this 'dedication' and hard training on the young children involved.

There is an increasing interest amongst teachers in curricular planning and many are seeking more precision in establishing curricular objectives. Where applicable, these may be stated in behavioural terms, but we remain fairly flexible in our approach to establishing these, bearing in mind the advice of writers like Kenneth Richmond [8] who has said, "Like it or lump it, education is an activity which people engage in without being absolutely sure what it is they are trying to do. It is, therefore, a disservice to planning to pretend that routes leading to desired outcomes can be laid down in advance. It is an even greater disservice to pupils to disguise the fact that the learning process is hedged about with uncertainties, since living with uncertainty may well be reckoned the ultimate aim of education".

Content

Although so far the lack of central government control has been stressed, perhaps at this point one should mention the latest publication on physical education by Her Majesty's Stationery Office. It is entitled, *Movement – Physical Education in the Primary Years* [5] and was produced in 1972. Giving advice on content, it sets out its recommendations under six headings: Gymnastics, Dance, Games, Athletics, Water Sports and Outdoor Activities. These are indeed the major aspects of physical education programme content in the primary years (in fact of all our P.E. programmes).

Quoting from this, "We might say a child is moving gymnastically in his clambering, balancing, rolling, swinging, etc. In his trials of strength and skill lie the origins of athletics; whilst play associated with bats and balls, chasing and dodging, and the urge to out-play an opponent develops into games. Similarly water play develops into swimming. When feeling overflows into movement, when movement is used as a form of expression, or when it is indulged in for its rhythmical qualities, it assumes the nature of dance, whilst the springs of drama are found in impersonation, imitation and in the playing out of situation and relationships".

Outdoor activities, the sixth area, is seen to include walking, simple expeditions on foot, camping, boat work, riding, skating and skiing;

this latter activity usually requiring travel abroad although there are an increasing number of artificial ski slopes being used by school children.

Obviously it would be possible to spend a great deal of time expanding this area of content but it must suffice to note that the influence of Rudolf Von Laban's work has been very strongly felt in indoor work and there are moves to extend the use of 'movement' terminology to the teaching of games as well. Texts mentioned in the references (e.g. (1, 6, 7)), will provide a selection of further reading on different aspects of programme content.

Organisation and Methods

Time allocation

There is no longer in England any statutory amount of physical education laid down for schools. In a publication by the national Schools' Council *Physical Education 8 – 13* [9], the recommendation is made that, "Schools should aim at one period of P.E. per day or its equivalent. The weekly allocation can be blocked if longer games periods are required. The timetable should be sufficiently flexible to allow variations of time in good or bad weather".

The recommendation is similar to that put forward by the British Association of Organisers and Lecturers in Physical Education in its booklet, *Physical Education in Schools* [3]. Again one period a day is specified, allowing a working time of at least 30 minutes and it goes on to say, "Given good indoor facilities, the periods should be allocated as follows: gymnastics and dance (indoor) 3, games (outdoors) 1, swimming 1.

"It does not necessarily follow that this scheme should be adhered to rigidly through the year". Obviously at certain times athletics will become a feature of the programme, probably in the summer months.

Methods

Effective methods are partly related to the nature of the programme content and also to the personality of the teacher. Equal success can often be obtained by different teachers, using different methods. On the other hand there are some general features of modern methods which are worthy of comment. These are the emphasis on:

Challenge – the setting of tasks for the children which are realistic and realisable, with effort.

Clear Guidance – and feedback – when the teacher contributes it is from a basis of knowledge and observation; feedback is as precise and as immediate and individual as possible.

Great encouragement – given as individually and as specifically as possible so that the child knows he has done well and how close he is to even greater success.

Achievement and satisfaction – for both the child and the teacher, the methods should provide a 'diet' of success and satisfaction.

Enjoyment is quoted as an aim of physical education by some experts but (important as it doubtless is) in my opinion it is an aspect of method that it should be most seriously considered.

Psychological research tells us that children *can* learn under threat of punishment but evidence appears conclusive that children learn as well *if not better* under the stimulation of pleasure/enjoyment – and, more particularly, of satisfaction following achievement. This satisfaction, plus the pleasure which most children find in pure physical activity and in pleasing social relationships between pupils and between the teacher and pupils, produces a most effective learning atmosphere.

Percy Jones, the driving force behind the excellent gymnastics which some of you may have seem demonstrated by the British primary school team in Brussels last July, has written recently about improved class-teacher relationships [4]. He notes that "learning has become a more enjoyable experience because of the following factors:

1. The child is now allowed to develop as an individual
2. Frequent opportunities are provided for exercising choice.
3. The teacher recognises individual problems and that progress is an individual matter.
4. Stimulation and encouragement are more frequently given.
5. Coaching methods are more varied and effective.
6. There is an informal and pleasant atmosphere of purposeful endeavour.
7. A sense of achievement is more often experienced by each child.
8. Each pupil copes adequately with the situation in which he is placed.
9. Each child enjoys a sense of adequacy and security.
10. Each child is purposefully and actively employed.

11. Teachers are less detached and are more approachable".

This is a useful summary of modern pupil-teacher relationships.

Evaluation

This element has been left until last because at present it is perhaps the least developed aspect of the curricular process, certainly in primary schools. This is not to say that teachers are not continually evaluating their pupils' and their own progress in a subjective manner; but so far, the rigorous application of the tests and more scientific evaluation procedures have had little impact in English primary schools. The current trend towards the identification of behavioural objectives will doubtless lead to more careful consideration of the likely outcomes of the programme, and a greater awareness if they are not being achieved; but it seems doubtful, and in my view largely undesirable, that any amount of time and effort will be spent testing rather than teaching primary school children in the relatively limited time which is available.

References

1. Anderson, M. E., *Inventive movement*, W. R. Chambers, London, 1970.
2. Andrews, J. C., 'The curricular aims of physical education', The Philosophy of Physical Education Conference. *Report of A.T.C.D.E. Section*, September, 1970.
3. B.A.O.L.P.E., *Physical education in schools*, Methuen, London, 1970.
4. Bilbrough, A. and Jones, P., *Developing patterns in physical education*, University of London Press, 1973.
5. Dept. of Education and Science, *Movement – physical education in the primary years*, H.M.S.O., London, 1972.
6. Frith, J. R. and Lobley, R., *Playground games and skills*, A. C. Black, London, 1971.
7. Morrison, R., *A movement approach to educational gymnastics*, J. M. Dent & Sons, London, 1969.
8. Richmond, W. K., *The school curriculum*, Methuen & Co. Ltd., London, 1971.
9. Schools' Council Working Paper 47, *Physical education*, 8–13. Evans/Methuen Educational, London, 1971.

5

Evaluation in the Everyday Teaching of Physical Education*

Introduction

Curriculum theory is in grave danger of creating its own mystique, so cutting itself off from day-to-day work in schools, leaving the majority of practising teachers feeling that there is little connection between the models, and esoteric language of the theorists and the 'real world' of teaching in which they operate. This essay attempts to bridge what is, in some ways, an ever widening chasm.

Accepting that evaluation is a topic of enormous proportions and importance in curriculum theory, it is interesting to ask oneself: how much does the normal physical educationist, working full-time in a school, know about evaluation and actually engage in objective measurement?

To obtain a clearer but still subjective impression, one might pick up a standard North American text such as *A Practical Approach to Measurement in Physical Education* by Barrow and McGee [2], flick through its 600 pages, and ask oneself: how many teachers do I know who are

* A revised version of a paper first presented at the International Congress on Evaluation, held at the University of Jyvaskyla, Finland, in July, 1976 and first published in the *FIEP Bulletin*, vol. 46, no. 3, pp. 57–65. July-September, 1976.

using, in any way at all, any of the many excellent suggestions for more objective testing of the product and process of physical education, and for the classification and grading of pupils?

Despite the inclusion of study units entitled 'measurement and evaluation' (or something similar) in most teacher training courses, fairly widespread and long term personal observation would seem to suggest, that in Britain at least, such testing and measuring is quite often completely missing or simply interpreted as the awarding of marks – where forced to – and as the writing of periodic reports for parental consumption. Recently there has been a growth of testing in various skill and performance areas to grade children for externally instigated and validated certificates awarded by national governing bodies of sport. The Amateur Athletic Association's 'Five Star' award scheme is a typical example of one of these. Of course school standards and some local and national proficiency awards have been well used for many years. Some but by no means all teachers keep adequate written records of their pupils' performance and progress.

Perhaps this is unusual and the situation in Britain is very different from that in other countries. For example, in a discussion of technical aids to evaluating performance, Nixon and Jewett [12] report that in the United States, "Instant playback television is being used extensively as a teaching aid in physical education classes. Teachers are enthusiastic in their support of this assistance". One must ask: just how extensive is this 'extensive use?' and also wonder: how durable will be this new enthusiasm? Will instant playback portable television become a standard teaching aid for all specialist teachers of physical education, in all schools? Even if this happens in the U.S.A., will it be possible on a world-wide scale? It seems doubtful, at least in the foreseeable future.

Later in the same chapter, Nixon and Jewett [13] note: "The increasing application of technology to education has led many to express concern about the possibility of 'dehumanising' education". This is not yet a major problem in Britain.

For economic reasons alone the march of technology is likely to be slow and there is still a widely held belief that teaching is essentially a human activity; an art as much as science. As recently as 1971 Kenneth Richmond [15] wrote in a book on *The School Curriculum*, "Like it or lump it, education is an activity which people engage in without being absolutely sure what it is they are trying to do. What is more arid than an educational practice which found no place for inspired guesswork, for unexpected flair, or for acts of faith!".

But perhaps one can over-exaggerate the distance between theory and practice; between the introduction of new technology and its widespread application, and between the art and science of teaching. Certainly physical education teachers in Britain are engaged in almost continuous evaluation. To sort out how this can be so in face of the preceding observations, needs recourse to some basic definitions.

Definitions

The phrase, 'everyday teaching of physical education', will immediately conjure up the correct impression for many, but to avoid any possible misunderstanding, what is meant is the daily teaching of schoolchildren of primary and secondary school age in lessons within the timetable under the heading of physical education. In other words, it covers the full contribution of the physical educationist to the school curriculum – defined by Kerr [8] as, "all the learning which is planned and guided by the school, whether it is carried on in groups or individually, inside or outside the school".

It may also be necessary to mention that physical education is normally defined as a process (Andrews [1]) but the words are also commonly used to label subject courses, for example in teacher training colleges, or, as in this case, to name a subject area of the school timetable. As long as one is clear about such subsidiary uses, no confusion need arise.

The practising teacher will know only too well what is meant by day-to-day teaching. However, despite his training (the memories of which tend to fade more quickly and completely than many would admit), conceptual differences between testing, measuring, grading, assessment and evaluation are likely to be less clearly appreciated. Moreover all theories do not use the same words with quite the same meaning.

For the purpose of this discussion, *testing* is the application of a specific measuring device (a test), on a particular occasion or occasions. It is normally assumed that the person being tested knows of the test and is involved in some form of response.

Measurement is the means by which, as precise and objective as possible, data is obtained. Such data is most often quantitative and expressible in numerical form. It may then be treated by appropriate statistical procedures. Additionally, for example, where there is a panel of expert judges used, **qualitative factors** may also be measured. Morehouse and Stull [10] point out that measurement scales differ and that statisticians employ four major categories — nominal, ordinal, interval and ratio scales.

These they differentiate as follows:

1. Nominal Scales – in which it is possible to place the variable in a

discrete category only, for example, categorisation by sex or nationality.

2. Ordinal Scales – in which results can be set out along a given scale but no exact amounts of difference can be ascertained. For example, tests requiring a 'strongly disagree, disagree, agree, strongly agree' type of response fall into this category.
3. Interval Scales – in which there is a consistent interval on the scale but no true zero point; and finally,
4. Ratio Scales – in which intervals are the same throughout the scale and there is a true zero point. Distances and times, for example, can be measured in this way.

These differences are mentioned because Wheeler [16] in his book *Curriculum Process,* notes that "While it is relatively easy to measure a change in a student's height or weight or . . . in his speed of running or his strength of grip, both the process and the scale of measurement involved are quite different for most other behaviours with which the school is concerned". It is true that one can make ratio scale measurements of time, weight, height, strength and distance but physical educationists must beware of any assumption that this is their only sphere of interest. There are at least as many and no less important aspects of physical education which can only be approached through ordinal measures, or perhaps cannot yet be measured at all.

Moving on to consider 'evaluation', Helen Eckert [3] in a book devoted to *Practical Measurement of Physical Performance,* writes, "Testing is a pointless exercise unless evaluation and the use of the test scores that have been collected also occur". Evaluation is thus seen to be the process which gives real point and meaning to testing and measurement and to the data collected.

A simple definition by Wheeler 1967 [17] is that adopted for the remainder of this paper: "Evaluation, then, involves judgement with respect to some criteria". Some years later [19] he went on to write: "Evaluation is the process of coming to conclusions about the educational enterprise. While it may be considered under numerous headings and may be seen to serve diverse purposes or ends, it is neither measurement nor assessment . . .. It is judgement with respect to explicit criteria". To complete this brief series of definitions, the term 'assessment' will be reserved for the process of investigating the status of an individual or group with respect to intended curricular outcomes. This investigation may include measurement and result in the ranking (grading) of individuals with respect to what they can do, or know, others in the group, or more widespread norms.

Evaluation, as defined, pervades the entire curricular process and teachers of physical education, whether involved in objective testing or not, must be continually involved in evaluation, albeit in an informal, unstructured and perhaps almost sub-conscious manner. It is this evaluation which is universal and it is the quality of this evaluation which must be improved if any widespread long term progress is to be made.

Evaluation in the Curricular Process

There are now many quite sophisticated models of the curriculum process available, but for the practising teacher it will often suffice to increase his awareness of the different elements of the process and their interdependence. A start can be made by introducing a simple design distinguishing four elements: aims and objectives, content, organisation and methods, and evaluation.

Elements in the Curriculum Process
(after Tyler)

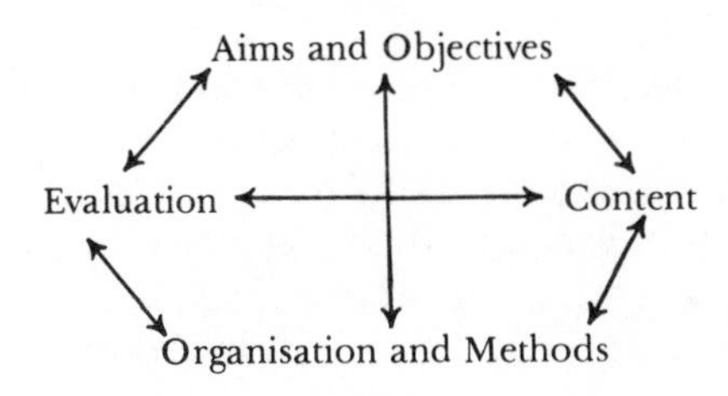

Fig. 5.1

From the particular point of view of emphasising the scope of evaluation, this is better than the equally common circular model of the curriculum process shown in Figure 5.2, put forward by Wheeler [18] in 1967.

Although this model adds some further valuable ideas such as the possible existence of an intervening stage between objectives and content selection – the stage of deciding on what learning experiences are required before rushing to decide content–from an evaluation point of view it could perhaps suggest to the unwary that evaluation only takes place at phase 5, which, even if it is then applied to all preceding phases, could be seen to be too long delayed – concerned only with changing objectives if necessary and so restarting the cycle. As has been emphasised already, evaluation is best considered as an on-going, all pervading process, judgements needing to be made at and about every stage of the curriculum process.

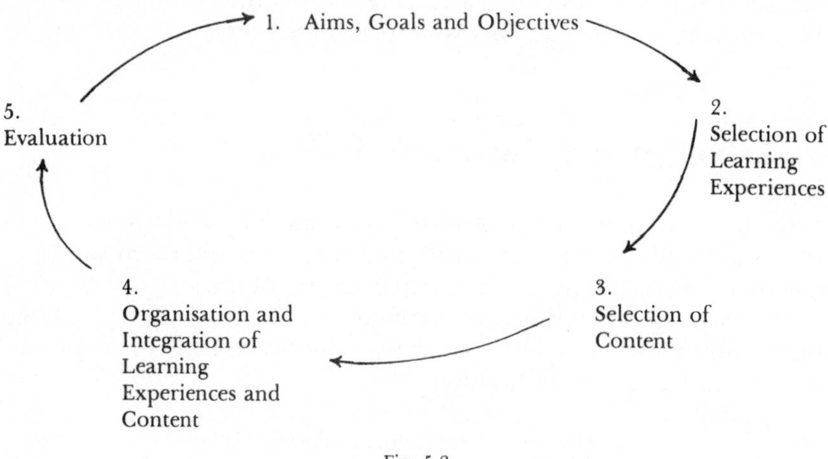

Fig. 5.2

If one can encourage the practising teacher to think more often and more clearly about these different elements, and accept that he or she has a series of value judgements to make – and, if necessary defend, then the results should greatly enhance the conception and implementation of his physical education programme.

Some physical educationists have been heard to complain about the constant need to justify their work. In fact this stimulation is both necessary and beneficial: it makes one constantly examine and restate the case – exposing, sometimes painfully – the bases, facts, dogmas, and value judgements on which daily employment depends.

Accepting that evaluation 'involves judgement in respect to some criteria', then the building, refinement and strengthening of these criteria are of fundamental importance to the process. On the quality of the implicit and explicit criteria used, will ultimately depend the quality of the evaluation and the day-to-day practice which results.

To narrow the discussion it is proposed to comment on just four aspects of the teacher's work.

Evaluating Pupils and their Progress

Various diagnostic tests have been created to help the teacher take a more individual and personal look at the many children he meets each working day. Seven periods a day, each having about 30 children per period, gives a total of over 200 a day, in 'unstreamed' groups, and this would not be an excessive estimate in many British schools.

The sorting out of this situation in practice is normally achieved, not through the application of aptitude and ability tests but by on-the-spot decisions made in the gymnasium or on the games field. Height or perhaps general physique may be used to fix apparatus groups or games teams; children's friendships may decide partners and team choices; expressed interests may be taken into account where choice is possible, or diversity of activity is necessary in order to cope with numbers; quite arbitrary initial groupings are then modified as children begin to react and progress differently.

The keys to the success of this apparently haphazard process are the knowledge and experience of the teacher. These are often founded in the 'apprenticeship' situation during teacher training, where school practice is organised under the critical but helpful eye of a college tutor.

Many teachers who have tried to use diagnostic tests have abandoned them after a short while because of the amount of time involved, because of the rigorous test conditions which have to be created if tests are to be valid, objective and reliable; and the feeling, emanating from both the pupils and their own consciences, that physical education time is short and precious and the administration of such tests – important as they may be – is not the most attention-holding and valuable use of the limited time available.

Before one rushes to criticise this picture, and it is wide open to criticism by anyone with a tidy, analytical scientific approach, one should stop and ask if, in the final analysis, a more rigorously test-controlled physical education programme would be significantly more successful.

The evaluation of pupils' progress can be improved in two simple ways without increasing the work-load of the physical educationist, who, according to a recent survey by Kane [7] already puts in on average an additional eight hours of unpaid extra-curricular service each week.

The first of these is to move away from the somewhat dull, onerous task of producing summative end of term or year marks, towards a system of more continuous formative and summative assessment. Whenever progress is achieved, this is recorded – the steps forward being noted by teacher and pupil alike. This need not take much time and it moves evaluation out of the examination atmosphere, into the day-to-day life of children and teachers alike.

The second recommendation is linked with the first, in that continuous assessment necessitates some sort of pupil record system. This should contain, for example, personal information, a photograph, records of interests and achievements (in and out of school time) and progress made in curricular activities. Rather than looking to produce a national, all-purpose record card, which will not fit the many different teaching situations, each school P.E. staff should design its own, its accuracy and updating should be the joint responsibility of the teachers and children. Where the system of physical education is heavily centralised, then a recommended format could be issued, capable of being locally modified.

The aim should be to produce a card which can be quickly and accurately completed without a lot of written comment; one which children can fill in themselves for eventual checking and additions, where necessary, by the teacher. The design, content and use of such records should be part of every college measurement and evaluation course and head-teachers, parents and visiting officials should be able to see such records.

Evaluation as Learning Feedback

Evaluation plays an important role in promoting learning. According to Wilhelms [20] "the test of an evaluation system is simply this: does it deliver the feedback that is needed, when it is needed, to the persons or groups who need it?"

Physical education is fortunate in that it can utilise accurate (ratio) measurement. Provision for this can be made without the outlay of vast sums of money. What is needed is extra effort by groundstaff and more attention to detail by equipment manufacturers and designers of physical education facilities. For example, as well as height calibration on high jump and pole vault stands, there should be distance measures built into every long jump and triple jump pit; all throwing areas in field athletics should be marked to give an instant and fairly accurate read off of the result of each throw, without recourse to tape measuring; running tracks and swimming pools should all have appropriately sized and calibrated clocks, so placed that performers can check their times at a glance. School standards, qualifying distances, regional and national records, etc. can be marked – so contributing to better on-going evaluation of attainment and progress by teachers and pupils alike.

In addition to such quantitative measures, the pupil needs the teacher's evaluation of style, effort, progress, technical improvements needed, and attainment. The more precise this feedback can be, the more immediate, the more it stresses the key points and is given in language appropriate to the particular child – the more effective it will be.

Again the criteria against which such evaluations are made will only be formed by thorough training, experience and forethought. Practising teachers need to be continually reminded of the importance of improving this aspect of their teaching. Evaluation as an aid, rather than a process of sitting in judgement on pupils, should be the prevailing atmosphere.

Self-evaluation and Motivation

Just as the basic idea underlying this essay is to improve the teachers' self-evaluations and other critical judgements, so too must pupils' self-evaluations be stimulated. The practical proposals already made will also serve to guide pupils' self-evaluation. Similarly the use of pre-specified lesson objectives, dealt with later, will also help.

Wilhelms [21] tells us that, "Much of the real evaluation, too often unnoticed, goes on within the individual pupil .... It can lead him forward to precisely calibrated learning efforts on an ever-broadening front . . . or it can strain and distort him, narrow his vision and purpose, and bring him little but a sense of defeat".

Aiding pupils' self-evaluation is at the very heart of education and the feeling here is that real help for children will come, not from exposure to an ever increasing battery of objective tests, but from the increased awareness amongst teachers of the need for care in evaluation of individuals and even greater sensitivity in communicating their evaluations to children.

The Pre-selection and Communication of Objectives

In a short essay it is impossible to go into the arguments for and against the behavioural objectives approach to programme planning. Perhaps one may accept, however, Hirst's [5] point that, "There can be no curriculum without educational objectives. Unless there is some point to planning the activities, some intended educational outcome, however, vague this might be, there is no such thing as a curriculum".

Certainly not all valuable objectives can be stated in behavioural, measurable terms. Audrey and Howard Nichols [11] in a practical guide to *Developing a Curriculum* underline "the futility of introducing new courses based on a wide range of objectives and then examining only a limited number . . .". What can come from this on-going discussion to benefit the practising teacher? If one turns to research such as that done by Merrill [9] on the 'Effects of the Availability of Objectives and/or Rules on the Learning Process', it seems that having clear objectives, known to the participants, did have "orienting and organising effects, which dispose students to attend to, and organise relevant information and thus facilitate performance on criterion-test items constructed in accordance with the objectives".

It also seems reasonable that in stating more precisely lesson objectives, the teacher will need to do some thoughtful preparation – never an easy thing in day-to-day teaching, where one can get too deeply immersed in the daily round of class organisation, instruction, equipment problems and the thousand and one other aspects of the teacher's role. It may even serve to move these more fundamental thoughts up the list of priorities. Where objectives are communicated to pupils and become their objectives, then a great step forward has been made in the teaching/learning process, even if performance does not yet match intention.

Where behavioural outcomes can be built into statements of objectives (for example, where the desired outcome is for each child to swim a certain distance, inside a certain time, using a certain stroke) then evaluation is relatively straightforward. However as Hogben [6] says, "If we wish to assess and evaluate beyond this, different models are needed; models that will tolerate less specific objectives, and which will deliberately cater for student achievement (and reward) at different levels and in diverse directions. This is not a plea for the outright rejection of clear statements of intention in favour of vague, grand-sounding educational goals. Rather it is a plea for more flexibility . . .".

Concluding Remarks

To sum up, this essay has sought to point to ways of improving the evaluation which is already present in all schools – that going on within each teacher and child.

It is not the intention to criticise the development and introduction of specific tests and measures; indeed, much valuable work remains to introduce more valid, reliable and objective tests (vital for research) in many areas of physical education. The point is that so far very few such tests seem to be in general use in schools. Is this likely to change?

In 1971 Harlen [4] wrote, "Information has to be gathered economically; the luxury of tests which take a long time to prepare or administer, however thorough they may be, can not be afforded". The problem of introducing more objective testing without further reducing precious teaching and pupil practice time is highlighted in the 1971 Schools' Council Survey on *Physical Education in Secondary Schools* (Kane [7]), which confirmed that average class time for physical education in Britain is now only about two to two-and-a-half hours per week, depending on the age of the children and the type of school. Of course shortage of time may not be such a problem in some other countries. Przeweda [14] reported in the April, 1976 issue of the *FIEP Bulletin* that, "time given to motor activities organized at school is expected to increase to at least six hours per week" in Poland.

Taking a realistic view, the most productive way of improving day-to-day evaluation by practising teachers seems to be, at least in the short term, to make a strenuous effort to make teachers more conscious of where their value judgements are (or should be) involved and to help them make even more explicit, the criteria against which such judgements are made.

In times of great change, teacher training institutions must continue to provide a sound basis for each new generation of teachers to build the background of values, which will ultimately decide the quality of evaluation and everyday teaching. Seen in these terms, improved evaluation is as much in the hands of philosophy as of science.

References

1. Andrews, J. C., 'Physical education and education'. B.A.O.L.P.E. *Bulletin of physical education*, vol. 8, no. 3, pp. 21–27, July, 1970.
2. Barrow, H. M. and McGee, R., *A practical approach to measurement in physical education*, 2nd ed. Lea & Febiger, Philadelphia, 1971.
3. Eckert, H. M., *Practical measurement of physical performance*, p. 21. Lea & Febiger, Philadelphia, 1974.
4. Harlen, W., 'Some practical points in favour of curriculum evaluation', *Journal of curriculum studies* **3**, 1969 p. 131.
5. Hirst, P. H., 'The contribution of philosophy to the study of the curriculum'; in Kerr, J. F. (ed.), *Changing the curriculum*, p. 41. University of London Press, 1968.
6. Hogben, D., 'The behavioural objectives approach: some problems and dangers', *Journal of curriculum studies,* **4**, p. 47. 1972.
7. Kane, J. E., *Physical education in secondary schools*. Macmillan, London. 1974.
8. Kerr, J. F., 'The problem of curriculum reform', in Kerr, J. F. (ed.), *Changing the curriculum,* p. 16. University of London Press 1968.
9. Merrill, P. F., 'Effects of the availability of objectives and/or rules on the learning process', *Journal of educational psychology*, vol. 66, no. 4, pp. 534–539.
10. Morehouse, C. A. and Stull, G. A., *Statistical principles and procedures with applications for physical education*, pp. 10–11. Lea & Febiger, Philadelphia 1975.
11. Nichols, A. and Nichols, S. H., *Developing a curriculum*, p. 84. Allen & Unwin, London, 1972.
12. Nixon, H. E. and Jewett, A. E., *An introduction to physical education,* 8th ed., p. 264. Saunders Philadelphia, 1974.
13. *ibid.*, p. 266.

14. Przeweda, R., 'A vision of physical education in Poland', *FIEP Bulletin*, vol. 46, no. 1, p. 13. 1976.
15. Richmond, W. K., *The school curriculum*, p. 185. Methuen, London, 1971.
16. Wheeler, D. K., *Curriculum process*, p. 268. University of London Press, 1967.
17. *ibid.*, 268.
18. *ibid.*, 31.
19. Wheeler, D. K., 'Curriculum concepts and conceptual clarity', *Journal of curriculum studies*, vol. 6, no. 2, p. 113. 1974.
20. Wilhelms, F. T., 'Evaluation as feedback', in Hooper, R., (ed.), *The Curriculum: context, design and development*, p. 323. Oliver & Boyd, Edinburgh, 1971.
21. *ibid.*, 321.

6

A Terminology for Curriculum Change*

In a 1970 Schools' Council publication the United Kingdom Secretary of State for Education and Science, Edward Short [10], assured us that "Our system of education is geared to constant review and renewal". This may be thought to suggest that there exists a steady, planned and rational approach to curriculum change. However, in 1968, Maclure [6], reporting on an international conference, also organised by the Schools' Council, described a seminar dealing with Rational Planning in the Curriculum which was "periodically airborne in as many different directions as there were participants", and when it wasn't airborne, "theoretical discussions tended to get bogged down in terminology and definitions". Woodring [12], introducing an American book on *New Curricula* writes, "Changes in the schools do not proceed at a steady pace. Educational reform, like all social reform, comes in waves, with long periods between the waves in which reforms are re-examined, re-evaluated, and sometimes modified or rejected". Hoyle [2], talks about "the rational planning implied in the term development" and also "the relatively unplanned and adaptive 'drift' which has characterised so much curriculum change in the past".

Is education in Britain geared to review and renewal? What is meant by 'review and renewal' in the Minister's statement? Could it be that constant review and renewal is a purely British attribute and that

* A revised version of a paper first published in India in *Naya shikshak/Teacher today*, vol. 17, no. 3, pp. 12–17. January-March, 1975.

'waves of reform' only sweep North America? How valid is Hoyle's distinction between 'development' and 'drift?' How much of the curriculum which actually exists in many schools has evolved as a chance result of interplay between planned development and drift over a long period? Have the problems of terminology encountered in the Rational Planning Seminar been solved since 1967?

Language is primarily a means for communication, and there is a danger in getting "bogged down in terminology and definitions" and hence communicating nothing. No doubt Mr. Short would claim his words were being examined too closely, and would wish to qualify them, if one challenges seriously his implication that there exists an integrated 'cog' in the educational system of this country, which has some kind of fixed relationship with the whole, and which maintains review and renewal procedures as constant features. On the other hand, the discussion of curriculum change seems laden with words which are used loosely to mean the same thing – often, one feels – because the speaker or writer has an inbuilt belief that to use the same word twice in a sentence is to employ 'bad English'. This essay attempts to build a personal rationale by which to regulate the use of the many terms which are, or could be, employed in such a discussion.

As a point of departure one may examine the words used on the first page of Kerr's [4] book, *Changing the Curriculum.* Here he writes of 'curricular renewal', 'rate of change', 'fundamental developments', 'reform', 'persuasive innovators', 'real progress', 'curriculum making', and 'modifications to the curriculum'. If one adds to these from other sources [13] the words 'review', 'restructuring,' 'renovation', 'deterioration', 'revolution and drift', then the vocabulary is not yet exhausted but one is beginning to build up a list of at least some of the words in current use.

One of the many problems in sorting out in which context these words are best employed, is that encountered in much of curriculum theory, namely that most of the literature is of North American origin. At the international conference already mentioned, Maclure [7] comments that the North American party "included among their number distinguished professors of education who had grown up in a tradition in which it was respectable and important to discuss curricular matters in theoretical terms. They came armed with a language in which to do it. They were 'ready and eager to conceptualise where the English were only prepared to follow their noses". Later he says, "the English retain a perverse proprietary attitude to the English language. They are prepared to tolerate the Americans using it if they must, but on points of meaning they find it remarkably difficult to accept North American usage as having the same validity as their own" [8].

It is with this in mind that one has to examine the language of curricular change, so it is pleasing to be able to start from a point of apparent international agreement – at least between two books published in the same year on different sides of the Atlantic – on what constitutes the curriculum. Kerr [5] puts forward a modified version of a definition by two Americans, Herrick and Tyler [1]. The curriculum is "all the learning which is planned and guided by the school, whether it is carried on in groups or individually, inside or outside the school". This is very similar to that given by Thomas, Sands and Brubaker [11]. Their definition of the curriculum being, "all the intended learning goals, experiences, teaching materials and evaluation techniques which educators plan and/or use". It is this wide view of the curriculum which is adopted for this discussion of the terminology of curriculum change.

The term *curriculum change* is selected as that which can encompass all other terms to be discussed. It can cover alterations for either better or worse, it has no speed connotations, it can involve quantitive differences or even the complete substitution of one curriculum for another. Hoyle [2] uses it and relates it to its wider context: "Curriculum change is a variety of educational change which, in turn, is one form of social change".

Let us examine some of these terms. Mr. Short wrote "constant review". A **review** generally entails a restrospective survey of what has happened previously or an inspection of the situation at present. In **curriculum change,** a review can take place at any point but it is more likely to take place at certain times; for example, at the end of a term, a school year, or under the stimulus of an inspection. It has much in common with what is often called 'evaluation' in curriculum theory. A number of review points are normally included in the curriculum process. It is possible to have 'constant review' in theory but in practice this tends not to occur.

Progress is seen as the advancement of the curriculum. This can be simply the achievement of successive stages in a curriculum, with little overall change in what is being done from year to year. Perhaps the best term for any change related to this type of curriculum progress is 'maintenance'. This entails keeping the curriculum serviced and in working order, preserving what has been done in the past and repeating it in the future. If this is not done then the curriculum will retrogress. Deterioration (in general), depreciation (loss of value) and degeneration (falling away from former high standards) are all forms of retrogressive change which can afflict the curriculum.

When a curriculum is deteriorating, a change is required which might best be described as *reform.* Although in some ways reform means simply to change for the better, in common parlance some thing requiring reform is thought of usually as being bad in some way. For this reason, in this account, 'reform' is reserved to describe the rescue operation; the return to former high standards. Thinking for a moment, using a property analogy, a number of words are used to describe returning something to its former glory; 'rebuilding', if partial or total collapse has taken place, 'repairing' or 'restoring', 'renewal' or 'renovation'; all these words imply a process of making something **as new** again. For this reason, in curriculum discussion, all these terms are perhaps best used to describe aspects of reform following retrogressive change.

There are occasions in curriculum change when a satisfactory curriculum may be changed, it is hoped, for a better one. All changes for the better could be termed *improvements* and even changes from less-than-satisfactory states. Reforms are part of a continuum of improvement. If one accepts that normally curriculum planners are not going to set out to make a curriculum worse (although this may be the final result), then these types of changes for the better can be termed 'planned improvements'; or better, 'planned developments'. The word 'development' is preferred because it has stronger associations with bringing out the latent potential, strengthening, expanding and elaborating processes, which many planners would feel very much in line with their aims.

The least drastic of possible developments on the progress/improvement scale is that of curriculum modification. Here changes are slight, for example, a change in the amount of material included in a curriculum or a change to a more frequent feedback of comments to pupils whilst teaching.

Beyond this stage more apparent changes may be made by degrees of restructuring. This involves changing the relationship between parts of a curriculum and changing the emphasis between and within parts. In as much as 'restructuring' means that something new is formed, this is a form of innovation. However, it is only when new aims, content, methods, etc., are introduced hand-in-hand with restructuring that the degree of innovation becomes greater. This is why, where a different structure is imposed on a curriculum without the introduction of any new factors, the degree of innovation is often more apparent than real.

Occasionally one hears of revolutionary changes in curriculum taking place. Here the changes are usually drastic, thorough and complete. What follows sets out to be fundamentally different from what went on before. Revolution could be said to lead to total innovation. This may follow from a start in 'planned development' but the nature of revolution is such that it comes as easily, if not more so, as a reaction following severe deterioration.

Finally, one comes to two rather difficult terms – 'drift' and 'evolution'. 'Drift' in curricular terms, would appear to describe rather aimless curriculum change, some maintenance being effected but the overall direction being largely determined by numerous external forces. For this reason it is seen as often contrary to planned development and likely to lead to deterioration rather than improvement. In its wanderings it may occasionally be that considerable improvements are obtained, but more by chance than good judgement.

Curriculum evolution is seen, lastly, as the long term aspect of change; the cumulative change in curricula occurring through long series of curriculum changes. For example, it could be in terms of curriculum evolution that one might consider the differences between the curriculum offered to a ten year old child in Britain today and that offered, for instance, to a child of ten, one hundred years ago.

It is highly unlikely that the usage recommended here will meet with general agreement, particularly in view of international semantic differences, but it is interesting to note that it is possible to draw what appear to be fairly logical distinctions between how these terms could be used. It seems that the largest number of terms applying to approximately the same operation are those concerned with reform. Other words could relate to quite different types of curriculum change.

A delightful picture is conjured up by Maclure [9] who writes, "the group struggled to sort out its conceptual small change". This article represents a simple attempt to sort out the coinage of words associated with change in the curriculum.

References

1. Herrick, V. E. and Tyler, R. W. (eds.) *Towards improved curriculum theory*, p. 59. Chicago University Press, 1950.
2. Hoyle, E., 'How does the curriculum change'?, *Journal of curriculum studies*, vol. 1, no. 2, 1969 p. 132.
3. *ibid.*, p. 132.
4. Kerr, J. F., *Changing the curriculum,* p. 7. University of London Press, 1968.
5. *ibid.*, p. 16.
6. Maclure, J. S. (ed.), *Curriculum innovation in practice,* p. 11. H.M.S.O., 1968.
7. *ibid.*, p. 4.
8. *ibid.*, p. 9.
9. *ibid.*, p. 71.
10. Short, The Rt. Hon. E., 'A question of quality. School and Innovation 1870–1970', Supplement to *Dialogue*, p. 2, the Schools' Council Newsletter, February, 1970.

11. Thomas, R. M., Sands, L. B. and Brubaker, D. L., *Strategies for curriculum change*, p. 6. International Textbook Co., 1968.
12. Woodring, P., 'Introduction in Health', R. W. (ed.) *New curricula*, p. 2. Harper Row, 1964.
13. Note – In making a rapid survey of the range of terms used to describe curriculum changes, three books were examined in addition to those quoted above.

(a) Schools' Council, *The new curriculum*, H.M.S.O., 1967. A collection of extracts from many previous Schools' Council publications on the subject.
(b) Rosenbloom, P. C. (ed.) in *Modern viewpoints in the curriculum*, McGraw-Hill, 1964, Contributions by 31 Authors.
(c) Martin, W. T. and Pinck, D. C. (eds.), in *Curriculum improvement and innovation*. Robert Bantly Inc., 1966. Contributions by 32 authors.

SECTION 2

Socio-Psychological Aspects of Physical Education

7

Motor Learning Theory and the Practice of Teaching *

Introduction

The problems of relating *theory* and *practice* are not new, nor do they exist exclusively between motor learning theory and its applications in teaching, but unless educationists are prepared to accept that a gap can, and in many cases *does* exist between theory and practice, then little progress is likely to be made towards more effective teaching and learning.

Loretta Stallings [19] comments in the preface to her book *Motor Skills: Development and Learning* (1973) that "many theories and concepts are now available which, if made the subject of systematic study, can contribute to the improvement of instruction. Unfortunately, progress along the continuum from advances in knowledge to educational practice is not automatic". She has produced her book "to help to bridge this gap by providing the practitioner in the field with selected concepts of skill development and a framework for their systematic application in practice".

The problem is not only one for the practitioner. Robert Wilberg [23], addressing the 3rd World Congress on Sports Psychology in

* A revised version of an opening address first given at the International Congress on Psycho-Motor Learning at the Free University of Brussels, Belgium, in November, 1976 and first published in the *FIEP Bulletin*, vol. 46, no. 4, pp. 39–46. October-December, 1976.

Madrid in 1973, outlined the problems faced by physical educationists who have become involved in research topics such as memory, personality and psycholinguistics. He stressed the increasing specialisation necessary even *within* sub-areas of the field of motor learning, and said that whilst he might feel competent to evaluate research in the sub-area which he defines as 'human performance', he admitted, "I am completely out of my depth in the other three areas of socio-cultural psychology, psychological growth and development, and sport psychology".

If Dr. Wilberg has such problems, the inexperienced student-teacher is even more likely to encounter difficulties. De Cecco [7] points out that, "If the student wants to pursue the madness of asking how we should conduct instruction ..., he soon finds himself pursuing the basic research even though his chief interests are more practical than theoretical".

Cratty [6] describes the gap as one 'between people': perhaps contrasting two types more starkly than one would normally meet them in everyday life. He tells us that, "The thoroughly rehearsed practitioner armed only with tricks, teaching methods and skills is usually less ready to cope with new theories, nor can he explain the rationale for what he is doing". On the other hand, "The 'pure' theoretician may often be handicapped but in a different way. He may know *why* he should do something, be able to handle the jargon or to construct philosophical outcomes, but be unable to cope with the real world of children movement and objectives".

Let us look in a little more detail at some of the problems and perhaps suggest at least a few ways in which we can try to overcome them; both individually and as a profession.

Different Theoretical Orientations

In a thought-provoking article published in the July, 1974 *Bulletin of Physical Education*, Eric Saunders [14] put forward the view that *theory* and *practice* are seen in different ways by different groups of people within physical education. He picks out three archetypes "in which the characteristics of one are deliberately contrasted with characteristics of the others". The teacher or practitioner he calls Practicus, the teacher trainer, Academicus and the researcher, Empiricus.

Practicus has developed his theory by acquaintance with children, knowledge that has not come by detached observation and theorising alone, but by direct handling of groups of children in the swimming pool, on the field, in the dance studio, or in other activity settings. He tends to regard new ideas as impractical and be reluctant to change. Practicus also has a firm conviction that experience is the cornerstone of informed practice so that he has a tendency to regard what he does as natural and common sense.

Academicus is usually found in colleges or in universities, and spends part of his working life training teachers. He usually stresses the way Practicus should act in educational settings and bases his theories upon some notion of what constitutes good educational practice .... His theories are not grounded in practice .... However, Academicus can offer useful strategies to solve many of the problems encountered in school, although it is common knowledge amongst practitioners that every teaching problem may present a unique situation to be worked out on the spot by each individual teacher.

Finally, Empiricus usually works in colleges and universities and unlike Practicus he is more comfortable when making detached observations, than in debating or recommending courses of action. He attempts to be objective and *value free* in his analysis ... and often irritates and confuses the practical person by an excessive use of jargon. Furthermore, it can be argued that in reality the analysis of teaching behaviour must take place in natural rather than laboratory situations, so that the problematic nature of effective teaching can be appreciated. These factors are often overlooked by Empiricus so that he fails to indicate that the perspective of his own single discipline is an inadequate basis from which to solve any type of practical problem.

Implications

Ignoring for a moment the latter comments about the multi-factorial and interdisciplinary problems of research into teaching, let us concentrate on some implications of recognising that these types exist, at least in part; and on some suggestions for improving relationships between them.

The first is to 'recognise yourself'. (How many of you, I wonder, were considering your own position as I sketched in the types?)

The second is to accept that *all* these theoretical standpoints have value and can be complementary to each other. The inter-dependence of the types needs to be emphasised rather than the differences.

The third implication is for a more systematic assessment of the particular contributions that each can make – and also of the dangers inherent in too rigid adherence to one perspective only – and then for an attempt to be made to fuse the best from each.

The fourth is to accept that very different personalities may be better suited to and may seek to work in different roles. This acceptance has further far-reaching implications: for example, for the type of students we attract and accept into initial training courses; for different kinds of course; for the content options within, and routes through courses, and the final qualifications offered in physical education; and for the positions which are created in colleges and universities and the kinds of people who are appointed to fill them.

From this it is also clear that where there is to be a marked change of position or role for an individual, then some retraining may well be necessary.

Finally, now more than ever before, there is a need for the emergence and recognition of a fourth type – one who can bridge the gaps between Practicus, Academicus and Empiricus – who can be an acceptable colleague to all three and can help to translate and communicate between them. Following Saunders' terminology we might call him Pracapiricus.

The first major point is, therefore, that the gaps will remain, and perhaps even grow, unless in the future we look very carefully at *the people* who are to work in physical education. This will mean looking at our criteria for student entry into physical education studies, continuing to fight for the acceptance by the authorities that the background studies necessary for improved physical education are academically demanding and needful of high quality research in college and university settings; and, ensuring that more examples of the hybrid type 'Pracapiricus' are given the chance to flower, particularly in the teacher training situation. It is here, in my view, that people with good practical experience and expertise must work alongside the researchers. There should be the possibility of early retraining when they are appointed and there must be time allowed for them to perform their vital tasks of translation and communication.

Problems Within Theory

So far, theory has been treated as if it is a unified whole but, as we are well aware, 'theorising' is a more precise process – or it can be – than simply 'talking about rather than doing' – which is how some people see it; even some of our colleagues. There are problems within the theory area itself.

To theorise there is obviously a need for **'definition of terms'** and the creation of basic frameworks in order to classify known and assumed information. We can then make inferences, we can generalise from related observations, we may put forward hypotheses and test them, so moving into the realms of research. We can attempt to predict. We can develop models which show causal relationships and, eventually, large over-arching theories can be constructed which have attendant sub-theories.

Accepting that theorising proceeds, in simple terms, by describing, explaining and predicting, then we can see that it must be an integral part of anything other than a completely haphazard teaching/learning process. We must ask, however: is motor learning theory at the stage where it can yet fulfill these roles to the full?

Stones [20] points out that "experimental investigation into the nature of learning has developed only in this century and that as recently as the period 1940–1961 only five papers on the application of learning theory were published in the three main journals in the field of educational psychology". Of course the count may have been inaccurate and the sample restricted to three English language journals, but the conclusion that the field is a relatively new one is inescapable.

Since 1961 there has been much more work in the motor learning field. Singer [16] has reported that, "In the 1960's, man's quest for the mastery of space resulted in further inquiries into man's motor behaviour under unusual circumstances. Industrial technologists, vocational researchers, and physical educators have always been concerned with motor learning, and their contributions to the research literature have increased tremendously in recent years".

Despite this there still remains much to do before motor learning theory can fulfill *all* the functions ascribed to theory in my previous statements.

In his book, *Human Behavior: Exploring Educational Processes*, Cratty [4] writes that he has at times "attempted to place new ideas into cogent wholes formed by a mosaic of facts assimilated. In this manner, a series of 'special models' have been constructed, frameworks for understanding which have proved helpful in various ways". He goes on to admit, however, that "some of the models presented are naïve and at times may lack coherence when reviewed by the reader", although they are useful. This indicates, I would suggest, that theorising has hardly reached the level of sophisticated model building, let alone the generation of over-arching theories which one day may become metamorphosed into 'laws'.

Terminology

At a very basic stage of theorising, that of *definition*, motor learning still has a great deal of work to do. Whilst sharing the practitioners' irritation with much of the jargon used in so-called scientific discourse, I realise that the situation is by no means a simple one. If one uses everyday words for something which needs precise definition then there is the likelihood that this will result in confusion and impede the intended clarity. On the other hand if new words are coined by different theorists for essentially the same thing, or the same words used for similar but significantly different things, then again the result is likely to be confusion, irritation and lack of understanding. These problems are compounded by international language differences and different cultural contexts.

I can suggest no easy answers. I would only plead that each of us, in trying to communicate – and that is surely the purpose of language whether it is written or spoken – should attempt to make as clear as possible what we mean when we use certain terms. Where there is a term commanding widespread use, then let us use it. Too often one has the feeling that some people introduce their own terminology simply to be different; to form their own clique of those who communicate in the 'in' language. Others may get so bound up in their own ideas and quest for knowledge that they would not even accept the need for communication and they ignore the possibility of the useful application of their theory.

Wilberg [24] has advanced the idea of the International Society for Sports Psychology, establishing a committee "whose purpose would be the cataloguing and defining of word terms considered to be acceptable to all member countries". If, or when, this is established, it could do something to close the gap between different researchers in different countries – it remains to be seen if it could also help to close the language gap between theorists and practitioners.

I will leave the final words on promoting mutual understanding to Jerome Bruner [3] who says, "discovering how to make something comprehensible to the young is only a continuation of making something comprehensible to ourselves in the first place ... understanding and aiding others to understand are both of a piece". Do we work at it hard enough?

The Applicability of Research

There are two more problem areas which merit comment at this stage, the first concerns the applicability of animal research in the study of human behaviour, and the second, the problem of which is more valuable – *pure* or *applied* research.

Writing in 1966, Stones [21] said: "In the study of the application of learning theory to school, much remains to be done since the bulk of experimental work has been done with animals and this necessarily means we must pay a good deal of attention to animal learning. Elsewhere he has written [20], "Man is an organism; more specifically he is an animal . . . we can, by studying the ways in which other animals learn, gain insight into the way man himself learns". I would accept that provided there is 'critical caution in application', which Stones stresses, then at times the gap between 'the rat lab' and teaching children can be bridged to some advantage.

Rushall and Siedentop [13] in their book entitled *The Development and Control of Behavior in Sport and Physical Education* (1972), made, in many ways, a pioneer attempt to bridge two of the gaps already mentioned. Their aim was to employ "the theories and principles of the operant school of psychology . . ." and they presented a specific application of the general operant model. We know that the early work of the father of operant psychology, B. F. Skinner, as an experimental psychologist, was predominantly with infra human subjects'. They thus set out to demonstrate the potential use of a broad theory in the applied situation. In this case the theory selected was based on laboratory investigations with non-human subjects. Hill [9] has pointed out that many psychologists are dissatisfied with Skinner's ideas and "have chosen other paths".

Although very interesting as a theoretical work written to influence practice, I am not yet aware that Rushall and Siedentop have had any great influence on the practice of physical education teaching in Great Britain.

In a paper given to the 18th International Congress of Applied Psychology in Montreal in August, 1974, Dr. Robert Wilberg [24] again commented on "the lack of meaningfulness" of much of the basic research conducted "when the application of the results has been attempted". He picked out examples where authors "interpret basic research with a familiarity and clarity not readily available in other works". However, he went on to say that, "Unfortunately, complete familiarity and understanding with research fact amounts to only one half of the . . . problem. The other half . . . that of application in specific teaching, sport and/or competitive circumstances, often goes unfulfilled". So far, he concluded, "Only a handful of authors in psychology have been able to come to grips with the . . . problem".

The solution to this problem is again difficult but it could be partially solved if researchers would recognise their practical limitations and avoid what Wilberg describes as their "Insensitivity towards the very population they are attempting to reach". The inclusion in research teams of people with, for example, the necessary practical knowledge of the activity being researched, should be an accepted practice. However carefully a research team is constituted and goes ahead with its work, once a research project is carried into the multi-variable situation of everyday teaching, it is a considerable strain, if not an impossibility, to maintain sufficient experimental control to obtain results of any real significance.

The result has been either that such research has been written off as worthless, even before it is finished, or that the researcher has withdrawn to the laboratory where he can control the situation to a greater extent. John Whiting [22], who has had much experimental experience in England, has stated, "laboratory studies have been useful in drawing attention to those characteristics of skilled performance which are worthy of attention. There is still a need however, for making the transition from rigidly controlled laboratory experiments . . . to field type experiments in actual game situations . . .".

Singer [18] sees both laboratory and field research as necessary and *complementary* means of increasing our understanding of human behaviour. In the matter of bridging this gap, the responsibility seems firmly in the hands of research workers and those who select and finance research projects.

Interpreting Research

A necessary aid to crossing the gap between *practice* and *theory* is at least a working knowledge of basic statistics. Somehow a realisation of the importance of this knowledge too seldom communicates itself to physical education students in training.

In the light of the general theme of this chapter it is amusing to find that Reichmann [12] in his book *The Use and Abuse of Statistics*, says, "There is a real gulf between the statistical and non-statistical world of ideas, and the statistician often finds it difficult to project his ideas across that gulf. This is partly his own fault in that his jargon, like all scientific terminology, tends to intensify the difficulties". It seems we are not alone with our problems, but that problems in statistics may also be added to ours in as far as we use statistical methods and language in our discussions!

As well as establishing the worth of any particular piece of evidence, we also have the problem of conflicting evidence. In yet another of his numerous publications, Cratty [5] reminds us that, "Determining what is truth poses formidable problems. Must a finding be echoed in numerous research studies, or will a single investigation's findings suffice when attempting to establish the truth? What is the truth when conflicting findings are available?"

With my own students, my response is to produce a framework for consideration of existing evidence* and discuss its worth as far as possible; to give general guidelines for practice where these are indicated; and, to note where conflicting evidence exists or no firm evidence is available. The honesty of showing the inconclusiveness of the evidence on which we advocate work in some areas of practice, seems to me to be essential.

We obviously need care in selecting which new ideas we attempt to translate into practice. Dr. Pierre Seurin [15] the F.I.E.P. President, in his Opening Address at the 1976 Congress on Evaluation, staged in Finland, warned against the dangers of new ideas too quickly taking on the mantle of scientific fact. Cratty [5] has also questioned whether a single research finding can establish truth. I could not leave this point without drawing your attention to what has become almost a public scandal in Britain in 1976. You may have heard the charge that the late Sir Cyril Burt, "father of British educational psychology . . . published false data and invented crucial facts to support his controversial theory that intelligence is largely inherited".

On October 24, 1976, the front page of *The Sunday Times* [8] stated, "The accusation has far reaching implications. Not only were Burt's ideas fundamental in influencing British education for half a century – from the late 1920's right up to his death in 1971 – but they also inspired public controversy over race and intelligence, which has been led in Britain by Professor Hans Eysenck and in America by Professor Arthur Jensen".

It goes on to report that "Burt was so eminent in his lifetime that his work was accepted without question, escaping the usual processes of scientific scrutiny". It is largely through statistical methods that his honesty is now being questioned.

My only comment here is to note the great difficulties in establishing 'truth' for the practitioner who wishes to base his work on a sound theoretical footing – and to marvel at how even the mighty can mislead or be misled.

In Conclusion

In closing I would like to acknowledge a few facts of the situation as it stands and to express a brief word of thanks.

* A typical example of this type of framework and summary, was published in the proceedings of the 1976 Israeli seminar on Motor Learning in P.E. and Sport. In it, I establish a simple analysis by which to highlight possible breakdown points in the process of verbal instruction during day-to-day teaching in physical education [2].

1. Firstly, we must accept that there will always be a time lag between the birth of new ideas, their verification, and their acceptance and widespread implementation.

2. Secondly, we must accept that 'a research explosion' has taken place in recent years in the motor learning area and that, in common with many other areas of study, it is becoming increasingly difficult to stay in touch with all the work which is being published. There is a very real danger of thinking one knows more than one does and, in trying to retain an overall perspective, running the risks of over-simplification and misinterpretation. Recognising these dangers is at least a step towards avoiding them.

3. Lastly, I would like to acknowledge the work of many of the physical educationists and others who *have* set out to bridge the gaps for us over the past years. In this respect I must mention the publication in 1963 of *Skill in Sport* by Barbara Knapp [10] which has had a lasting influence on the content of specialist physical education teacher training courses in Great Britain. Drs. Whiting and Kane have also reached international audiences with their research work and published material.

Looking to the United States, I have already referred many times to the numerous publications of Robert Singer and Bryant Cratty. In addition there are straightforward texts like those of John Lawther [11] on *The Learning of Physical Skills* and that of Loretta Stallings [19] mentioned earlier, and Richard Alderman's [1] *Psychological Behavior in Sport*, published in 1974.

Perhaps worthy of special mention is yet another attempt to work through the complete process of translating theory into practice by Singer and Dick [17]. In a joint work, published in 1974, they examine "a systems approach to the teaching of physical education".

I do not pretend to have mentioned all the 'bridging' publications or all the authors involved, for example I have entirely neglected the many excellent journal articles and I have not referred to any of the works of my European colleagues. However, I offer my sincere apologies to anyone who feels offended by not being mentioned ... and my thanks go to all, whether mentioned or not, for the important work so far carried out.

Much more remains to be done. I hope this congress* will provide the opportunity for further fruitful communications.

* International Congress of Psycho-Motor Learning-Free University of Brussels, Belgium.

References

1. Alderman, R. B., *Psychological behavior in sport,* W. B. Saunders, U.S.A., 1974.
2. Andrews, J. C., 'Problems of verbal instruction in physical education', in Proceedings of the 1976 Seminar on Motor Learning in Physical Education and Sport, Wingate Institute, Israel.
3. Bruner, J. S., *Towards a theory of instruction*, p. 38. Belknap Press, Harvard University, U.S.A., 1966.
4. Cratty, B. J., *Human behavior: exploring educational processes*, pp. 14–15. The University Press, Texas, U.S.A., 1971.
5. Cratty, B. J., *Psycho-motor behavior in education and sport*, p. 147. Charles C. Thomas, Illinois, U.S.A., 1974.
6. Cratty, B. J., *Remedial motor activity for children*, pp. 11–12. Lea & Febiger, Philadelphia, U.S.A., 1975.
7. De Cecco, J. P., *The psychology of language, thought and instruction*, p. vii. Holt, Rinehart & Winston, London, 1969.
8. Gillie, O., 'Crucial data was faked by eminent psychologist', *The Sunday Times*, p. 1. London, October 24, 1976.
9. Hill, W. F., *Learning: a survey of psychological interpretations*, p. 79. Methuen, London, 1964.
10. Knapp, B., *Skill in sport*, Routledge & Kegan Paul, London, 1963.
11. Lawther, J. D., *The learning of physical skills*, Prentice-Hall, U.S.A., 1968.
12. Reichmann, W. J., *Use and abuse of statistics*, Pelican Books, London, 1964.
13. Rushall, B. S. and Siedentop, D., *The development and control of behavior in sport and physical education*, Lea & Febiger, Philadelphia, U.S.A., 1972.
14. Saunders, E. D., 'Theory and practice in physical education', *Bulletin of physical education*, vol. 10, no. 3, pp. 13–21. B.A.U.L.P.E., July, 1974.
15. Seurin, P., 'Opening address', 1976 Congress on Evaluation at Jyvaskyla, Finland. *FIEP Bulletin*, vol. 46, no. 3, 1976.
16. Singer, R. N. (ed.) in *Readings in motor learning*, p. vi. Lea & Febiger, Philadelphia, U.S.A., 1972.
17. Singer, R. N. and Dick, W., *Teaching physical education: a systems approach*, Houghton Mifflin Co., Boston, U.S.A., 1974.
18. Singer, R. N., *Motor learning and human performance* (2nd edition), p. 5. Macmillan, New York, 1975.
19. Stallings, L. M., *Motor skills: development and learning*, p. vii. Wm. C. Brown Co., U.S.A., 1973.
20. Stones, E., *Educational psychology*, p. 53. Methuen, London, 1966.
21. *ibid.*, p. 17.
22. Whiting, H. T. A., *Acquiring ball skill*, p. 104. G. Bell and Son, London, 1969.
23. Wilberg, R. B., 'The direction and definition of a field', *Trabajos cientificos, tomo III*, p. 221. Proceedings of the 3rd World Congress of the International Society of Sports Psychology (I.S.S.P.). Madrid, 1973. Madrid, 1975.
24. Wilberg, R. B., 'An analysis and application of game and human performance theory to sport and competition', in Whiting, H. T. A. (ed.), *Reading in sports psychology 2*, pp. 122–137. Lepus Books, London, 1975.

8

Individual Differences Amongst Children*

A Brief Survey with Reference to Physical Education

Introduction

It has become something of a cliché in educational writings that almost all accounts of teaching and learning pay at least lip service to 'the individuality of the child'. This individuality is so often taken for granted nowadays that it is perhaps necessary, from time to time, to re-underline the obvious.

In this essay some of the more obvious sources of individual differences are referred to – without apology – whilst perhaps some of the less obvious ones are considered as well. Although the main area of reference throughout is to physical education, implications often go beyond the bounds of 'subject areas'.

Finally, even in the teaching of physical activities there is much (some would say 'too much') use of language; hence the attention

* A paper prepared for the course entitled 'An integrated approach to physical education', St. Paul's College, Cheltenham. September, 1977.

given to 'language differences'. Before this, however, some more tangible variables can be examined.

Age

The age of the child is of obvious importance in the teaching and learning situation, particularly in the early years at school. Generally, when the layman talks of age he is referring to 'chronological age' but we need to remind ourselves this is only one aspect of age. Tanner [39] for example, gives *four* different ages for assessing what he calls *developmental age*. Briefly these are:

1. **Skeletal age** – found by examining X-ray photographs, usually of the hand and wrist, against other photographs showing criterion stages of development.
2. **Dental age** – based on the examination of teeth and the development of their roots.
3. **Morphological age** – 'shape age' – based on measures of height, weight and shape, etc.
4. **Secondary sex characteristic age** – this method of assessing age only becomes useful at, and after, the onset of puberty.

These measures depend on the processes of growth, development and maturation and are all aspects which show the developmental (or physiological) age of the child, One may also meet the notion of the 'psychological' or 'mental age' of a child and this is examined later.

Growth, Development and Maturation

The terms *growth, development* and *maturation* refer to changes in the human organism which are related, but are *not* the same. **Growth** is defined here as 'quantitative change leading to measurable variations in body size and proportion'. **Development,** on the other hand, is a much wider term including not only the physical changes which take place but also the effects of many other factors. It is possible, for example, to speak of mental development, social development, personality development, etc. Finally, the term **maturation** is used to refer to changes taking place in the anatomical and physiological complexity of the child. Knapp [21] writes that this is "the physiological ripening of an organism and refers to that part of development which results from causes other than specific activity or functioning. Maturation therefore in no way depends on exercise".

It is likely that in work with children of school age, even where a particular class has a fairly narrow chronological age range, the range of individual differences due to variations in growth and maturation will be considerable. Attempting to teach a skill before the child has reached the necessary minimum maturation level for that skill is largely a waste of time and may be harmful to future progress. Difficulties will almost certainly be encountered.

In some cases these difficulties are obvious. For example, few would try to teach a child who can hardly stand, how to kick – which involves balancing on one leg whilst swinging the kicking foot. Not so obvious perhaps is the example of the parent trying to teach a four-year-old how to catch a tennis ball. The necessary reaction potential and hand-eye co-ordination may not be present for the acquisition of such a relatively complex skill. The reaction of the child to the ball continually hitting him on the chest (or nose), perhaps to the ill-concealed displeasure and impatience of the parent, and so linked within a general atmosphere of 'failure', may be harmful to the development of this skill in later years. Similarly on a wider developmental scale, the teacher who tries to organise full-side major team games with six- and seven-year-old children in the upper infant school, is obviously overlooking the limiting factors working against the success of such a venture which arise purely from the age and stage of development of the children.

Critical Periods in Skill Learning

Whilst accepting the evidence by Dusenberry [15] and Gagné and Fleishman [17] that prematurational practice is largely a waste of time, there are some indications that children who have been deprived of experience at certain 'break-through' periods are sometimes clumsier than others who have made some early experiments and failed. There do appear to be certain *critical periods* during which activities are best introduced and most easily acquired. Evidence for this appears to be somewhat limited but Tanner [39] reports that in animals it has been found experimentally that there are periods during which a particular stimulus from the environment will evoke a particular behaviour in the animal but if not evoked in this limited period it may never appear. If there are similar periods in human development then it would seem important that appropriate skills should be introduced in them.

It is not proposed to go into greater detail in this brief discussion of the development of physical attributes. Let it suffice then to note that amongst the factors which will vary with age are: size, shape and tissue composition; strength, endurance and mobility. These terms will be familiar to the majority of physical educationists, the last three being used here in the way defined and discussed by Munrow in 1963 [30].

Basic Abilities

Another approach to the study of individual differences is to be found in the work of Gagné and Fleishman [17]. They postulate the existence of a series of *basic abilities*. "These basic abilities are relatively enduring characteristics of individuals, in which people differ appreciably from one another, and which affect performance of a great variety of specific human tasks". They define such an ability as "a general trait of an individual which determines the limit of performance he attains on many different tasks". Their work on the physiological bases of abilities, on the rate of development of abilities and on their identification, distribution and measurement, provides an analysis which could be useful in approaching the study of these factors in a teaching/learning situation. Some of the divisions which they suggest are as follows:

"1. Abilities supporting **discrimination** – individual variations in ability to distinguish between small changes in various dimensions of physical stimuli.

2. Abilities related to **identification** – e.g. perceptual speed; closure abilities – speed of closure and flexibility of closure.

3. **Spatial abilities** – spatial orientation and spatial visualisation.

4. **Auditory identification abilities** – e.g. auditory rhythm discrimination, and auditory perceptual speed.

5. **Memory** – supported by a group of abilities related to an individual's performance on tasks requiring the retention of different kinds of material for different lengths of time. These abilities include: associative memory, rote memory and meaningful memory; memory span abilities and visual memory.

6. **Motor abilities** – e.g. multiple limb co-ordination, fine control precision, response orientation, individual reaction time, speed of arm movements, rate control, fine manipulative abilities and gross motor abilities.

7. **Conceptual and thinking abilities** – an important set of abilities

concerned with the learning, retention and use of concepts. Examples include, verbal knowledge, word fluency, numerical ability, concept fluency, discovery of principles, general reasoning, seeing implications and consequences, symbol manipulation, logical evaluation and practical judgement."

They complete their fairly lengthy coverage of these thinking abilities with this caution. "We have described only what seems to be the most important and representative basic abilities in this area. Perhaps, too, further study will lead to their revision as we learn more about their generality. In any case, abilities related to thinking are less distinct than those in certain other areas; that is, they are likely to be more highly correlated with each other. However, the abilities we have described should provide an inkling of some of the complexities of the thinking process, as well as the variety of ways people can differ in these performances" [18].

Sex

At this point it is appropriate that some mention should be made of sexual differences between children as variables in the teaching/learning situation. This, however, need not be an extended consideration if one accepts the views put forward by Knapp [22] in *Skill in Sport.* She finds that sex differences are not a sure divider amongst young children (there being equally large differences *within* one sex as there are *between* the sexes. It appears that quite often differences that do appear are very likely 'culturally determined' by social pressures that indicate which are the more acceptable female activities, and the 'more feminine'. However, she goes on to state: "Major sex differences in physique also arise at adolescence and in so far as these affect initial ability for any particular activity they influence the speed at which any new skill is acquired".

Intelligence

What is intelligence? Is intelligence measurable? These are questions which have exercised psychologists and educationists for many years. The notion of 'measurable intelligence' has certainly held considerable sway in educational thought and administration in Britain, and if indeed 'general intelligence' does exist and has been successfully measured, then this has been a major factor in determining at least the overall grouping of children presenting themselves for P.E. lessons, particularly at secondary school level. School populations and class groups have been formed on the basis of intelligence tests. Many writers would claim that intelligence is *not* something which is quantifiable. A typical view is that one shows intelligence by acting intelligently, just as one shows stupidity by acting in a stupid manner. Despite the number of intelligence tests which have been extensively used in the past, it appears that the present tendency is towards a decreasing use of such measuring instruments. If there *is* something definable as 'general intelligence' then it is possibly a composite measure of verbal, memory, numerical and thinking abilities, such as those already mentioned in describing Gagné's and Fleishman's ideas on basic abilities. In as far as verbal and thinking abilities influence the teaching and learning situation in physical education, some further study of these, and particularly individual differences with regard to language ability, appears to be important.

Individual Differences in Language Behaviour

Carroll [9] reports the results of a number of researches which have established (generally by factor analysis techniques) "the existence of a number of more or less independent dimensions of ability in the domain of language behaviour". These he lists as:

1. **Verbal Knowledge** – knowledge of structure and vocabulary. This is highly correlated with the concepts of the individual – at least in as far as these are symbolised by words.
2. **Abstract Reasoning Qualities** – some work appears to suggest that there may exist differences within individuals to reason inductively, deductively, and also in serial order.
3. **Ideational fluency** – the ability to call up as many ideas as possible on a given topic.
4. **Word fluency** – the ability to think of words with certain formal characteristics, for example starting with the same letter, etc.
5. **Fluency of expression** – given an idea, the ability to put it into grammatically acceptable words and constructions.
6. **Grammatical sensitivity** – ability to recognise grammatical constructions and to perform tasks which particularly require this, e.g. translation.

7. **Naming facility** – the rapid response with names to items, etc. when presented.
8. **Oral speed ability** – to speak effectively and coherently.
9. **Articulation ability** – individual differences in speed of articulation.

This list is not claimed to be exhaustive and it is obvious that some of these abilities will be called upon in the teaching/learning situation more than others. The analysis is useful in that it allows additional differentiation within the very wide term of 'language ability'.

Group Differences in Language Behaviour

Other interesting dimensions of language behaviour are encountered if the consideration is moved from that of *an individual* child to that of *a group* of children. Two are considered here, *sex* and *social background.*

Mussen, Conger and Kagan [32] report that sex differences are noticeable in language development. It appears that, as infants, girls generally surpass boys in all aspects of language, such as, onset of speech, vocabulary size, sentence construction in terms of length and complexity, and general comprehensibility of speech. However, with increasing age these differences become less marked. Girls are not consistently superior beyond the age of three.

Social Class Differences

A number of studies [5, 7 and 14] have looked at the relationship between social class and language development. It seems possible that many of the differences in general intelligence between social classes previously 'discovered', were really a result of language deprivation. It is interesting to consider, therefore, whether social class, via its effect in this case on language development, has great effect on the ability of a child to profit from verbal instruction and also if differences between the social class of the teacher and his pupils may bring socially based communication problems in the use of language.

Bernstein [7] has been one of the most consistent investigators in this area and his analysis in terms of 'codes' of language could be helpful for those teachers seeking further insights into this problem. He differentiates between *an elaborated* and *a restricted* code of language. In the case of the elaborated code, the speaker selects from a relatively wide range of alternatives and his speech is therefore less predictable. In using a restricted code "the number of these alternatives is severely restricted and the probability of predicting the pattern is greatly increased". He continues, "The codes themselves are functions of particular forms of social relationships, or more generally, qualities of social structures".

Clarke [11], commenting on Bernstein's work, reports that the **restricted code** is mainly found in the lower socio-economic groupings of the population, whilst the middle and upper-class groups also possess an *elaborated code*. According to Clarke the **restricted code** is characterised by "non-analytical 'here and now' statements". It is usually 'direct' and 'concrete', using, what he calls 'heavy-duty' verbs.

The **elaborated code,** on the other hand, is *analytical* and *explanatory* and draws on a wider and more precise vocabulary. Nisbet (1953) [33] has put forward the view that "Limitation of opportunities for verbal development is therefore likely to exercise a depressive influence on ability to score in a test even of general mental ability". He tested this and found it to be generally true in some quite large scale research with children in Aberdeen. As well as social class factors operating here, he found that the size of the family was an important factor – although this in itself may be seen as a social factor. Certainly Bernstein [5] in a comment on Nisbet's work in 1961, sees this connection because he adds, "It should be remembered that as family size increases, the lower the socio-economic level".

These investigations are of obvious importance because, firstly, they throw some doubt onto the validity of intelligence testing as a mass grading and selection method and, secondly, for the teacher, they highlight one of the possible reasons for difficulty in communicating with the learner. As Bernstein says [6] "The child learns his social structure through its language, and this processing of learning begins when he can respond to, but not make, verbal signals. Language, spoken language, powerfully conditions what is learned and how it is learned, and so influences future learning". His argument is that the process of education operates very much in a middle class atmosphere and its language is very much that of the elaborated code. This gives an advantage to children of middle and upper class backgrounds whilst the children from the lower socio-economic backgrounds are required to work in what is virtually a foreign language. In contrast, however, when 'talking sport', the physical education teacher may have a key to a fairly specialised language which has wide communication value, in the social sense, than that associated with many other academic subjects.

Personality

Another source of individual difference – itself a tremendous complex of interacting variables – is that of the *personality* of the learner. (This is also true, of course, of the teacher.) Cattell [10] has defined personality as, "that which tells what a man will do when placed in a given situation". Many of the personality studies involving learning, teaching and performance of skills in physical education have looked for correlations between an aspect of P.E. and one of the personality testing instruments designed by either H. J. Eysenck in Britain, or R. B. Cattell in the United States. For a survey of the results of some of these findings see Andrews (1970) [2] and Whiting et al. (1973) [40].

An example of the formation that has been gained in these studies is that found by Whiting and Stembridge who investigated the personality of 43 persistent non-swimmers [2]. They found that these students were significantly more introverted and neurotic than normal, according to their results on the Maudsley Personality Inventory. Whiting then extended the study to 1,340 boys aged 11–12 years and similar results were found. (This later study used the junior version of the M.P.I.)

Skills in P.E. and the situations in which they are normally practised differ greatly. Obviously if a situation is stressful, as in rock climbing or learning to swim, then it may well be that the anxious child is more adversely affected and unable to benefit from verbal, or indeed any, instruction. It could mean that the child is unable to participate at all.

Anxiety, Stress and Fatigue Factors

Closely related to considerations of personality are those of anxiety, stress and fatigue. Most personality theories attempt to measure *anxiety* as a personality trait; Eysenck, for example, uses this as a major dimension under the heading of neuroticism. All people need a degree of anxiety because it is related to alertness (or level of arousal). However, in learning and performance situations *too high* a level of anxiety has been found to inhibit the pupil. In dangerous situations (not necessarily in P.E.) for example in battle, it has been found that anxiety builds up before the activity is attempted, but that this is often reduced by physical activity and concentration on the task. However when it is finished the anxiety level often builds up once again. Whether anxiety is helpful, or can be kept within workable bounds, depends partly on the nervous threshold of the person and partly on the stress placed on them by the situation.

Two types of anxiety are sometimes differentiated, 'harm anxiety' (where physical damage to the body is feared) and 'failure anxiety' (where the danger is in not being able to measure up to one's own or, more often other people's, expectations). Sometimes these are in opposition, for example, where a timid boy is faced with tackling a fast-moving heavier boy during a game of rugby football.

Anxiety operates to increase the tension levels in the body, **tension** in these circumstances being defined as a state of muscular contraction, caused by an emotional state or, perhaps, increased physical activity.

In this discussion **stress** is defined as an internal reaction to an external situation "considered threatening by the organism" [13]. Both the *stable* and the *neurotic* person can be subjected to stress; it is unlikely, however, that their behaviour under stress will be the same. A final interesting point about stress is that it is not only an *individual* phenomena it can also affect *groups* of people. Stress, it appears, is catching and it could be, for example, that in teaching rock climbing, stress is communicated from teacher to pupil, or vice versa, by verbal communication, even without the climbers being able to see each other on the rock face.

Even a fairly common-place term like 'fatigue' provides difficulty when it comes to finding a working definition. The problem is that *fatigue* may be a specific or a general condition of the whole person. This links closely with the description of endurance by Munrow [31]. He puts forward the idea of three levels of endurance:

1. **Local** – based on the endurance capacity of particular muscles or muscle groups.
2. **Athletic** – which involves a speed factor, and has a basis in the efficiency of the cardio-respiratory system.
3. **Expedition** – no speed factor but a great time factor and including physical hindrances such as hunger, heat etc., based on the total energy of the individual.

S. H. Bartley [4] in *Fatigue-Mechanism and Management,* prefers to refer to states of physical tiredness as degrees of *exhaustion* and *fatigue* is reserved for a more general state. "Fatigue is an experienced self-evaluation". It is characterised by aversion to activity, expressed in bodily feelings, in feelings of inadequacy, or futility and the desire to escape. It depends not only on how a person feels – the degree of exhaustion of his system – but also on how he assesses the situation in which he is placed. It is claimed that strong motivation can delay the effects of fatigue but that a pessimistic evaluation of a situation, leading to inability to carry on, often comes before muscular exhaustion. This has obvious significance in understanding for example, expedition leadership in adverse conditions and also leads the discussion on to a more general consideration of 'arousal' and other aspects of 'motivation'.

Motivation

The term *motivation* has a long and involved history in psychological writings. Bindra [8] records that it crept into the writings of functionally minded psychologists in the 1880's and that Sully in a book called *Outlines of Psychology*, written in 1884, said "that the desire that precedes an act and determines it is to be called 'its moving force, stimulus or motive'". Lindsley [25] taking part in the Nebraska Symposium on Motivation in 1957 said, "Motivation is generally defined as the combination of forces which initiate, direct and sustain behaviour toward a goal". He goes on to examine various concepts such as 'needs' and 'drives' before coming to what is perhaps the most useful contribution for this examination; the postulation of a continuum of psychological states with correlations shown between the electro-encephalographic monitoring of the electrical activity within the brain, states of awareness, and behavioural efficiency.

Cratty [12] makes the distinction that "motivation is a broad term referring to a general level of arousal to action. Motives on the other hand, are specific conditions which affect performance and contribute to the general motivational level". Motivation in fact, permeates the whole of the learning and performance situation and because of this some writers like Holding [20] prefer to avoid using the term as much as possible.

Some motivation theorists' ideas may be of use to the practising teacher, however, one of these being Lewin's [24] 'level of aspiration theory'. Knapp [23] points out, "The level of aspiration of a learner is important for it has been found that the good student is one who tends to set a level of aspiration just a little above past achievements. He therefore gets the satisfaction of attaining his goal but he then immediately raises his sights".

Theories of general arousal have been examined by Alluisi [1] and he concludes that these "may have relevance to the autonomic-linked* behaviour (such as variations in motivation, in level of induced ten-

*The autonomic nervous system – including the sympathetic and parasympathetic systems – is the controlling system for movements of the heart, the bronchi, the pupils of the eyes, the alimentary tract, the bladder, and the sphincter muscles. It is responsible for the tone of blood vessels, and it regulates the secretion of numerous glands.

sion, and in degree of wakefulness)". Certainly findings so far appear to support the statement of Furth and Youniss [16] that, "Inhibition (or control) of generalised arousal is a prerequisite to selective responding or attending".

Motivation, generally, is a vast variable which needs to be considered, when looking at the individual child. The effects of praise, reward, blame and punishment need careful examination with regard to the contribution of the teacher, although he need not be the only source of these.

Another idea, that of the existence of 'optimum tension levels' being possible for each individual in each learning or performance situation, might be used to 'explain' otherwise unexpected performance changes – for example, by the individual who is able to 'raise his game' in the face of normally superior opposition whilst the acknowledged favourite 'ties up' on the very big occasion. The social pressures of performing in front of a group of one's peers, or of members of the opposite sex; considerations of children's 'task involvement' in certain situations as opposed to their 'ego-involvement' in others (when 'ego involved', an activity is more important to them and the way they see themselves); these, plus the vital encouragement that comes from knowing just how one is progressing in any task (K.R.); all these are considerations which fall under the general heading of motivation.

Attention and Attitudes

The concept of *attention* would appear to be a broad term which takes into account arousal theory and also, according to O'Connor [34] includes, "Focussing on certain aspects of current experience and neglecting others. Interests, motives and perceptual set or expectancy, influence what is selected for attention".

She goes on to define an *attitude* as "A readiness to respond in a particular manner to some circumstance or idea". Certainly the recognition of the existence of attitudes and their role in education has led to a large increase of interest in this sphere and moves to establish instruments by which attitudes may be measured. Peel [37] wrote in 1956, "An attitude is an enduring organisation of motives, perceptions and emotions with respect to some aspect of the individual's world". He goes on to note the relationship between some personality theories and attitudes; where personality is defined "as a constellation of social attitudes".

Morris [29] puts forward the view that attitudes are "dispositions of people towards other people, towards things or indeed towards anything that can be conceptualized, real or imaginary". In further discussion the distinction is made between *positive* and *negative* attitudes.

In this paper such factors as attitudes to school in general, to P.E. in particular, to physical contact, to changing for P.E., to achievement, to oneself*, parental attitudes and those of other members of staff, are seen as among those having considerable influence on the teaching-learning situation.

Achievement has been a particular study of McClelland [26; 27; 28] and he sees this as one of the fundamental areas of human need and one in which again there are considerable individual variations.

The notion of 'achievement' figures in the 'level of aspiration theory' already mentioned, and Oliver [36] has successfully demonstrated the value of raising levels of aspiration in work with children classed as educationally sub-normal.

Handicaps

It is proposed to complete this brief coverage of some of the variables which a child may bring to the teaching/learning situation, with some mention of the problems of handicapped children. One reason for this is that difficulties which are highlighted in more extreme cases are often present in part, but are less easily recognised, in children who would be described as 'normal'.

It is not possible to deal with *all* handicaps, but perhaps some examples may serve to highlight potential benefits of looking into this area even for teachers of 'normal' children.

Stones [38] underlines the remarks made about *language deprivation* earlier in this study. He notes, "The question of linguistic disability is one of the key problems in the field of backwardness". Links are obvious here between the work of Bernstein, Luria, Vigotsky, Piaget, and Bruner, all of whom stress the importance of language in the building up of abstract conceptual thought.

The generality of this problem and of the application of some of the work at present being done for handicapped children is stressed by O'Connor [35], "In the field of backwardness, localisation of speech difficulties is proceeding and the mechanics of input or perception, and immediate memory are beginning to be understood . . . there is good reason to be hopeful . . . that such investigations will aid teachers

* Sometimes discussed under the heading of 'self-concept'. For a discussion of this with relation to P.E. see Arnold 1970 [3].

not only at the levels of severe subnormality but also with normal pupils".

Language development in *deaf* children – those who are born deaf or who lose hearing before they learn how to speak – is generally delayed. Although it has been found that such children can acquire concepts, compare sizes, and remember sequences, etc., the levels attained are well below those possible with the use of language. Whilst the specialised teaching needed with deaf children is outside the scope of this essay, mention of loss of hearing is made here to underline the vital roles that language, and in particular the spoken word, play in all normal teaching-learning circumstances.

One might sum up, therefore, by saying research concerning language difficulties, as with other studies of the handicaps of children, is not only assisting the progress of special education and the extension of man's knowledge of brain function, it is also likely to be a worthy area of study for the teacher concerned with normal children in normal school situations.

Concluding Comments

There have been numerous publications dealing with individual differences amongst children. This summary does not pretend to be all-inclusive nor profound but perhaps in looking again at some of the differences – in age, sex, growth, development, maturation, abilities, language, social class, personality, anxiety, fatigue, motivation, attention, attitudes, and handicaps – at least some may become more sensitive in dealing with children as a teacher in a teaching-learning situation.

References

1. Alluisi, E. A., 'Attention and vigilance as mechanisms of response', in Bilodeau, E. A. (ed.), p. 210. *Acquisition of skill*, Academic Press, London, 1966.
2. Andrews, J. C., 'Personality, sporting interest and achievement', *Educational review,* University of Birmingham, 1970.
3. Arnold, P. J., 'Physical education, creativity and the self-concept', *Bulletin of physical education*, vol. 8, no. 1, pp. 15–19. B.A.O.L.P.E. 1970.
4. Bartley, S. H., *Fatigue-mechanism and management*, Thomas, 1965.
5. Bernstein, B., 'Social class and linguistic development', in Halsey et al., *Psychology of language, thought and instruction*, p. 290. Holt, Rinehart & Winston, London, 1961.
6. *ibid.,* p. 307

7. Bernstein, B., 'Social structure, language and learning', *Educational research*, 3, pp. 163–176, also in De Cecco, J. P. (1969) *Psychology of languge, thought and instruction*, p. 101. Holt Rinehart & Winston, London, 1961.
8. Bindra, D. and Stewart, J., *Motivation*, p. 9. Penguin Books, 1966.
9. Carroll, J. B., *Language and thought,* p. 67. Prentice-Hall Inc., U.S.A., 1964.
10. Cattell, R. B., *The scientific analysis of personality*, Penguin Books, 1965.
11. Clarke, A. D. B., 'Intelligence', in Morris, J. F. and Lunzer, F. A. (eds.), 'Development in learning III', *Contexts of education*, p. 58. Staples Press, London, 1969.
12. Cratty, R. J., *Movement behavior and motor learning*, 2nd ed., p. 149. Lea & Febiger, U.S.A., 1967.
13. *ibid.*, p. 165.
14. Deutsch, M., 'The disadvantaged child and the learning process', in Passow, A. H. (ed.), *Education in depressed areas*, pp. 163–180. New York Teachers' College, 1963.
15. Dusenberry, L., 'Training in ball throwing by children three to seven', *Research quarterly*, 1, pp. 9–14, 1952.
16. Furth, H. G. and Youniss, J., 'Sequence learning: perceptual implications in the acquisition of language', in Wathendunn, W. (ed.), *Models for the perception of speech and visual form*, p. 344. M.I.T. Press, 1964.
17. Gagné, P. M. and Fleishman, E. A., *Psychology and human performance,* p. 44. Holt, New York, 1959.
18. *ibid.*, p. 132.
19. Gates, A. I. and Taylor, G. A., 'An experimental study of the nature of improvement resulting from practice in a motor function', *Journal of education psychology*, 17, pp. 226–236, 1926.
20. Holding, D. E., *The principles of training*, p. 8. Pergamon, London, 1965.
21. Knapp, B., *Skill in sport*, p. 71. Routledge & Kegan Paul, London, 1963.
22. *ibid.*, pp. 89–91.
23. *ibid.*, p. 118.
24. Lewin, K. et al., 'Level of aspiration', in Hunt, J. M., (ed.), *Personality and the behavior disorders*, vol. 1. Ronald, New York. 1944.
25. Lindsley, D. B., 'Psychophysiology and motivation', in Jones, M. R. (ed.), *Nebraska symposium on motivation*, pp. 44–105. Nebraska University Press, U.S.A., 1957.
26. McClelland, D. C., *The achievement motive*, Appleton, New York, 1953.
27. McClelland, D. C., *The achieving society*, Van Nostrand, Princetown, 1961.
28. McClelland, D. C., 'The urge to achieve', *New Society*, vol. 9, no. 229, pp. 227–229.
29. Morris, J. F. and Lunzer, E. A. (eds.), in 'Development in learning III', *Contexts of education*, p. 209. Staples Press, London, 1969.
30. Munrow, A. D., *Pure and applied gymnastics*, 2nd ed. Edward Arnold, London, 1963.
31. *ibid.*, p. 146.
32. Mussen, P. H., Conger, J. J. and Kagan, J., *Child development and personality*, 2nd ed., p. 194. Harper Row, London, 1963.
33. Nisbet, J., 'Family environment and intelligence', Halsey et al. in *Eugenics review*, XLV 31–42, p. 274. 1953.
34. O'Connor, K., *Learning: an introduction*, p. 131. Macmillan, London, 1968.
35. O'Connor, N., 'Backwardness and severe subnormality', in Foss, B. M. (1966) (ed.), *New horizons in psychology*, p. 332. Penguin Books, 1966.
36. Oliver, J. N., 'Pilot investigation into the effects of circuit training on

educationally sub-normal boys', *Research in physical education*, vol. 1, no. 1, p. 11. P.E.A. 1966.
37. Peel, E. A., *The psychological basis of education*, p. 240. Oliver & Boyd, London, 1956.
38. Stones, E., *An introduction to education psychology*, p. 310. Methuen, London, 1966.
39. Tanner, J. M., *Growth at adolescence*, p. 36. Blackwell, Oxford, 1955.
40. Whiting, H. T. A., Hardman, K., Hendry, L. B. and Jones, M. G., *Personality and performance in physical education and sport*, Henry Kimpton, 1973.

9

Problems of Verbal Instruction in Physical Education*

Introduction

Verbal instruction, for the purpose of this paper, is defined as a teacher's verbal communication, using a language of vocal symbols possessing arbitrary conventional meanings, transmitted through the organs of speech, with the objectives of stimulating, controlling and modifying a pupil's behaviour.

In his book, *Language and Thought* published in 1964 Carroll [4] wrote, "It seems almost too obvious to say that language functions in interpersonal communication – in conveying information, thoughts and feelings from one person to another and in providing a means by which people control each other's behaviour".

However, when one examines these 'functions' in schools and colleges, one realises that whilst verbal communication is basic to much teacher/pupil interaction, this process is so taken for granted that it is relatively little studied and its many complexities are often overlooked in teacher training and day-to-day teaching.

* A revised version of a paper presented at the International Seminar on Motor Learning in Physical Education and Sport, held at the Wingate Institute, Israel, in April, 1976 and published in the Seminar Proceedings, pp. 121–126, edited by Dr. Uriel Simri, in September, 1976.

Perhaps this is not really surprising, despite the fact that education as a whole is a kind of communication. Barnes and Shemilt [2] note that, "although this communication constitutes a large part of every teacher's professional activity, we cannot expect teachers to be highly aware of its nature. Like everyone else they are more aware of the people they communicate with, and of their own purposes, than of the act of communicating".

Observation of physical education teachers in training, as well as of lessons taught by qualified teachers, confirms the amount of verbal instruction used in what is usually considered a 'doing' rather than a 'talking about' teaching/learning situation. One sees all too frequently the physical education teacher who talks too much, at the wrong time, perhaps when the pupils cannot possibly hear, or when their attention is distracted, or in too complicated or otherwise inappropriate language. Lawther [8] has remarked, "Teachers are very fond of verbal explanations. However when talk interrupts needed practice time, it may actually be a handicap to the learner".

It is hoped that the simple analysis which follows may highlight at least some of the possible breakdown points in this process of verbal instruction and may help to raise their consideration to a higher level of importance amongst practising teachers. Potential researchers will also find many important questions as yet unanswered.

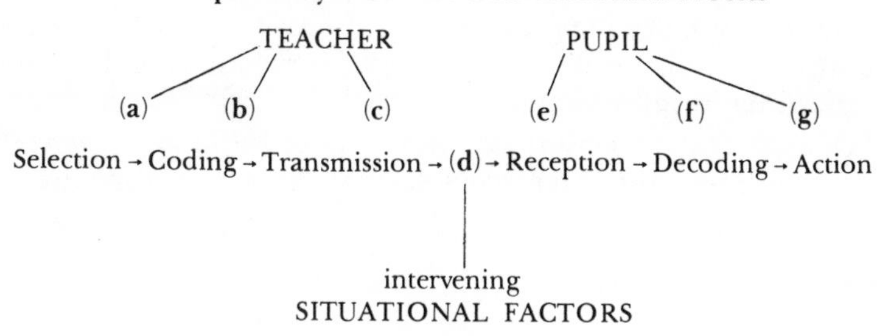

Fig. 9.1

The remainder of this chapter will be devoted to a brief look at the problems of a *teacher's* selection, coding and transmission of verbal instructions, of a *pupil's* reception, decoding and translation into action of these instructions, and of the possible intervention of *situational factors* which may either aid or impede communication.

Selection

It is at the selection stage that one might assume that the teacher, as the result of training and experience, should be able to choose quite easily from the almost infinite range of perceptual-motor tasks, those which are educationally valuable and applicable to the pupil.

However, even if in this discussion, one sets aside the educational value judgements needed, there are still many selection difficulties remaining.

For example, in teacher education, it is normally considered that the teacher's own level of motor skill and repertoire of skills are important determinants in generating instructional material. However the exact nature of the relationship between teaching physical education and the personal practical performance of the student/teacher is still in question.

Where the teaching of motor activities is attempted by verbal means then two types of behaviour are involved; verbal behaviour and motor behaviour. These types are related but they are *not* the same thing. Holding [6] emphasises this when he points out, "We cannot adequately describe all we can do, and we can not do all we can describe".

Student teachers need to be continually reminded that there is no direct relationship between, for example, a criterion performance of a particular skill, the teacher's own variable performances, and the mental image or images which the teacher may use as a basis for generating verbal instructions. Indeed the very existence of such images, or their nature – visual, verbal, kinaesthetic, or some combination of these – could be in question.

Further aspects of selection are those of the *extent* and *complexity* of the information which the teacher selects to code and transmit.

Coding

Coding, like all other stages, is an intricate area, still needing research. It must suffice here to note that there have been numerous and different approaches to analysing the coding and content of verbal messages [2; 3; 5; 9; 10; 11; 12; 14; 15; for examples].

In 1965, Miller [10] wrote, "Language is the prime example of rule governed behaviour, and there are several types of rule to consider. Not only must we consider *syntactic* rules for generating and grouping words in sentences; we must also consider *semantic* rules for interpreting word combinations. Perhaps we may even need *pragmatic* rules to characterise our unlimited variety of belief systems. Only on the assumption that a language user knows a generative system of rules for producing (and interpreting) sentences can we hope to account for the unlimited combinational productivity of natural languages".

Whatever the analytical divisions used, whether it be into 'phones' Dalrymple-Alford [5], or 'units' Vygotsky [15] or 'bits of information' Johnson [7], in practice the physical education teacher needs to select and arrange words to convey meanings in accordance with pragmatic rules. Different cultural, regional, socio-economic, general educational, and personal practical backgrounds will combine to make coding (and decoding) a very individual and probably inaccurate matter.

Transmission

Although tone and sound volume are often integral parts of conveying meaning, in teaching physical education it is sometimes in purely *signal* attributes that verbal instruction breaks down.

The signal properties of a word or words are quite commonly used in P.E. Children sometimes react to these as much as to the semantic content. For example, a young sprinter, held on his 'mark' for a practice start, would 'go' whether the word 'go', 'yes' or even 'stop' was given in an executive manner.

In many familiar teaching situations the pitch, speed and sound volume of instruction may determine whether a child receives the coded message or not. Whilst acceptable variations in signal properties can be high, extremes are likely to cause breakdowns in communication.

Situational Factors

Situational factors can either be of help or hindrance.

In most cases the situation provides *the context* through which meanings may be interpreted. This context may compensate to a certain degree for inaccurate selection and coding by the teacher, and for other adverse environmental factors, such as partial loss of the instructions being transmitted due to distance, noise, wind, etc.

Information theorists call *redundant* those parts of a message which can be lost without loss of meaning. The context may make some verbal material redundant or at least compensate for losses in transmission due to adverse environmental conditions.

Mehrabian and Reed [9] also propose that a concept of "optimal information processing rate *which is extermally imposed*" (i.e. determined by situational factors) may be appropriate in assessing what they call 'communication channel attributes'.

Situational factors are certainly important in everyday teaching. Good class organisation can combat many adverse environmental conditions but some are built into specialised facilities. (One sometimes wishes swimming pool architects could be required to teach for a day in the acoustic bedlam which they too often design!)

Reception

Reception can be seen to depend on at least three major sets of variables: firstly those of *attention*; secondly, those involving the efficiency of the appropriate *sense organs*, and; thirdly, those concerning pupils' *attitudes*.

The concept of **attention** would appear to be a broad one which takes into account 'physiological arousal' and, according to O'Connor [13] leads to "focussing on certain aspects of current experience and neglecting others. Interests, motives, and perceptual set or expectancy, influence what is selected for attention". She goes on to define an **attitude** as "a readiness to respond in a particular manner to some circumstance or idea". The receptiveness of the learner is obviously of great importance.

Clearly difficulties with the reception organs, such as partial deafness, cause a complete breakdown in communication, but other language difficulties, for example associated with children categorised as 'retarded', may also make the successful reception of verbal instruction less certain.

Decoding

Some of the problems of handicapped children may be at the decoding stage but even without the presence of a handicap, this is yet another point where instructional process may break down.

Decoding involves the attachment of meanings to, and perhaps the building of images from, the instruction received. This process entails the use of the pupil's linguistic ability, prior experience and habitual language code. Bernstein's [3] research has shown that the language codes employed by teachers and pupils can differ markedly. It is as well to remind oneself from time to time that even where teacher and pupil are really trying to communicate, the image in the mind of the teacher may be very different from that which the child creates from the teacher's instruction. Moreover such positive cooperation is not always present.

Action

Finally, even if instruction has passed successfully through every stage mentioned so far, there is still no automatic translation into motor action. The pupil (or teacher) may 'know' how to do a skill; may have a clear image of it – may be able to describe it accurately and in detail – but may still be unable to perform it. How often one hears the learner say, "I know what I want to do, I just can't do it". Sometimes learning is a matter of more trials, feedback in the form of 'knowledge of results', and further instruction. Sometimes successful action may be denied by anatomical or physiological limitations, or perhaps held back by the lack of necessary equipment and/or facilities.

Concluding Remarks

No formal conclusions are called for in a simple discursive paper like this, other than to re-emphasise that the process of verbal instruction may break down at any of the stages mentioned – and to note the analysis was brief and incomplete.

The hope is that students and practising teachers may, as a result of seminars on motor learning such as this, become more knowledgeable and sensitive in their everyday work.

One day, instead of the slightly angry (or resigned) response of the teacher who says, ". . . but I just *told* you how to do it!" to a pupil who patently failed to do what he was told, one may notice an increasing sense of wonder and appreciation amongst physical educationists that verbal instruction is as successful as it is.

References

1. Andrews, J. C., 'Language and communication in learning and teaching skills in physical education', Unpublished dissertation for M.Ed. degree, University of Birmingham, 1971.
2. Barnes, D. and Shemilt, D., 'Transmission and interpretation', in *Educational review*, vol. 26, no. 3, p. 213. Published by School of Education, University of Birmingham, June, 1974.

3. Bernstein, B., 'Social structure, language and learning', *Educational research*, no. 3, pp. 163–176. 1961.
4. Carroll, J. B., *Language and thought*, p. 4. Prentice-Hall, U.S.A., 1964.
5. Dalrymple-Alford, E., 'Psycholinguistics', in Foss, B. M. (ed.), *New horizons in psychology*, pp. 152–166. Penguin Books, England, 1966.
6. Holding, D. H., *Principles of training*, p. 70. Pergamon, London, 1965.
7. Johnson, D. M., *Psychology: a problem solving approach*, p. 144. Harper, New York, 1961.
8. Lawther, J. D., *The learning of physical skills*, p. 64. Prentice-Hall, U.S.A., 1968.
9. Mehrabian, A. and Reed, H., 'Some determinants of communication accuracy', *Psychological bulletin*, vol. 70, no. 5, pp. 365–381. 1968.
10. Miller, G. A., 'Some preliminaries to psycholinguistics', *American psychologist*, no. 20, pp. 15–20. 1965.
11. Morris, C., *Signs, language and behavior*, Prentice-Hall, New York, 1946.
12. Mussen, P. H., Conger, J. J. and Kagan, J., *Child development and personality*, 2nd ed. Harper & Row, London, 1963.
13. O'Connor, K., *Learning: an introduction*, Macmillan, London, 1968.
14. Rommetveit, R., *Words, meanings and messages*, Academic Press, London, 1968.
15. Vygotsky, L. S., in De Cecco, J. P. (ed.), *Psychology of language, thought and instruction*, pp. 56–60. Holt, Rinehart & Winston, London, 1969.

10

Personality, Sporting Interest and Achievement*

Introduction

This essay examines research into the relationship between measures of personality, and interest and performance in certain sporting activities. Consideration is confined to work using personality tests established by H. J. Eysenck and by R. B. Cattell. Although other tests have been used, the majority of attempts to relate a measure of personality with sporting interests and achievements have utilised a questionnaire designed by one of these researchers.

Personality is defined by Cattell [6] as "that which tells what a man will do when placed in a given situation". Allport [1] defined personality as "what a man really is". In fact, defining personality is one of the many difficulties which have beset research workers in this field. Anastasi [2] warned that "continuing development is hampered by special difficulties associated with the concept of personality. As a consequence the measurement of personality is to be regarded as tentative".

Despite this kind of reservation, personality testing became increasingly popular during the 1960's. In individual cases the results

* A revised version of a paper first published in *Educational review,* vol. 23, no. 2, pp. 126–134, in Birmingham, England. February, 1971.

obtained from personality questionnaires can only be considered as starting-points for closer (sometimes clinical) study; but, used to find a picture of personality trait distribution within fairly large groups, it is claimed they provide useful and fairly accurate information.

Personality Testing

The work of both Eysenck and Cattell is based on a study of personality traits, for example, dominance, aggression etc. Whiting [43], writes that a classification into traits is "devised to bring some form of order into the diverse acts of behaviour". Trait psychology has a considerable history and many works in common use describe behaviour in terms of different traits. Cattell reduced a list of approximately 4,500 'trait words' to about 170 by putting together those which most people would consider are synonymous – such as 'worrying' and 'anxious', 'rigid' and 'unbending', etc. He then arranged them in clusters of similar words and contrasted them with other clusters which appeared to be their polar opposites. Finally, by subjecting his work to a system of factor analysis, he 'discovered' the existence of 16 first-order factors; really clusters of traits and their polar opposites, joined to form a series of scales.

Eysenck [19] says, "Traits are not observable; they are inferred (as any kind of determining tendency is inferred). Without such inference, the stability and consistency of personal behaviour could not possibly be explained. Any specific action is the product of innumerable determinants, not only of traits but of momentary pressures and specialised influences. But it is the repeated occurrence of actions having the same significance that makes necessary the postulation of traits as states of being. Traits are not at all times active but they are persistent even when they are latent . . .".

Eysenck and Cattell differ in the emphasis which they place on personality factors – that is clusters of traits. Cattell uses a system of 16 first-order factors and where there is a correlation found between sets of these factors he generalises to a second-order level of 'types'. Cattell has arrived at two main second-order factors which he calls 'extraversion' and 'anxiety'. Similarly Eysenck has picked out two major dimensions (types in Cattell's system) of 'extraversion' and 'neuroticism'. Recently he has added a third major dimension – 'psychoticism' [22]. There is considerable agreement between the two theorists on 'extraversion', but their concepts of 'neuroticism' and 'anxiety' do not coincide so closely.

Whiting [43] sums up the situation when he points out, ". . . it is largely a question of preference and utility whether a particular theorist concentrates on 'traits' or 'types' – on first-order or on second-order factors. Eysenck puts emphasis on types and Cattell on traits. This does not mean that Eysenck ignores traits or Cattell types".

The Tests

All the tests mentioned attempt to measure personality objectively by using questionnaire techniques. Eysenck's main tests are the Maudsley Personality Inventory (M.P.I.) and the Eysenck Personality Inventory (E.P.I.). Both these have Junior versions (J.M.P.I. and J.E.P.I.). There is a recent revision of the E.P.I. which includes the extra major dimensions of psychoticism. It is possible that this will prove to be an improvement in terms of reliability and validity on the E.P.I. as well as giving further information. Eysenck claims that with the E.P.I., using a test/re-test reliability method, $r = 0.85$, which is quite high for this type of measurement instrument.

Cattell's test is generally known as the 16 Personality Factor Test (16 P.F.).

Methods of Reporting Results

Both theorists talk in terms of continua and classify a person as being at a certain point on a continuum between polar extremes. Eysenck uses three axes which he claims are independent, that is, it is not possible to predict a reading on one scale from knowledge of a score on another scale. Most of the work so far reported has been done with the M.P.I. and the E.P.I., and in both cases scores may be shown plotted on a two-dimensional model. By contrast, when recording results on the 16 P.F., 'profiles' are often produced which show up marked differences extremely clearly. A series of profiles can be superimposed for direct comparison.

This is only a very brief description of general work concerned with defining and testing personality and a selection of the considerable writings of Eysenck and Cattell should be consulted for further information. [See references 5; 6; 13; 14; 15; 16; 17; 18; 19; 20; 21; 22.)

Personality and Sport

The main purpose of this essay is to examine attempts to relate personality test results with aspects of sport. Many avenues of investigation are open. Flanagan [23] for example, says, "Certainly to the physical educator it seems important to have some understanding of why some individuals prefer to respond to certain types of activities, while other individuals may be reached by activities of quite different types". Initial interest in a sport, the learning of the skills involved, amount of participation and achievement have all been studied. Occasionally some pattern has appeared in the results but in many cases insufficient research has been completed and the evidence at present is somewhat conflicting.

Experimental Findings

Using Eysenck's Tests

In 1961 Stone [37] found, after examining top English athletes with the M.P.I., that they were significantly more extraverted than the normal population and Whiting [40] supports this by suggesting that, other things being equal, extraverts are more likely to "reach the top" in athletics. Dimsdale [11] found that a small sample of athletes, respresentative of a wide range of ability in athletics (the sample included club and county athletes as well as junior and senior internationals), scored more highly than Eysenck's normal English population on both the extraversion and neuroticism scale using the E.P.I.

However, it appears from work by Nias [33] at Loughborough College of Education, that most physical education students are quite highly extraverted – more so than the reported scores of the international athletes, so that whilst extraversion may be highly correlated with interest and participation, it may not be a vital factor in determining success at higher competitive levels. Brooke [4] found average neuroticism and very high extraversion in 118 Loughborough P.E. students. Comparing their scores with Eysenck's normal population Nias says, "we may conclude the average P.E. student is more extraverted than 70% of people in general". If true, this has considerable implications for the relationship between teachers of P.E. and their pupils and also between many coaches and their protégés.

Using the M.P.I., Knapp [31] established that a sample of 46 top-class tennis players were more extraverted and less neurotic than a sample quota of 1,800 ordinary English people but that the differences between the means were not significant. She concluded that "although there is a preponderance of individuals with extravert tendencies, there are also a considerable number of outstanding lawn tennis players who are introverted". Six of the forty-six were, in fact, more than one standard deviation from the norm towards the introversion end of the continuum.

Rasch and Mozee [34] found (in spite of a quite common belief that many men who engage in weight-lifting and body-building, do so for reasons connected with the possession of a certain personality type) that after testing 69 competing weight-lifters and body-builders with the M.P.I. as a total group they did not deviate from the norm for the population and neither did they suffer significantly from each other as sub-groups.

Whiting and Stembridge [42] used the M.P.I. to investigate the personalities of 43 persistent non-swimmers. They found that these students were significantly more introverted and neurotic than normal. The study has been extended, using the J.M.P.I. to 1,540 boys aged 11 and 12 years and the same results were found. In discussing the results Whiting suggests that introverts are more likely to be put off by early unpleasant experiences in learning to swim, particularly if they also score highly on the neuroticism scale.

Using the 16 P.F. Test

Many researchers have preferred to use the 16 P.F. test as they claim that it yields more information.

Hendry [25; 26] tested 30 potential international swimmers. He found them bright, outgoing, emotional but realistic. As a group he found them to be very similar to the general population. This is confirmed by another study by Hendry and Whiting [27]; and Entwhistle [12] sums up the situation as he finds it after a detailed examination of the present research. In his view, "no particular 'swimmers' personality' exists. A variety of personalities is found in swimming at all levels .... Participation in competitive swimming is not dependent on possessing a certain personality type". On the other hand, Hendry did find that many girl swimmers tended to be introverted, and Rushall [35], whilst not agreeing with Hendry, claimed to have found distinctive types of personality after relating the results of 16 P.F. tests on 300 swimmers to their performance records. For example, he found his top male swimmers to be highly individual and self-centred. The evidence about swimming, certainly beyond the persistent non-swimmer stage, appears to be somewhat confused at present.

Kane [30] has examined the personalities of three groups of soccer players, professionals, young professionals and amateur internationals, and found considerable similarities between their 16 P.F. profiles which led him to say [38], "It would seem that there is some reason for suggesting a 'footballer type' ". He found that the factors significantly represented were as follows (in order of importance); emotional integration, extraversion, toughmindedness, ruthlessness, radicalism and general intelligence. He found also that they were significantly less dominant factor (E) as a group, and comments that whilst high dominance is normally associated with ability in individual sports "apparently, professional team players must be reasonably able to conform in the interests of the team".

Another interesting supposition by Kane is that due to slow emancipation of women, only a certain personality type tends to come forward, be selected and 'reach the top' in women's sports. He compares female swimmers and athletes and finds a similar 16 P.F. profile [38] but he sounds a note of warning that later work, concerned with lawn tennis, tends to support Knapp's negative findings and confuse the picture [29].

Athletics has also been studied by Cureton and Heusner [10], who found that a sample of former champions was significantly different from the norm. They were more dominant (E), less inhibited (F), more confident and free from neurotic tendencies (O). This was also found with a group of 40 outstanding young English athletes [28], but intergroup differences became more apparent when the group was subdivided according to their events. For example, throwers and sprinters were found to be highly extravert, while middle distance runners scored lowest on extraversion. Hardman [24] in a study of many sports found that cross-country runners were generally intraverted and quite different from other groups participating in active athletics.

Werner [39] studied American football players and found them more sociable, group dependent and conventional, dominant, enthusiastic, adventurous and tough when compared with a non-athletic group. Kroll and Peterson [32] compared the profiles of winning and losing American football teams and found significant distinctions between the teams' intelligence (B), adventurousness (H), confidence (O) and will-power (Q3). The higher scores were obtained in all these aspects by teams with a consistently good record of wins.

Cockerill [7] found a relationship between dominance and successful, as opposed to run-of-the-mill golfers. He wondered which was the cause, and which the effect in this situation! Other studies have looked at rugby footballers [36], table tennis internationals [43] and gymnasts [3]. In this latter work Boscoe found that the gymnast was significantly "brighter and more intelligent (B), calmer and more mature (C), more conventional and serious (M), more confident, critical and experimental (O) and more controlled and exact (Q3)".

Other researchers have sought to examine performance in stressful situations. Brooke [4] examined physical performance and pain perception without coming to definite conclusions, but Costello and Eysenck [8] demonstrated that the extravert has a marked superiority in pain tolerance and Whiting [41] concludes that "the extravert would be able to express more of his strength where pain was a limiting factor". Cratty [9] points out that "personality of the performer also influences his susceptibility to the audience effect".

Summary and Implications

There has been considerable research in this field but more is needed before positive statements can be made. Confusion remains in a number of areas where conflicting results have been obtained.

There is some evidence of a relationship between a stable extravert personality and high-level performance in sport. High dominance appears to be an important factor in individual sporting achievements.

In view of the many exceptions that have been found it is vital that the teacher and/or coach should not treat all individuals included in activities alike but should make suitable adjustments in their approach to teaching and coaching individuals.

There is some evidence for the existence of certain 'sporting types'. Also certain activities appear more attractive to different personalities. For this reason a wide programme of differing activities should be offered in secondary schools to cater for this factor.

Personality factors are an important consideration where sportsmen or children are taking part in activities in a stressful situation, whether the stress be caused by physical danger or the presence of an audience.

Finally, the physical education teacher should realise that he is probably different in personality from approximately 70% of the community. What is sauce for the goose may not be sauce for the gander!

References

1. Allport, G. W., *Personality, a psychological interpretation*, Holt, p. 510. 1937.
2. Anastasi, A., *Psychological understanding*, Macmillan, New York, 1961.
3. Boscoe, J. S., *The physical and personality characteristics of champion male gymnasts*, Report to Colleges of P.E. Association Conference, 1962.
4. Brooke, J. D., 'Extraversion, physical performance and pain perception in P.E. students', *Research in physical education*, 1, no. 2, 1967.
5. Cattell, R. B. and Eber, H. W., *Handbook for the 16 P.F. questionnaire*, 1957.
6. Cattell, R. B., *The scientific analysis of personality*, Penguin, 1965.
7. Cockerill, I., 'Personality of golf players', in Whiting, H.T.A., *Acquiring ball skill*, p. 90. Bell, 1969.
8. Costello, C. L. and Eysenck, H. J., 'Persistence, personality and motivation', *Perceptual and motor skills*, 12.
9. Cratty, B. J., *Movement behavior and motor learning*, 2nd ed. Lea & Febiger. 1967.

10. Cureton, T. K. and Heusner, L., *Personality traits of champion and former champion athletes*, Research Study, University of Illinois, 1952.
11. Dimsdale, A., 'Two personality dimensions of a small sample of British athletes', *Bull. of Brit. psych. soc.,* 21, 1967.
12. Entwhistle, P., 'Personality traits of competitive swimmers', unpublished paper, University of Leeds, 1968.
13. Eysenck. H. J., *Dimensions of personality*, Routledge & Kegan Paul, 1950.
14. Eysenck, H. J., *Scientific study of personality*, Routledge & Kegan Paul, 1952.
15. Eysenck, H. J., *The structure of human personality*, Methuen, 1953.
16. Eysenck, H. J., *Sense and nonsense in psychology*, Penguin, 1957.
17. Eysenck, H. J., *Manual of the Maudsley personality inventory*, University of Liverpool Press, 1959.
18. Eysenck, H. J., *Diagnosis of anxiety and hysteria*, Routledge & Kegan Paul, 1959.
19. Eysenck, H. J., *Crime and personality,* Routledge & Kegan Paul, 1964.
20. Eysenck, H. J. and Eysenck, S. B. G., *Manual of the Eysenck personality inventory*, University of Liverpool Press. 1964.
21. Eysenck, H. J., *Fact and fiction in psychology*, Penguin. 1965.
22. Eysenck, H. J. and Eysenck, S. B. G., 'A factorial study of psychoticism as a dimension of personality', in *Multivariate behavioural research*, 1968.
23. Flanagan, L., 'A study of some personality traits of different physical activity groups', *Research quarterly*, 22, p. 312. 1951.
24. Hardman, K., 'Personality differences between top-class games players of lesser ability'. Paper to British Society for Sports Psychology Conference, 1968.
25. Hendry, L. B., 'Personality – the coach and the swimmer', *British swimming coaches association bulletin*, 42, 1966.
26. Hendry, L. B., 'The personality traits of British swimmers', *British swimming coaches association bulletin*, 46, p. 1. 1967.
27. Hendry, L. B. and Whiting, H. T. A. 'Social and psychological trends in national championship swimmers – a three year replication study', *International journal of sports medicine*, 1968.
28. Kane, J. E., 'Personality and physique of athletes', *Physical recreation*, 34, 1960.
29. Kane, J. E. and Callaghan, J. L., 'Personality traits in tennis players', *British lawn tennis*, July, 1965.
30. Kane, J. E., 'Personality description of soccer ability', *Research in P.E.,* 1, p. 1. 1960.
31. Knapp, B., 'The personality of lawn tennis players', *Bull. of Brit. psych. society,* October, 1965.
32. Kroll, W. and Peterson, K. H., 'P.F. profiles of collegiate football teams', *Research quarterly,* 36.
33. Nias, D. K. B., cyclostyled notes for P.E. students Loughborough College of Education.
34. Rasch, D. J. and Mozee, G., 'Neuroticism and extraversion in weight trainers', *Journal of association of physical and mental rehabilitation*, no. 6. 1963.
35. Rushall, B. S., 'Preliminary personality work with swimmers', *British swimming coaches association bulletin,* 44. 1967.
36. Sinclair, E., 'Personality of rugby football players', in Whiting, H. T. A., *Acquiring ball skill,* p. 93. Bell, 1969.
37. Stone, P., 'Is the athlete different in personality to the non-athlete?', Paper at British Association of Sports Medicine Conference, 1961.
38. Warburton, F. W. and Kane, J. E., 'Personality related to sport and physical ability', *Readings in physical education*, Physical Education Association, 1966.

39. Werner, A. C., 'Physical education and the development of leadership', Proceedings of colleges of P.E. association annual conference. 1958.
40. Whiting, H. T. A., 'Personality and the athlete', *A.A.A. coaching newsletter*, May, 1963.
41. Whiting, H. T. A., 'Personality and sports medicine', *Physical education*, 56, no. 168. July, 1964.
42. Whiting, H. T. A. and Stembridge, D. E., 'Personality and the persistent non-swimmer', *Research quarterly*, 36, p. 3. 1965.
43. Whiting, H. T. A., *Acquiring ball skill*, p. 87. Bell, 1969.

11

Some Socio-Psychological Considerations of the Teacher of Physical Education*

Introduction

It is probably useful to start this paper from a fairly wide sociological viewpoint because, although all children by law find themselves in school, only a small percentage of these children go on to become teachers.

Studies [6] made of the social origins of teachers suggest that an examination of this factor may provide a partial explanation for the development of different role definitions amongst teachers. Furthermore, "the teaching profession acts either as a favourite stage in upward mobility or as a second-choice occupation for university educated individuals". 'Upward mobility' here relates to movement up the scale of social classes, the 'upward mobile' usually being ready and eager to embrace the norms and attitudes of the new group.

Formerly many teachers came from 'working-class' backgrounds and for a while, different groups, with different social backgrounds were clearly discernible in different sectors of the educational system. Latterly Floud and Scott [5] report that, "the picture of the changes in

* A revised version of a paper first published in the *Asian journal of physical education*, vol. 1, no. 1, pp. 35–41. Taipei, Taiwan. January, 1978.

the pattern of recruitment to the various types of school lends some support to the view that there is a breaking down of 'caste' lines between the different types of school and more resemblance than hitherto in the social background of the teachers in them. In all types of school, the largest group of teachers entering is now drawn from non-manual families". These families would generally fall into the 'lower middle class' category.

Class Values and Attitudes

The fact that many teachers may be drawn from a relatively narrow strata of the community as a whole, and that as a group they are essentially aspiring to middle class status and ready to adopt middle class values and attitudes, is likely to affect the ease of communication between them and large sections of the school population.

'Middle class values and attitudes' are thought to include those of ambitiousness, seeking self-improvement through occupation, seeking individual responsibility, valuing academic achievements, long term planning and postponement of gratification, control of aggression, respect for authority, respect for property, courtesy, and constructive use of leisure time.

A glance through the list should pinpoint at once some possible areas of conflict between a teacher holding these values and a child from a social background where these are *not* the accepted norms for behaviour!

Hoyle [9] writes of the problem of "teacher and pupil 'talking past each other'". In some respects physical education is less prone to these problems than other areas of the curriculum, much of the language of sport, for example, being widely used across social class bounds. This is true, however, only to a limited extent and the underlying traditions of rugby football, as opposed to those of soccer are very much class based. This is also true of such concepts as 'the spirit of the game' and 'sportsmanship'. These concepts reflect essentially middle class values.

Again Hoyle [11] talking about the role of the teacher, says, "A teacher's actions are determined partly by his own personality and partly by the expectations which are held of him *as a teacher*. But even within the teaching profession, roles are differentiated according to authority, function, attributes such as age, sex and qualifications, and informal social status. Each of these generates different sets of expectations. Moreover, teachers perform their roles differently according to the type of school in which they teach and the sort of district in which it is situated".

A number of studies have been done on the personality of teachers in general and, being such a large group, they tend to show a fairly normal range of distribution. However, particular studies with physical education students show that on Eysenck's introversion – extraversion scale, physical educationists may tend to be quite highly extravert as a group. Some authorities claim, more strongly, they are different from about 70% of the children they teach [1].

The Concept of Role

Looking more closely at the concept of *role,* one can examine three aspects. Firstly, a position or **status** is indicated; secondly, there is a **pattern of behaviour** associated with the role, which is independent of the person who actually occupies it; and finally, there is a **pattern of expectations** held of the occupant which will include ideas of what he *should not* do as well as what he *should.* Two other concepts are of particular interest from role theory; that of **role set** – the group of people who have expectations of the teacher and whose expectations have significance for the teacher; and that of **role conflict.** Conflict may occur in a number of situations; for example, where two different roles of the same person are in opposition (teacher versus father), where expectations of different members of the role set are in opposition (children versus headmaster), or where the expectations of the role are in conflict with an individual's personality needs (need for acceptance and affection versus necessity to retain social distance, impartiality, authority, etc.).

It is not possible to go deeper here into this fascinating area of studies, but in considering the effectiveness of any individual as he teaches a class, small group, or individual, it may be enlightening to consider the status of the teacher in that situation, the expectations of the child or children (who will be members of the teacher's role set) and whether the particular programme content and the manner/method in which guidance is given, includes anything likely to cause 'role conflict' for the teacher or for the learner.

Members of the role set also have considerable influence on what is considered to be the main, or most important, part of a teacher's rather diffuse role. Heaton [8] looked particularly at the role of the male physical education teacher working with boys in secondary schools. He categorised the specific role of the P.E. specialist into five areas: moral/social education; giving knowledge of techniques and skill in performance; general physical development; organisation and administration; and, aesthetic education. Questionnaires were circulated to sixth form schoolboys, students, teachers, head teachers, L.E.A. organisers of P.E., and college of education lecturers in P.E. The result, perhaps somewhat surprisingly, was that there was a large measure of agreement that *the first priority should be given to moral and social education*. In his discussion of results, he reports, "The only group not to give this a first choice is the sixth form group who show conflict with their teachers". If such conflicts can be discovered then it may be that another variable in the teaching/learning situation may be appreciated and, perhaps, controlled.

Authority

The authority of the teacher is recognisable at two levels. At the **national level** there is the aspect of delegated authority which gives the individual teacher a large measure of autonomy in the classroom or gymnasium. Baron and Tropp [2] have compared the problems of teaching in the United States of America and England. They conclude, "The greater authority of the teachers in the English educational structure and their insulation from external pressures is reflected in the classroom situation. There is less need for the British teacher to seek *the consensus of his pupils*. Parents are either active or passive supporters of teachers in their disciplinary problems".

Certainly before any instructional roles can be engaged in, the teacher must have authority at the level of **class control.** Hoyle [10] says, "Ability to control his class is also basic to the expectations held of a teacher by his colleagues, and from the point of view of the head teacher, a teacher's competence is assessed in the first place on his ability to maintain order". The necessity to maintain this aspect of control may severely limit the kind of instruction which a teacher can give. Whereas 'being one of the boys' and 'speaking their language' might well facilitate immediate communication, it is certain that it would stir-up some role conflict which might in the long run lead to less effective teaching, or even the total breakdown of the teaching situation. Any innovations involving substantially different pupil-teacher relationships thus need to take into account the prevailing authority structure, role conflicts (effects on other members of staff and their teaching) and long-term effects on the whole pupil/teacher relationship.

The Teacher as a Leader

"The role of leadership of a group is one example of the relationship between individual and group and is of special interest to the teacher since he has to lead his pupils" Peel [16]. Lippitt and White [14] investigated the effects of three different kinds of leadership: 'authoritarian', 'democratic' and 'laissez-faire', on the activities and attitudes of groups of boys.

Their main findings were that the work of the *authoritarian* led group was more constructive than that of the *laissez-faire* group, but less constructive than that of the *democratically* led group. Work fell off in this group when the leader was absent. The intra-group attitudes tended to be aggressive.

The *democratically* led group was more cohesive and approaches to the leader were friendly and non-competitive in contrast to those in the authoritarian group where they were submissive and attention demanding.

The *laissez-faire* group was least constructive; frustration caused by ignorance led to considerable problems. They were highest in aggression of all the groups.

Harding [7] has criticised the too facile interpretation of this experiment as proving that democratic leadership is more effective than autocratic. Each pattern offers a different set of advantages in different situations. Hoyle [12] underlines this by saying, "The first point is that the appropriateness of leadership behaviour in the classroom is relative to the nature of the group and to the task in hand". A teacher may successfully adopt one leadership style with children from certain home backgrounds which would not work with children from other backgrounds. Certainly outside the classroom (and sometimes well outside the confines of the school), the physical education teacher will have to be very adaptable in his leadership behaviour. "The skilful teacher can play the role of comedian, kindly uncle, confidante, or any other informal role, but yet retain the capacity to return with ease to a more detached role without losing the goodwill of his pupils" [12].

Work on a combination of factors which include notions of personality, role and leadership style, has led to the postulation and identification of a series of *teaching styles*. Although these have not been fully developed for physical educationists, it could be that this will prove an area of useful development which could then be correlated with the effectiveness of teaching particular skills, in particular ways, in particular situations, etc.

Imitation

Before leaving the general effect of the teacher on the learner, it is necessary to mention the possibility of **imitation.** The gross imitation of movements, of mannerisms and attitudes, is a potent factor in the teaching situation and needs to be considered in any analysis of the effects of teaching. The pupil may still learn more from seeing and imitating the total behaviour of the teacher than from learning just what the teacher wishes to convey.

Interaction Between Teacher and Class

Some of the problems of the relationships between the teacher and (particularly) his class have been analysed by Parsons [15]. He expresses these as a series of 'dilemmas' which the teacher must face before he can act. They are: affectivity versus affective neutrality (the emotional tone of the relationship); specificity versus diffuseness (how specific the role is – instruction or socialisation?); universalism versus particularism (how does one person judge another – as an individual or against universal standards?); quality versus performance (orientation on the basis of a quality such as age or sex, or on the basis of performance and achievement); self-orientation versus collectivity orientation (does the teacher put his own or the profession's interests first?).

This type of analysis leads to a clearer understanding of the teaching situation, which is one of interacting human beings, and some such classification of the teacher's particular solutions may be useful in looking in some detail at teaching staff. Quite sophisticated means of 'interaction analysis' have now been developed [4; 17; 19].

Perhaps the simplest of all classifications of teacher behaviour is that which draws on terminology at present in use in physical education. Taking one division as **formal** teaching (e.g. command-response) and another as **informal** (e.g. conversational) teaching and adding to these the notions of **direct** teaching (e.g. expository) and **indirect** teaching (e.g. using discovery methods) one could arrive at a simple classification of teachers' styles into four categories.

Formal – Direct
Informal – Direct
Formal – Indirect
Informal – Indirect

Perhaps the most unlikely of these is the third – the combination of 'formal and indirect' – but having heard a middle-aged teacher employing just such methods in teaching 'modern educational gymnastics', it certainly exists!

The Teacher's Voice

Although in general considerations of the ease of hearing voices of different pitches it is usually stated that (all other things being equal), it is as easy to hear the 'soprano' as it is to hear the 'bass', experience shows that in teaching physical education, certain voices are more effective than others. Too low pitched voices, for example, in indoor gymnasia (some of which are notoriously badly designed acoustically) tend to get lost in the background noise caused by the activity of the class. (The modern tendency is not to stop the whole class every time instruction is given to a group or to an individual.) Another factor which causes considerable trouble and needs very careful timing and enunciation, is met in class teaching in halls and swimming pools where there is an appreciable *echo*. Training and experience are both beneficial in combating such problems and teachers can be helped to speak loudly without strain where necessary and to articulate clearly. In some ways it is unfortunate that in a mood of 'avoiding meddling with a student's natural speech and accent', some important work that was done on voice and speech in colleges of education in the past, is now left undone.

Starkweather [18] has studied the amount of information which the voice carries *about the speaker*. "In addition to that which is coded as linguistic content, the total communication in a face-to-face interaction includes important vocal behaviour as well as the information contained in verbal content and in non-verbal gestures and expression. Some people (children in particular?) appear to be very sensitive to vocal information and use cues from a speaker's voice to make inferences about his personality and his emotional state of the moment." Lieberman [13] likewise has studied the effects of intonation with particular reference to the relationship between intonations and the syntactic processing of speech – but he notes, "The emotional aspects of intonation are *extra-linguistic* since the listener must know the behaviour of a particular talker in order to decode correctly the acoustic signal. One talker may signal anger by speaking in a quiet, low-pitched voice, whereas another may speak in a loud, high-pitched voice". This is obviously quite true but it does not completely contradict Starkweather because the listener *does* make assumptions about the speaker from the pitch and intonation of the speaker's voice, but as

Lieberman reminds us, without some further knowledge of the behaviour of that person, the interpretation may, in fact, be erroneous.

The Teacher as a Motivator

Finally, in this brief consideration of the teacher, the 'working atmosphere' which he creates must be mentioned. This is often seen as a consideration within the scope of 'motivation' and in particular the affective state which is created – largely by the general relationship between the teacher and class – and particularly by his use of praise and blame, rewards and punishments. The important role of 'knowledge of results' must also not be overlooked in this situation.

It is generally assumed that a child will wish to please the teacher and this is probably so for most children, at least up to the age of about five or six years. Cratty [3] reports, "It is usually found that 'verbal punishment' elicits a heightened state of arousal resulting in a more rapid or more intense efforts. At the same time negative verbal exhortation tends to disrupt complex performance". He sums up by saying, "The influence of verbal exhortation upon performance is a function of the age of the performer, his past experience at the task, as well as the nature of the task. Similarly the previous relationships between individuals offering encouragement or disapproval and the performers also influences the effects of this kind of social motivation". Generally the effects of *praise* and *reward* have been found to be greatly superior to pain and fear in motivating the learning of children. They are certainly more ethical.

Closing Comments

Although the title of this essay referred particularly to the teacher of physical education, it should be obvious that many of the socio-psychological considerations included are of much wider application.

By tracing such strands as social origins, role expectations, personality, authority and leadership, and by considering the influence a teacher can have as a model for imitation, as well as a communicator – often through language – of knowledge, skills and attitudes, one can start to appreciate the great complexity of the 'teacher input' side of the teaching-learning process.

This leaves aside the equally, if not more, complex pattern of individual differences amongst the children he will teach.

References

1. Andrews, J. C., 'Personality, sporting interest and achievement', *Educational review*, p. 129, vol. 23, no. 2, Birmingham, 1971.
2. Baron, G. and Tropp, A., 'Teaching in England and America', in Halsey, A. H. *et al.* (eds.), *Education, economy and society*, p. 554. Collier-Macmillan, London, 1961.
3. Cratty, B. J., *Movement behavior and motor learning*, 2nd ed., p. 10. Lea & Febiger, U.S.A., 1967.
4. Flanders, N. A., *Analyzing teaching behavior*. Addison Wesley, U.S.A., 1970.
5. Floud, J. and Scott, W., 'Recruitment to teaching in England and Wales', in Halsey, A. H. *et al. Education, economy and society*, pp. 542–543. Collier-Macmillan, London, 1961.
6. Halsey, A. H., Floud, J. and Anderson, C. A., 'Teachers in schools and universities', *Education, economy and society*, pp. 527–626. Collier-Macmillan, London, 1961.
7. Harding, D. W., *Social psychology and individual values*, Hutchinson, London, 1953.
8. Heaton, J., 'The role of the male physical education teacher working with boys in secondary schools', *Bulletin of physical education*, vol. 8, no. 2, pp. 31–35. B.A.O.L.P.E., 1972.
9. Hoyle, E., *The role of the teacher*, p. 25. Routledge & Kegan Paul, 1969.
10. Hoyle, E., *ibid.*, p. 42.
11. Hoyle, E., *ibid.*, p. 57.
12. Hoyle, E., *ibid.*, p. 62.
13. Lieberman, P., 'Intonation and the syntactic processing of speech', in Wathen-Dunn, W. (ed.), *Models for the perception of speech and visual form*, pp. 314–319. M.I.T., 1964.
14. Lippitt, R. and White, R. K., 'An experimental study of leadership and group life', in Newcomb, T. M. and Hartley, E. L. (eds.). *Readings in social psychology*, Holt, U.S.A., 1947.
15. Parsons, T., *The social system*, Routledge & Kegan Paul, London, 1951.
16. Peel, E. A., *The psychological basis of education*, p. 240. Oliver & Boyd, London, 1956.
17. Pieron, M., 'La relation pédagogique étude par l'analyse de l'enseignement', *Teaching the teacher in physical education*, pp. 41–75. A.I.E.S.E.P. Year Book, Madrid, 1976.
18. Starkweather, J. A., 'Vocal behaviour as an information channel of speaker's status', 253–263 in Salzinger, K. and Salzinger, S. (eds.), *Research in verbal behaviour and some neurophysiological implications*, pp. 253–263. Academic Press, London, 1967.
19. Underwood, G. L., 'The use of interaction analysis and video tape recording in studying teaching behaviour in physical education'. *Evaluation in physical education*, pp. 24–34. N.A.T.F.H.E. Conference Report, 1976.

SECTION 3

Physical Education and Sport

12

Physical Education as a Basis for Sport*

Introduction

In one short paper it is clearly impossible to deal in great depth with such a complex topic. The writer of the preliminary notes sent out before this conference spoke of 'misconceptions', perhaps a few of these *may* be cleared up, at least to some people's satisfaction. The selected references used in this paper may also help others to follow up some of the points to their own conclusions. "Differences between sport and physical education" were also mentioned. These *do* exist and they need to be understood. Whether their analysis leads to divided positions or to communication and co-operation, is another question, depending for its answer partly on the people involved and how far they are prepared to value and accept other people's points of view.

Definitions and Relationships

Unfortunately some working definitions are needed even before any discussion can really start. Those adopted here may seem too simple,

* A revised version of a paper first presented as the opening address at the National Congress on Physical Education as a Basis for Sport, Sligo, Ireland, in April, 1977.

almost naïve: if this *is* so, it is not because the true complexity of the problems has been overlooked. The very need to start by defining terms, illustrates the diversity of current opinion and the lack of generally accepted terminology.

Singer [26] in a good discussion of terminology, mentions some blind men trying to describe an elephant. One at its leg, said "it is 'tree like'", another, near the trunk, said "it is 'long and thin'", another at its side said, "it is 'hard and wall-like'". One may need to be sure that the whole 'animal' is being viewed and one's definitions are not dominated by too close contact in a limited area.

With this warning in mind one can examine the concepts of physical education and sport. Firstly, **physical education:**

The term 'physical education' has been used variously. For example,

(a) to name *courses of study* in colleges and universities; some leading to professional life, others more 'academic' and less career-linked;
(b) to indicate a qualified *position for work,* as in the term 'physical education specialist';
(c) as a *subject heading for lessons,* including sports activities, in school curricula; and
(d) to indicate *a process.*

It is in this latter use that the real essence of physical education is to be found; the other uses indicate *areas related to the* central process of physical education. Of all the possible ways of considering the term, therefore, "Physical education is essentially a process, one of the family of processes which make up Education" [2].

This definition is in line with the consensus of international opinion put forward in the *F.I.E.P. World Manifesto on Physical Education* in 1970, which said: "Physical Education is the element in education which uses, in a systematic way, both physical activities and the influence of natural agents; air, sunshine, water, etc., as specific means" [10].

If this is accepted, it means that physical education must be valued on its contribution to acceptable educational aims: that is, through at least partial achievement of the aims of physical education.

Processes may be judged 'valuable' in their own right but it is fashionable (even in education), and probably correct, that the *product* of the process should also be questioned. The curricular aims of physical education give some notion of *the desired product.*

To talk of 'physical education as a basis for sport' may be to suggest that sport has a product relationship with the physical education process. This *may* be so, but if it is so, one still has to ask, "How much of physical education *does, can* and *ought* to go into this product?"

However, it may be that sport is best seen as separate from education; the process of sports participation having many similar, perhaps overlapping, aspects which would mean that again one could consider 'physical education as a basis for sport' in terms of the extent of supportive overlapping elements, without considering sport as something necessarily *built on* a basis of physical education.

Before pursuing these considerations further, one needs to examine the complex phenomenon known as **sport**.

How does one produce a simple sentence to define a phenomenon which includes such a vast variety of human behaviour, such different environments, such varied structures, and which is subject to such immense pressures as racism, politics, the demands of mass media and the entertainment industry, professionalism, etc. John Loy [19] making 'a definitional effort' in Ellen Gerber's book, *Sport and the Body*, reports that, "Sport is a highly ambiguous term having different meanings for various people". He then goes on to devote about ten packed pages to the complex problems of definition!

This is obviously a time-consuming discussion. In the same book Eleanor Metheny, having examined "This 'thing' called sport", concluded, there is a "professional need for a comprehensive taxonomic classification of sport-type behaviours – but time did not permit (her) to undertake the enormous task of composing one". So how does one proceed here?

The F.I.E.P. President, Dr. Seurin [25] introducing the joint debate between F.I.E.P. and the International Olympic Academy at Olympia in July, 1975 said:

> "Sport is
> **a game;** that is to say a free activity, which does not follow any utilitarian objective but which is developed within a set of . . . rules, and at the same time puts the individual to the test. The objectives are recreative and self-testing.
>
> Sport is
> **a contest;** against an opponent: an adversary, space, time, obstacle, or natural force. The objective is victory.
>
> Sport is
> **intensive physical activity;** the objectives of which are self-excellence and record breaking. Sport is a 'game of prowess'."

He goes on to claim that if a single one of these criteria is missing, the activity is not 'sport'. *Professional sport* is classed as 'a trade'. Other activities, less intensive from the physical point of view, such as walking, bowls, chess, etc., are classed as *recreational activities*.

This was a brave effort at brevity. It has obvious problems, for example, in that some of the activities which would meet all the criteria to be classified as sports, could also be categorised as recreational. However, those classified solely as recreations would *not* have all the attributes of a sport.

More recently, Professor J. M. Cagigal [7] has published a paper on 'Sport and Education' in which he makes an interesting differentiation between 'spectator sport' and 'sport as an individual activity'. He sees these as two tendencies in different directions which "influence and condition each other". Spectator sport he describes as, "sport of performance, competition and as a profession . . . moved and conditioned by powerful economic and socio-political forces". On the other hand, in *sport as individual activity* he includes, "the other aspects of sport, such as 'sport as a health pursuit', 'sport as active leisure', 'sport as recreation'", this approach he terms, sport-for-all.

Note that **sport-for-all** is differently defined in various countries. Sometimes it is contrasted with *Elite (competitive) Championship* sport; the 'for-all' offsetting the *exclusiveness* of the high level 'champion producing' (and possibly professional) nature of the other. However, 'sport-for-all' is also used as an *all inclusive* term, thus including sport for the elite of talented performers. The Sports Council in England and Wales has used this latter conception as the basis for its national 'sport-for-all' campaign.

There remain other problems of inclusion and exclusion as one meets up with arguments about whether blood sports, horse and greyhound racing, fishing and motor cycling are 'sports' at all. About many of these, the mass media seem in no doubt; the air-time and newspaper coverage given to some of these activities on 'sports' programmes and 'sports' pages would appear to settle the question pragmatically, publicly and beyond doubt.

One may note that the inclusion of sporting activities in school curricula could be interpreted as giving them a utilitarian purpose beyond that normally ascribed to sport. One might ask, "Is *School Sport*, really sport in the way that Seurin has defined it?" It would certainly seem to be a significantly different aspect of the total sporting spectrum.

Perhaps one can best summarise these various aspects as shown in Figure 12.1.

In considering physical education as a basis for sport, even at this early stage, the question is posed, "Which aspects of sport are we considering?" May there be priorities, and choices which have to be made? Perhaps one can look at the problems in another way. One approach could be to ignore for the moment the problems of the 'other

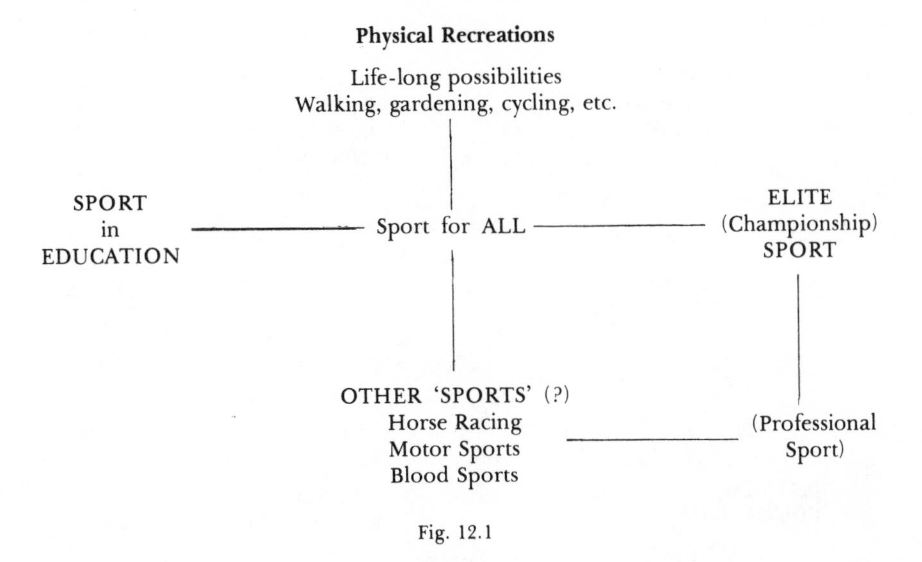

Fig. 12.1

sports' area; include 'sport in education' as a 'content-determining' and related part of physical education; include in community physical recreation, 'sport-for-all' in the sense that Cagigal has used it; and then look at relationships between physical education and community physical recreation; and their relationship in turn to top level championship sport.

Relationships Between Physical Education, Physical Recreation and Competitive Sport

Munrow [21] has pointed out that, "Standards in sport are sometimes likened to a pyramid. Broaden the base, it is argued, and the peak will rise accordingly. It is true, but by no means the whole truth. Coaching and competitions provide *throughout* the pyramid a re-inforcing structure which really determines the height of the peak in relation to a given base".

In 1972, Groves [14], wrote of two different ways of viewing relationships between physical education, physical recreation and competitive sport. In Figure 12.2 are some modified versions of the diagrams he used to express these views.

The first example depicts the notion mentioned by Munrow; that the broader the base of physical education and physical recreation (shown as different but overlapping to a certain extent), the more competitive sportsmen should be produced and, by selection from a

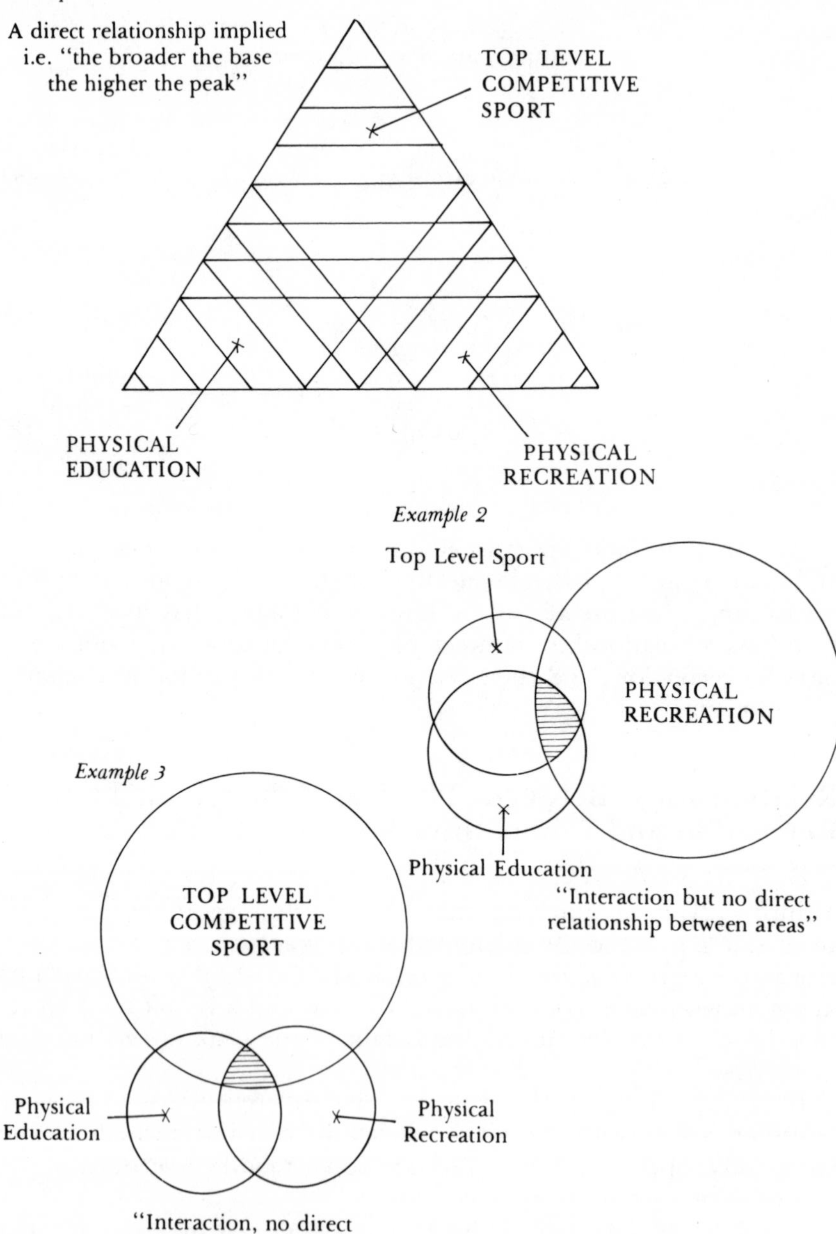
Example 1
A direct relationship implied
i.e. "the broader the base
the higher the peak"
TOP LEVEL
COMPETITIVE
SPORT
PHYSICAL
EDUCATION
PHYSICAL
RECREATION
Example 2
Top Level Sport
PHYSICAL
RECREATION
Physical Education
"Interaction but no direct
relationship between areas"
Example 3
TOP LEVEL
COMPETITIVE
SPORT
Physical
Education
Physical
Recreation
"Interaction, no direct
relationship, different
national priority"

Fig. 12.2

greater number, the higher the performance peaks reached. A direct relationship between the broad base and the peak is implied (note Munrow's warning about the competitive structure needed throughout the pyramid to assist this in reality).

In the second and third of given examples, the three areas are shown as *interacting* but not *directly* related in size. Example 2 depicts a hypothetical situation where there is little regular basic physical education in schools, but considerable (perhaps State provided) physical recreation. There is as yet, little participation in top level competitions such as the Olympic Games. In Example 3, one might say that there is not much going at all! What effort there has been, has been to try and find potential champions for nationalistic reasons perhaps. Money, coaching talent and facilities have been devoted to this cause, perhaps to the neglect of basic physical education in schools and community physical recreation. Such a system may well produce some talented athletes, perhaps even a few champions, without there being any depth of physical education and sports participation in that country.

Although the pyramid example illustrates what might be called 'traditional British thinking', there must be some doubt concerning its assumptions about an automatic relationship between increased total numbers involved and a resultant rise in the quantity and quality of top level performers. The size and importance of these areas may be unrelated. Other pressures are certainly at work! Time permits the mention of only a few.

Some Pressures and Problems in Sports Participation

Nixon and Jewett [23] in the United States are well aware of some current problems in sport and have written, "Full opportunity to participate freely in sport should be made equally available to all persons regardless of colour, race, or creed. Sport should be an area which provides for the democratic participation of all, without overtones of racism, prejudice, or inequality".

Unfortunately in practice it doesn't usually happen like that. From within the U.S.A. itself, for example, comes a comment from Mal Andrews [4] 'an African born in America'. In an article entitled 'Physical Education and Sports: business as usual vs. by any means necessary', he makes a very strong attack on white physical educators as racist agents. He says, "If white physical educators and coaches are going to relate to all people they got some dues to pay. They got to recognise differences between black and white people and they can start *now* by studying and living the real physical education, the 'psychoblackological' experience. Then maybe we can get on with what's PEOPLE in this world".

Secondly, if one believes that politics are not, or should not be, mixed up with sport, and that East Germany's successes in the Montreal Olympic Games were simply the result of better co-operation between community, schools and clubs, then listen to the General Secretary of the Socialist Unity Party of Germany welcoming the victorious athletes home; he said, "The 90 medals, 40 of them gold, which you have won are an expression of *conscientious political and sporting preparation*". Honecker [15].

Thirdly, if one needs any further evidence of some of the pressures *on*, and *within* sport, which may decide who can participate and at what level, then the recent publication, *The Politics of Race and International Sport: the Case of South Africa* by Richard Lapchick [18] published in 1975 provides ample food for thought.

Fourthly, if we move right up to date and closer to home, the March, 1977, edition of the *British Journal of Physical Education* contains two examples of the pressures on physical education from sport.

(a) John Anderson [1], a teacher, writes of the continuing problem of approaches to school boys from professional football clubs. Of course there have been attempts to control such approaches, but as he concludes, "the lure of the big time football is powerful, and it is questionable whether the management of clubs, being under great pressure to win and make a profit, is concerned about the welfare of its charges". Soccer is not the only sport looking for talent in schools.

(b) On the opposite page of that journal, Richard Palmer [24] a trained physical educationist with a Master's Degree in Education, writes, "Britain, with a sporting heritage next to none, is rapidly in danger of losing her standing in international sport .... We must examine our methods of teaching, identifying and nurturing talent as a matter of urgency. For the 1980 Olympics we can do little; for 1984 maybe we can have some impact. This is a matter for the P.E. profession". Don Revie made somewhat the same noises following the recent thrashing of the England soccer team by their Dutch masters. In Palmer's case, as he is now Deputy General Secretary of the British Olympic Association perhaps he is most influenced in his view by his particularly close contact with 'the elephant' or in this case, the 'mammoth' – the Olympic Games.

Fifthly, as a spectator throughout the Montreal Olympics, an overriding personal impression was of the sheer size of the operation and the supreme importance of 'the spectacle'. The athletes (and the fact that certain countries were not even represented and their top class competitors were missing), were minor flaws in the framework of the total Colossus. As a man and a knowledgeable spectator, one could not but share the thrills and disappointments, the drama and the beauty of the Games; but as a dedicated physical educationist there was a sense of overwhelming unreality and extraneousness about the whole experience.

Sixth and lastly, even turning to community recreation and away from top level competition, one still finds that such sport is not free of socio-political pressures. Isobel Emmett [9], for example, has noted, "Many studies in the field of *leisure and sport* fail to take account of the fact that some parties to the game have more power than others: some own, build, plan, design, restrict use, make rules, allocate resources to train for this but not for that, here, but not there; whilst others have little or no say in such matters and use, or are persuaded to use or not use, facilities, to spend their leisure time in these and not those ways". At every level, outside power groups seek to influence sport (and physical education as well) – primarily for their own purposes.

Physical education *can* provide a basis for sport. However, one needs to be clear, for what kind of sport? When demands are made on physical educationists to increase or otherwise modify their programmes in schools, one needs to ask, "What are the underlying motives for such demands?"

Physical Education as a Basis for Sport

Having suggested some of the pitfalls in definitions and problems inherent in a casual assumption that all people interested in the worlds of physical education and sport will automatically see eye-to-eye with each other, this discussion can turn to a more straightforward, and unashamedly P.E.-biased point-of-view about physical education as a basis for sport. Obviously many physical educationists will be totally familiar with the points raised, yet such points need to be made continually if they are to reach and be appreciated by those less knowledgeable about, and committed to, education and physical education.

Point 1

Physical education is primarily concerned with **education**, with the *person* being educated, and with its part in the *care* for that person as an *individual*, and as part of society as a whole.

At times this could mean that a school child, talented in a sporting activity, might have to be shielded from the demands of adult sport. Munrow [22] makes the point clearly when he says children should be, 'insulated' but 'not isolated'. Certainly talented children need to be protected from some external pressures, such as the worst aspects of professional sport's attitudes and practices. It is possible that a child might have to be advised, by a physical educationist, *not* to give too much time and effort to sport in contrast with other aspects of education during certain key periods. Protection should be from *all* attempts to *exploit* school children's talents, even from well meaning agencies and even if such protection means, in the long term, fewer World Cup successes, national anthems playing and flags being ceremoniously hoisted. Of course this is not a 'black-and-white' matter, judgement is required but the physical educationist has a great responsibility in such situations.

Conflicting pressures and philosophies can cause considerable 'role conflict' [5] amongst physical educationists. Paul Governali [13] of San Diego State College wrote an extremely interesting piece on 'The Physical Educator as Coach' in the July, 1972 *Bulletin of Physical Education*. The whole article really requires reading but for example, he notes, "The general purpose of physical education is to contribute to the student's total development, while that of intercollegiate athletics is, frankly, entertainment for the public and student body, personal glory for the players and coaches, and profit where possible". Later he says, "many colleges pretend that the purposes, methods, and objectives of athletics (this term covers many sports in the U.S.A.) are one and the same with those of physical education . . . some coaches accept ambivalence as part of the job". But, "Many coaches with conscience, those who *should* be teaching young people the way it *ought* to be, ultimately are forced out of coaching".

It is not suggested that such pressures, or at least such *high* degrees of pressure, exist as yet in England or Ireland. On the other hand, many will have witnessed, for example, school teams being driven 'into a match' by opposing physical education teachers; shouting their instructions from the touch lines and marshalling their players like toy soldiers in a mock battle. Some will have experienced the headmaster's displeasure at Morning Assembly as he read out news of yet another defeat on the games field on the Saturday before.

'Success at all costs' in sport can be its downfall. As Governali affirms, "to win is good, But in *educational sport* to *want* to win is a greater good". This kind of sentiment, more often expressed by physical educationists and sportsmen in the past, seems to carry with it nowadays the tag of 'old fashioned'. It is considered 'a luxury' and 'outmoded thinking' if the player, the team, the school, the country, is to do well.

Point 2

Of course one of the tenable aims of physical education [3] is to develop the **knowledge, skills** and **attitudes** to enable individuals to participate in recreative physical activities and sports in their leisure time, both whilst they are *still at school* and afterwards throughout their *whole life*. From physical education they should transfer to a process of active recreation with its potential benefits for health and happiness. But physical educationists need to teach well to achieve transfer. John Kane's [16] Schools' Council Survey of *Physical Education in Secondary Schools*, published in 1974, showed that male physical education teachers, placed "the opportunities given for acquiring appropriate physical pursuits for the enjoyment of leisure time" *first* in their list of teaching objectives; whilst women placed it *fourth* out of nine objectives. (The sample totalled 888 teachers.) The intention to stimulate post-school sport is obviously present in many teachers; even if transfer too often breaks down in reality. Emmett [8] has studied the relationship of school sport participation to adolescent sporting interests and she did not find a very high carry-over. Lack of facilities seemed an important factor; but again this is a complex problem.

Point 3

Knowledge gained in the process of physical education should facilitate communication and contact with agencies through which physical recreations can be followed up. Personal *skilfulness* and *successful* experience in physical activity should also provide a basis for potential future interests, and perhaps the necessary specific skill performance levels, to move on into the wider world of sport. Above all, positive attitudes to sporting participation should be created through physical education, but note that *attitude* development is a two-way process. Children's attitudes in physical education are very strongly affected by the attitudes demonstrated in adult sport. These are by no means always acceptable. Looking for priorities within the three; knowledge, skill and attitudes, Kelly [17] has written, "No amount of teaching of an activity can compensate for an attitude which is unhappy or warped".

Point 4

Physical attributes: mobility, strength, local and cardiovascular endurance, which are founded, developed, or enhanced through physical education, can obviously act as bases for sporting performance. But sport, as Dr. Erich Geiringer [12] has pointed out, can sometimes be, "*a threat* to physical and mental health". He quotes frightening statistics to support his view of the *damage* done in the name of sport. Not everyone it seems, supports the existence of an automatic link between sport and good health. Adapted physical education may be called on to repair some of this damage as well as to cater for people handicapped in other ways [6].

However, in short, and despite very many reservations, physical education, *can, does* and *should* provide a certain basis for sport.

Conclusion

In conclusion, it would be quite wrong to ignore what has been potentially the most significant event concerning the future of physical education and sport on a world wide scale: the First International Conference of Ministers and Senior Officials responsible for Physical Education and Sport, organised by U.N.E.S.C.O. in co-operation with the International Council on Sport and Physical Education, in Paris in April, 1976.

The *Conference Final Report,* U.N.E.S.C.O. [27], its recommendations, some of which are being discussed and adopted by the General Assembly of the United Nations, and the various activities which the conference has stirred up at national and international, professional and political levels, are already major contributions to the kind of discussions which should continue in the future.

To give some idea of the views put forward and confirming attention simply to the *recommendations**, one reads.

> "That, in order to fulfill the educational purposes of physical education and sport, national plans should be aimed at checking and eliminating the commercial tendencies which, largely fostered by professionalism in sport, hinder the wider development of sport and turn those who practise it into a type of merchandise.
>
> That, in order to ensure that physical education and sport really contribute to international solidarity and that all countries can participate in them without any barriers, the traditionally recognised principles which prescribe racial, political and economic discrimination should be confirmed.

*From *The role of physical education and sport in the education of youth* © U.N.E.S.C.O., 1976. Reproduced by permission of U.N.E.S.C.O.

That Member States recognise that the benefits of physical education and sport are the right of all people and especially children and youth, and that therefore:

(a) physical education and sport must be closely linked and formed as an integral part of the educational curricula and included in the country's legislation with that of the educational system of the country;

(b) programmes of physical education and sport should be provided also for persons who have special needs, including children who are not enrolled in school;

(c) due provision should be made in national programmes to meet the need for growing participation by girls and women;

(d) measures should be taken to promote the practice of 'sport for all', starting in school, in order to introduce the widespread practice of sport throughout life. Further that Member States should ensure that broad and diversified programmes of physical education and sport are provided, and therefore should: take into consideration the complementary nature of competitive sport aimed at excellence and high achievement on the one hand, and broad-based mass physical and sport programmes on the other, in the planning of national programmes".

The recommendations also observed, "that in the context of life-long education and the practice of sport beyond the age of compulsory schooling, it is important to give the child both a good background of general physical education and a liking for some particular sport to be practised as a matter of choice".

The importance of these words is not simply in their content – similar sentiments have been expressed at different times in the past – but in their context. These are recommendations and observations made on behalf of 101 Member Associate Member States of U.N.E.S.C.O. and as such these sentiments may well directly influence the governments of the world. There is a proposal to draft a United Nations Charter on Physical Education and Sport and an Interim Inter-governmental Committee has already been set up which will be actively promoting the future of physical education and sport; that is if it can avoid getting 'bogged down' in the problems of international competitive sport and political wrangling!

To sum up finally: physical education is and should be a basis for sport, but, to quote the closing words of the 1970 F.I.E.P. *World*

Manifesto on Physical Education [11], "The return on physical education is not defined in terms of victories won by top specialists but rather is measured by the improvement – more difficult to judge, certainly – it can bring to physical, intellectual and moral values by its social effectiveness, and, finally, the chance of well-being which it offers each individual".

References

1. Anderson, J. S., 'School boys and professional football clubs', *British journal of physical education*, p. 37, vol. 8, no. 2. P.E.A., March, 1977.
2. Andrews, J. C., 'Physical education and education', *Bulletin of physical education*, vol. 8, no. 3, pp. 21–27, B.A.O.L.P.E. July, 1970.
3. Andrews, J. C., 'The curricular aims of physical education', *The philosophy of physical education*, pp. 17–31. A report of two conferences. A.T.C.D.E. 1971.
4. Andrews, M., 'Physical education and sports: business as usual vs. by any means necessary', in McGlynn, G. H. (ed.), *Issues in physical education and sports*, p. 192. National Press Books, U.S.A., 1974.
5. Ball, D. W. and Loy, J. W., *Sport and social order*, pp. 444–445. Addison-Wesley, London, 1975.
6. Bennett, B. L., Howell, M. L. and Simri, U., *Comparative physical education and sport*, p. 62. Henry Kimpton, London, 1975.
7. Cagigal, J. M., 'Sport and education', *FIEP Bulletin*, vol. 46, no. 4, pp. 25–26. 1976.
8. Emmett, I., *Youth and leisure in an urban sprawl*, pp. 75–76. Manchester University Press, 1971.
9. Emmett, I., 'Masses and masters. A brief comparison of approaches to the study of work and leisure', in Haworth, J. T. and Smith, M. A. (eds.), *Work and leisure*, p. 78. Lepus Books, London, 1975.
10. F.I.E.P., 'World manifesto on physical education', *Bulletin of physical education*, vol. 3, no. 5, B.A.O.L.P.E. January, 1971.
11. F.I.E.P., *ibid.*, p. 20.
12. Geiringer, E., 'Sport as a threat to physical and mental health', *Bulletin of physical education*, vol 9, no. 3, B.A.O.L.P.E., July, 1972.
13. Governali, P., 'The physical educator as coach', *Bulletin of physical education*, vol. 9, no. 3, pp. 29–32. B.A.O.L.P.E., July, 1972.
14. Groves, R., 'Physical education, recreation and competitive sport', *Bulletin of physical education,* vol. 9, no. 3, B.A.O.L.P.E., July, 1972.
15. Honecker, E., *Sports in the G.D.R.*, facing p. 16. Montreal, 1976.
16. Kane, J. E., *Physical education in secondary schools*, p. 35. Schools Council Research Studies, Macmillan, 1974.
17. Kelly, J. J., 'Basic issues', in Sanborn, M. A. and Hartman, B. G. (eds.), *Issues in physical education*, 2nd ed. Henry Kimpton, London, 1970.
18. Lapchick, R. E., *The politics of race and international sport*, Greenwood Press, London, 1975.
19. Loy, J. W., 'The nature of sport: a definitional effort', in Gerber, E. W. (ed.), *Sport and the body*, pp. 44–53. Henry Kimpton, London, 1972.
20. Metheny, E., 'This "thing" called sport', in Gerber, E. W. (ed.), *op. cit.* p. 24.

21. Munrow, A. D., 'A discussion of principles', *Physical education*, p. 222. Bell, London, 1972.
22. Munrow, A. D., *ibid.*, p. 235.
23. Nixon, J. E. and Jewett, A. E., *Introduction to physical education*, 8th ed. p. 304. W. B. Saunders, London, 1974.
24. Palmer, R., 'A matter for debate?', *British journal of physical education*, vol. 8, no. 2, p. 36. P.E.A. March, 1977.
25. Seurin, P., 'Opening address', 1975 Joint F.I.E.P. – I.O.A. Conference. *FIEP Bulletin,* vol. 45, no. 4, p. 15. October/December, 1975.
26. Singer, R. N. (ed.) in *Physical education: foundations*, p. 33. Holt, Rinehart & Winstone, U.S.A., 1976.
27. U.N.E.S.C.O., *Final report*, First International Conference of Ministers and Senior Officials Responsible for Physical Education and Sport. U.N.E.S.C.O., Paris, 1976.

13

Physical Education and Olympism*

Concepts, Problems and Comments

Introduction

It would be easy to let the historic setting of Ancient Olympia overcome my better judgement and blindly follow the notion that to be present and taking part, rather than any result, is what really matters. I could set off now in an unequal race to present a paper on 'Physical Education and Olympism through the thoughts and achievements of Anglo-Saxon and Nordic countries', but this is an impossible task in the time allotted (like trying to run 5,000 metres in 10 seconds) and the result could only be unworthy of the setting, and the scope and richness of the thoughts and achievements of the countries mentioned.

Instead I have prepared a number of more personal comments which, nevertheless reflect my background in English physical educa-

* A revised version of a paper first presented at the joint meeting of the F.I.E.P. and the International Olympic Academy at Olympia, Greece, in July, 1975 and first published in the *FIEP Bulletin*, vol. 45, no. 4, pp. 65–74. 1975.

tion and teacher preparation as well as having foundation in the publications quoted and discussions with colleagues and students.

Definitions and Relationships

One of the prerequisites for clarity of thought and communication is to be as precise as possible in one's terminology. In an ideal world we might find a universally agreed terminology, but in its absence we need to be quite clear what we mean ourselves when we use certain terms and to try and make our usage clear to others. Here then are some thoughts on concepts basic to our present discussions.

Firstly, on education and recreation – these are seen as *dynamic processes*.

Education consists of not one but a family of processes which proceed towards an 'ultimate aim': not on a fixed totally predetermined pathway but in a general direction, susceptible to local variations, decisions being made along the way according to accepted criteria held in mind by the educationists. This ultimate aim in my view could be simply stated as, "a fully developed individual, able to identify with and contribute to a meaningful social, cultural and inanimate environment".

Recreation is also seen as a process; one in which the activities pursued are essentially self-chosen for intrinsic reasons rather than external rewards; participation providing a change – a diversion from other aspects of life – and leading to personal satisfaction in a fuller, healthier total life.

Physical education is one of the family of processes which together make up education; an important and integral part of that family – making both its unique and general supportive contributions to education as a whole through the pursuit of tenable aims of physical education [2; 3]. Its content is characterised by activities intentionally (and often systematically) involving the whole person in movement which is quite often (though not necessarily) of a 'sports' nature [6; 9; 23; 30].

Similarly **physical recreation** is part of the total recreation process; physical recreation making both unique and general contributions to the wider total field of recreation. The content of physical recreation is characterised by a large number of widely different physical activities, although individuals may participate in only one or a few to gain the full benefits. One of the aims of physical education is to develop the necessary knowledge, skills and attitudes to enable an individual to benefit from physical recreation [3].

Top Level Competition Sport and the Olympic Games

All physical activities engaged in educationally or recreationally need not be competitive but we recognise there is an element of competition which is vital to the existence of many sports. Competition properly regulated is educationally valuable.

In sports competition considerable further competitive stimulus is often added by the search for 'champions' at all levels. Within the scope of physical recreation as defined, it *is* possible to include 'top level championship sport', but the pressures inherent in the situation make its inclusion hard to maintain for all concerned. For the 'player' the recreational element may be replaced by a full time working dedication to 'the job' – which, almost incidentally, happens to be performing at a very high level in a physical activity. In such cases, material rewards and other extrinsic reasons for participation become by far the most important motivators, although vestiges of intrinsic motivation may remain.

The Olympic Games I see as World Championships, albeit surrounded with rituals and noble intentions, supposedly for individuals and groups of individuals but in fact having strong nationalistic overtones. The competitors participate for a multitude of intrinsic and extrinsic rewards, the exact mixture varying from person to person and country to country. Manifestly the International Olympic Committee has worked hard over the years – with varying amounts of success – to resist pressures from politics, commercialism and world wide audiences, as well as attempts by many of the competitors (and/or those coaching or financing them) to make a full time occupation of the pursuit of excellence at the highest level of Olympic performance.

Figure 13.1 shows the relationships discussed; including the tendency for top level sport and the Olympic Games to become 'work' for the competitor and entertainment for the masses.

Relationships between physical education, physical recreation and competitive sport at top level have been looked at differently by Groves [12].*

Historical Connections Between Olympism and English Education

Many writers [e.g. 7; 22; 29] have noted that English education had some part to play in the Olympic revival. In the 19th Century the so-

*For a closer examination of Groves' ideas see the *essay* entitled 'Physical Education as a Basis for Sport' *(Chapter 12)*.

called Public Schools (not in fact state schools but rather an ill-defined group of old established boarding schools for the 'sons of gentlemen' between the ages of nine and eighteen years, McIntosh [21]) exerted a tremendous influence both nationally and internationally. Thomas Arnold, Headmaster of Rugby School, was referred to by De Coubertin in 1894 as "the greatest educator of modern times". Lecturing some 35 years later in Paris and trying "to explain the facts clearly" about the Olympic revival, he claimed to have "superimposed on a passing Anglomania the immense prestige of antiquity" [7].

Peter McIntosh in *Sport and Society* [22] tells us that, "At its outset, then, the Olympic Movement looked back to ancient Greece for its ideal of physical prowess, and the enoblement of man in athletic contest. It looked to Britain and to Britain's Public Schools for a modern interpretation of the ancient ideals and it looked to Britain, too, for its organisational structure".

This latter point refers to the constitution of the International Olympic Committee in 1894: "the final arbiter in all matters concerning the Olympic movement. This committee" says McIntosh, "so strangely constituted and endowed with such power from birth, made no pretence to be democratic. It had much more affinity to the eighteenth century clubs which governed sports in Britain . . .".

My reason for mentioning these historical connections is not to make any nationalistic claim for credit for the revival of the Games; indeed McIntosh suggests that De Coubertin may have misinterpreted both the philosophy of the ancient world and Dr. Arnold's part in the growth of the games cult. "He was not interested in athleticism and it is the fault of Thomas Hughes' novel, *Tom Brown's Schooldays,* that Arnold has so often been credited or debited with the cult of organised games" [22].

What is important to me is that in looking back at the Public Schools in particular we can see the roots of concepts such as 'sportsmanship and fair play' as well as 'the amateur spirit' which still exist in both the Olympic Movement and in modern British physical education. Irrespective of whether these concepts were exported or not, we in Britain are now faced with a need to examine these ideals against the background of our changing society. We have had it made very clear to us in our own schools that these ideas are not necessarily 'eternal truths' but were in part at least, the products of a particular age and stage in the development of British society and its educational system.

Of course these concepts *do* exist internationally, so the review must be done against the background of not one, but many changing social backgrounds. This must make any review more complex – and international consensus perhaps impossible? We have found in Britain that we cannot automatically transfer concepts from one age to another,

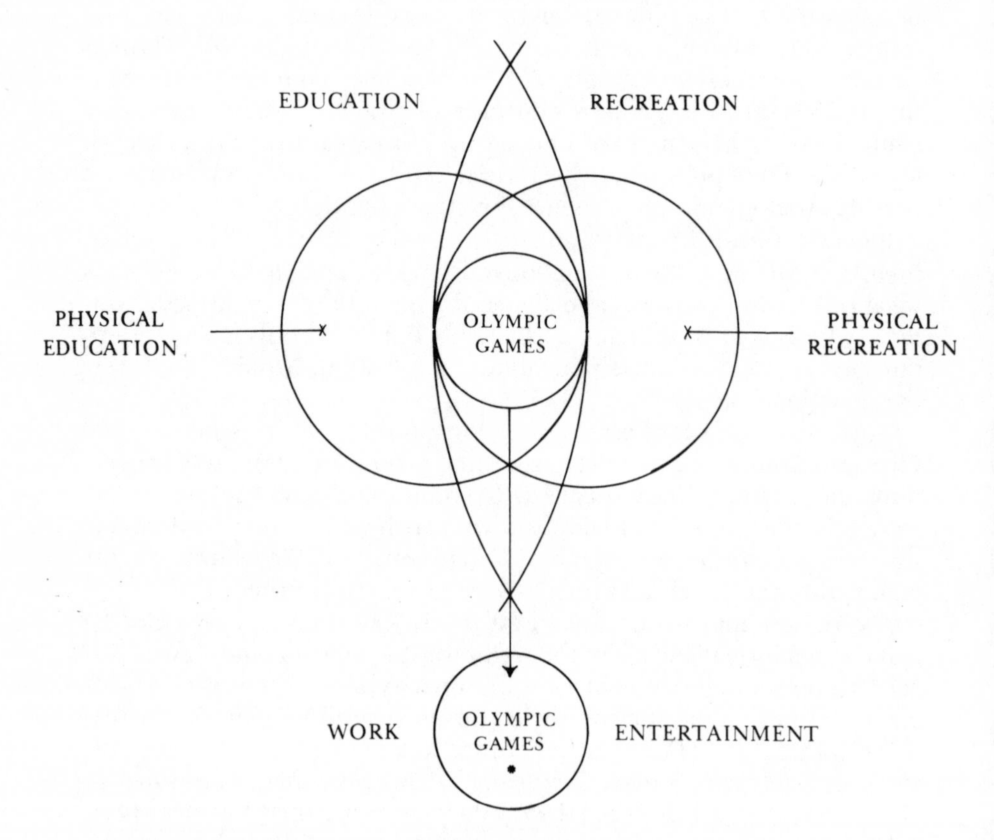

Relationships between Education – Recreation, Physical Education – Physical Recreation.

* Olympic Games shown tending to move into areas of Work and Entertainment.

Fig. 13.1

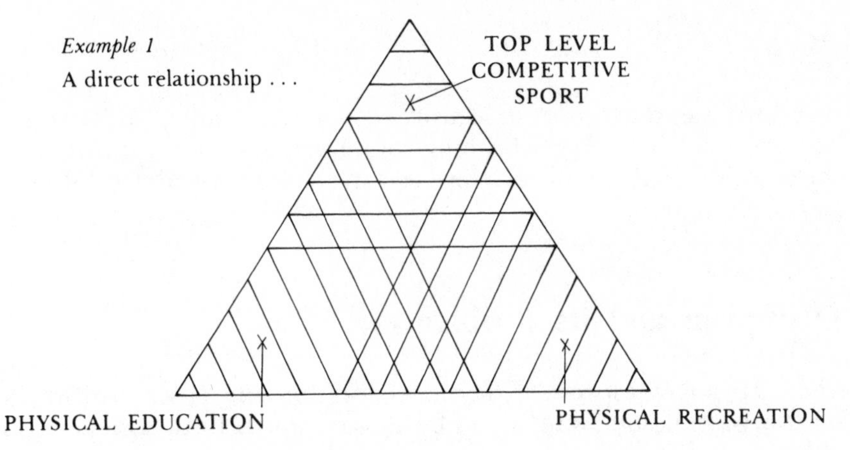
Example 1
A direct relationship . . .
TOP LEVEL COMPETITIVE SPORT
PHYSICAL EDUCATION
PHYSICAL RECREATION

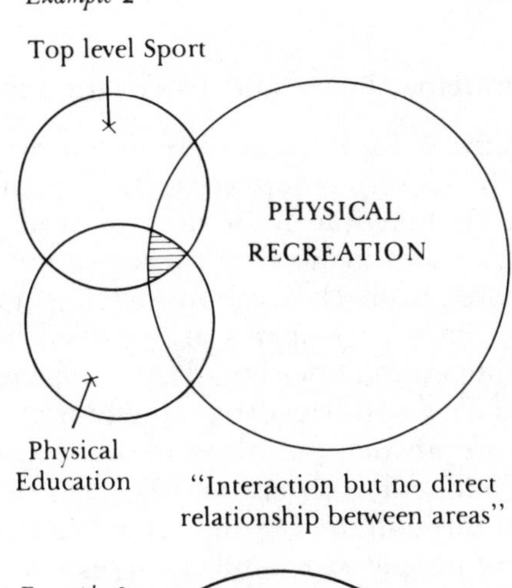
Example 2
Top level Sport
PHYSICAL RECREATION
Physical Education
"Interaction but no direct relationship between areas"

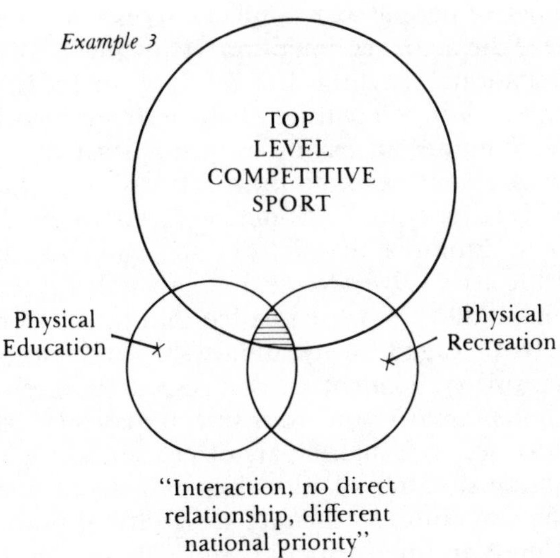
Example 3
TOP LEVEL COMPETITIVE SPORT
Physical Education
Physical Recreation
"Interaction, no direct relationship, different national priority"

Fig. 13.2

therefore we must not be surprised internationally, if we meet very great problems in establishing common ideas – say of sportsmanship – in widely different societies, existing simultaneously at different stages of evolution.

Olympism and its Problems

There are many aspects of physical education and Olympism which need urgent thought and action by all concerned. I can comment on only a few of these.

Respect for Opponents, Peace and International Understanding

What is our collective F.I.E.P.I.O.A. response to writers like Heinila [15] who tell us, "By its very nature competitive sport is not very well suited to perform the function of the dove of peace . . . Competition rewards few but frustrates many, and consequently, competition as a social process, is often justly classified in sociology under the heading of social conflicts. Since participants are labelled by competition as better or worse, competition does not offer very favourable conditions for mutual appreciation and friendship among participants".

Again, how do we answer the many critics, including many participants, coaches and other observers, who claim that international friendships formed through the Olympic Games are mainly due to the bringing together of people with similar interests and are formed *outside and in spite of* the actual competition? How much more effective, if at all, are international meetings like those of the F.I.E.P. and I.O.A. or the recent much less competitive Gymnaestrada held in Berlin?

One can quote numerous examples of the negative effects of international sport. A recent example from a British national newspaper, The *Daily Mail,* is fairly typical. "Someone forgot to tell the footballers of Tanzania and Ethiopia that it isn't the winning but the taking part which is the true Olympic ideal . . . so half the Ethiopian side ended in hospital, after the match ended in a brawl 15 minutes from time . . . . The battle raged for ten minutes". Surely no one can claim this was just an isolated incident, or that respect for one's opponent or international unity could result from such a match? Furthermore *one* such incident can set back many years of peaceful competition.

In such extreme situations faults obviously lie on many sides. For example as physical educationists are we guilty of putting too much stress on skill levels and performance, and not enough on developing the vital related knowledge and attitudes? Who should have taught these players more effectively?

Some would point to the fact that the game involved was soccer and put much of the blame on attitudes connected primarily with that game. This is too easy a way out. Following the wild scenes in Paris in 1975 after the European Cup Final, Brian Glanville [10] writing in *The Sunday Times* said, "Once again Britain's national game has landed the nation in disgrace . . .", but he did not criticise the game or the club, Leeds United, in isolation. He saw the game as "a depressing mirror to our violent society". Dr. Willee's article in the June 75 *FIEP Bulletin* [31] gives further examples of the problems of physical education and sport in modern industrialised societies.

A counter argument to all these doubts is that on balance the positive effects and successes of international sport far outweigh the negative incidents. Philip Noel-Baker [26] speaking from very many years' experience, is adamant that international sport, "is a powerful influence for better international understanding by which alone stable peace may one day be established". Such deep personal convictions based on long experience can not be overlooked but the 'balance sheet' needs constant and careful scrutiny.

Just Reward for Effort and Perserverance

Without doubt the high standards of performance at Olympic level require great personal effort and perseverance, and the rewards for champions are great. However we as educationists must be forever vigilant about the demands made on individuals, and in the final analysis I believe we would all agree that our concern should be for the *total* individual and not simply his or her *sporting* performance.

Even to reach Olympic qualifying standard and thus be able to take part may soon not be enough in Britain. John Le Masurier [19], our principal national athletics coach, wrote very recently that "suggestions have been made in the past that the British team should be more of an elite group and not overloaded with athletes who . . . have very little realistic chance of success beyond the first round. Selectors will naturally consider whether it is desirable in this day and age to retain the philosophy of De Coubertin or tailor it to the 1970's". Let us hope our 1976 selectors *do* retain the vision of the Games as something offering more to all participating than the chance to win a few medals. Success, it seems, is always relative, and is often bought at great personal price.

Mandell [20] in the conclusions to his book *The Nazi Olympics* warns us, "For most athletic activities only the young have either the physical or the uneroded spiritual capacity for total athletic efforts. And those who have snatched records since 1936 have done so by means of such intense focusing of their physical and psychic powers that in consequence they probably atrophy other youthful pursuits .... Each is a victim of his society's view of the athlete as a precious national (or local) resource ... the better the athlete, the more he is indeed a sap and a plaything of perverted ideologues and ambitious politicians". Hard words which we cannot ignore.

In his diary of the 1964 Tokyo Olympics, Christopher Brasher [5] himself an Olympic Gold Medalist, gave a broad assessment of another great athlete. "He is an unhappy, doubtful man, being torn in half. The half that is winning at the moment is sport, but ... it leaves him with a great doubt about his career – and in that he is a failure to all the tenets by which he was brought up. He failed the vital university entrance exams and, he failed in his alternative career as a quantity surveyor .... He is lazy, he does not like training, and he does not particularly like athletics; but when you are the greatest natural athlete in the world and you come from a small country ... there are pressures that keep you going". This athlete went on to take two gold medals in those Games, one in Olympic record time.

This example must also remind us that evaluation simply in terms of performance can favour the naturally endowed. Watching a marvellous demonstration of advanced canoeing skills by severely physically handicapped girls at the 1975 B.A.O.L.P.E. Conference, I was reminded of the question put by Andrecs [1] to the 1973 meeting of the International Olympic Academy. "Who measures the achievements of the blind man who can cope with life, who measures the will and efforts of the handicapped child? Their achievements are no less Olympic". In some cases I would say more so.

Amateurism and Nationalism

A pillar of De Coubertin's philosophy was that of amateur participation. What did this and does this mean? Professor H. A. Harris [14] in his classic work on *Greek Athletes and Athletics* wrote that we may "reject any picture of pure amateurism in Greek athletics at any period", and McIntosh [22] points out that in the ancient Olympics the "rewards for athletic prowess are seen to have been very generous indeed". Drees [8] suggests that fame and immortality were the desired rewards of ancient Olympic victors, so the 'star cult' in sport was by no means a 20th Century invention.

Keighley [18] in a wide ranging paper on 'amateurism and professionalism' concluded, "Once competition (after the Second World

War) became a question of national prestige, the amateur definition was irrelevant. No nation which believes its prestige is enhanced by athletic success will allow its athletes to be handicapped by financial circumstances except, many people feel, Britain. The old 'gentleman-amateur' concept was further reinforced in the 1950's by the brilliant Oxbridge athletes like Chataway, Brasher and Bannister".

Despite his gentleman-amateur tag, Chataway's opinion, published in 1968 in the book *War Without Weapons* [11] was also that, "By the early post war period the original Olympic concept of amateurism was almost dead . . . the time demanded by international sport was clearly incompatible with many kinds of employment".

In Britain increasing State subsidies have been called for by both the public and the sportsmen themselves. In the 1971 change to the new type Sports Council in England and Wales, we have seen a move towards more direct political intervention in and control of British Sport. The 1973/74 Sports Council *Annual Report* told us that, "Sport cannot divorce itself from governments, nor governments from sport" [28]. Of course, in many countries sport and politics are already firmly entwined and in an article entitled 'The Chinese Dragon Appears' Don Anthony comments that, "To secure the essential unity of world sport in the face of this development and to maintain the eternal values inherent in sporting conflict will not be easy" [4].

In view of this, those who would agree with Natan's [25] assertion that, "Nationalism is sport's deadliest enemy", will be pleased that at the close of Pooley and Webster's [27] survey of 'Sport and Politics', they conclude that "the International Olympic Committee still wields sufficient power to overcome national pressures". How long can this last? What can F.I.E.P. do to help?

The Future of the Games

Many in Britain feel that it is the very success and sheer size of the Olympic Games which may be their downfall. Ian Wooldridge [32] reporting in the *Daily Mail* on June 17, 1975, wrote, "One thing is certain. The Montreal Olympics, assuming that miracles of constructional engineering are actually achieved, will now be the costliest in all history".

The danger, when the balance sheets are finally revealed, is that they will finally convince all the cities of the Western World that the Olympic Games are about as desirable as an outbreak of bubonic plague. Certainly it does not seem possible that a British city will ever again be able to mount the Games in their present form. The view is also held in Britain that the high expenditure on recent Olympics reflects unnecessary efforts by municipal and national authorities to create prestigious 'bigger and better' facilities for each Games. The level of provision may be far beyond the requirements of the I.O.C. and certainly of the participants. In the end it is as always the spectators (including of course the world wide television audience) and tax payers who have to pay for the architects' and administrators' grandiose dreams.

Fair Play

I hope we agree that the future of all competitive sport depends to a large extent on a general acceptance of a fair play code. We must applaud I.C.S.P.E.'s [17] initiative in this sphere. Although this code has often been contravened, it has survived remarkably well considering the intense pressures it has encountered and the marked changes in many societies since it was first accepted.

Fair play is an attitude of mind and a form of self-control based on convictions which have their roots firmly in education and culture [16]. As this is so, physical educationists working in schools and particularly those preparing the teachers of the future, have a great part to play in sustaining and strengthening this attitude. Whilst perhaps we may need to wait for "sociologists and psychologists to reveal how universal the concept of fair play can be in the world and how different are the interpretations of the term" [17], I am sure that it rests largely in the hands of physical educationists, sportsmen and women, as well as sports administrators, to make sure that the fair play code is well taught, understood, adhered to, and if necessary, enforced.

Conclusions

"Modern Olympism, although separated from its glorious ancestor by many centuries of indifference to bodily things, is nonetheless developing along similar lines and passing through the same stages". When De Coubertin [7] wrote this in 1920, he was no doubt thinking mainly of the movement's growing influence and success. I hope he was not being too prophetic and that we will not soon see repeated the degradation and downfall of the Games as in ancient times. Will a historian of the future write as Harris [14] has done of the ancient Games, "the closing of the Olympic Games virtually brought to an end the history of Greek athletics. Even the most passionate lover of sport could scarcely wish that it had continued longer"?

You might say that many of the contemporary views I have

expressed appear to be rather too critical and pessimistic. I would not agree. What is needed, in my view, is not a barrage of rhetoric and unfounded, out-of-touch, lofty idealism, but a straight look into the face of problems by people who are committed enough to try to do something constructive about them. What are needed are stern efforts to maintain and strengthen those ideals, which are well-founded and relevant today, changes – perhaps swift 'surgery' – to minimise or cut out those aspects which are justifiably open to criticism; always reminding ourselves that the Olympic Games, for all our expertise, experience and interest, are not the property of physical educationists or even the I.O.C.

As individuals, as separate organisations and jointly, there are things we can start to do now or continue with renewed effort, they are:

1. We need to sort out our terminology and understand more fully the relationships between physical education, physical recreation and Olympism in various countries.
2. We must continue to advocate and advise on systems of national physical education which provide opportunities for a physically gifted elite – but not at the expense of basic physical education and sport for all people of all levels of ability, and not least for those struggling against physical and mental handicaps.
3. We must try to put competition and success more firmly into an educational perspective. As Munrow [24] has so wisely stressed, "Failure is not necessarily bad: within limits it is a valuable experience. What *is* bad is failure accompanied by a sense of rejection and this, of course, is a reflection of how people are treated as persons".
4. Through education we must forever be trying to bring ideal and actual competitive sports behaviour closer together. The teaching and unflinching support of *fair play* being a priority in this sphere.
5. As experts we must consider how far Olympic success can and should be used to evaluate national systems of physical education. We must be particularly wary of all attempts, even by well meaning agencies, to use Olympic success as the main motivator and/or the major evaluator of physical education and recreation in any country.

However much at times we feel we are swimming against a flood tide, we must struggle together and draw strength from one another. We must resist those many pressures which threaten to carry the Games wholesale into the world of mass 'gladiatorial' entertainment.

It means being convinced and convincing, vocal and literate, vigilant and outgoing.

There must be no pretence that problems do not confront the worlds of physical education and Olympism and, whilst one has great sympathy with De Coubertin when he thundered against "the myopic little people" who sought to question the future of his noble concept [7], it seems certain that if both physical education and Olympism are to survive, rhetoric alone will not suffice. We must ask questions, we need to be very clear about the various issues, we must face truths which are sometimes unpleasant. Above all, we must sort out our own differences of opinion and priorities so that together we can launch some *positive, united* action.

References

1. Andrecs, H., 'The Olympic idea and its realization in schools', *FIEP Bulletin*, vol. 45, no. 2, pp. 23–29, 1975.
2. Andrews, J. C., 'Physical education and education', *Bulletin of physical education*, vol. 8, no. 3, pp. 21–27. B.A.O.L.P.E. July, 1970.
3. Andrews, J. C., 'The curricular aims of physical education', *The philosophy of physical education*, pp. 17–31. A Report of Two Conferences. A.T.C.D.E., 1971.
4. Anthony, D., 'The Chinese dragon appears', *Sport and recreation*, vol. 16, no. 2, pp. 28–25. Sports Council, London, Spring, 1975.
5. Brasher, C., *Tokyo 1964: a diary of the XVIIIth Olympiad*, p. 9. Stanley Paul, London, 1964.
6. Caillois, R., *Man, play, and games*, Published in English by Thames and Hudson, 1962.
7. De Coubertin, P., *The Olympic idea: discourses and essays*, Carl Diem Institute, Köln, West Germany.
8. Drees, L., *Olympia: gods, artists and athletes*, Pall Mall Press, London, 1968.
9. Gerber, E. W. (ed.) in *Sport and the body: a philosophical symposium*, Lea and Febiger, Philadelphia, 1972.
10. Glanville, B., 'Football: a depressing mirror to our violent society', *The Sunday Times*, p. 27. June 1, 1975.
11. Goodhart, P. and Chataway, C., *War without weapons*, W. H. Allen, London, 1968.
12. Groves, R., 'Physical education, recreation and competitive sport', *Bulletin of physical education*, vol. 9, no. 3, pp. 33–38. B.A.O.L.P.E. July, 1972.
13. Groves, R., 'Education issues in sport and recreation', *Bulletin of physical education*, vol. 9, no. 3, pp. 9–11, July, 1975.
14. Harris, H. A., *Greek athletes and athletics*, Hutchinson, London, 1964.
15. Heinila, K., 'Sport and international understanding', vol. 44, no. 3, pp. 35–38. *FIEP Bulletin,* 1974.
16. I.C.S.P.E., *Mass media, sport, international understanding*, Report of International Seminar, Paris. June, 1971.
17. I.C.S.P.E., *Fair play*, U.N.E.S.C.O., House, Paris, 1973.
18. Keighley, J. S., 'Amateurism and professionalism', pp. 1–21. Unpublished paper, University of Birmingham, 1972.

19. Le Masurier, J., 'One year to go', *Sport and recreation*, vol. 16, no. 2, pp. 13–15. Spring, 1975. Sports Council, London.
20. Mandell, R. D., *The nazi olympics*, p. 287. British edition, Souvenir Press, London, 1972.
21. McIntosh, P. C., *Physical education in England since 1800*, G. Bell and Sons, London, 1952.
22. McIntosh, P. C., *Sport and society*, C. A. Watts, London, 1963.
23. Miller, D. M. and Russell, K. R. E., *Sport: a contemporary view*, Lea & Febiger, Philadelphia, U.S.A., 1971.
24. Munrow, A. D., *Physical education, a discussion of principles*, G. Bell & Sons, London, 1972.
25. Natan, A., 'Sport and politics', in *Sport, culture and society*, Loy, J. W. and Kenyon G. S. (eds.), Collier-Macmillan, Toronto, 1969. p. 205.
26. Noel-Baker, P., 'Sport and international understanding', *Royal Canadian Legion's coaching review,* vol. 4, no. 4, pp. 1, 2 and 12. March, 1967.
27. Pooley, J. C. and Webster, A. V., 'Sport and politics: power play', C.A.H.P.E.R. *Journal,* vol. 41, no. 3, pp. 10–18. January/February, 1975.
28. Sports Council, *Annual report*, Sports Council, London, 1973–74.
29. Seurin, P., 'Contribution de l'éducation au mouvement olympique', *La gymnastique volontaire*, no. 2, pp. 91–96. F.F.E.P.G.V., 1975.
30. Slusher, H., *Man, sport and existence: a critical analysis*, Henry Kimpton, London, 1967.
31. Willee, A. W., 'Physical education in the age of post-industrialization', *FIEP Bulletin*, vol. 45, no. 2, pp. 12–22. June, 1975.
32. Wooldridge, I., 'They are working 69 hours a week in a bid to win the biggest race of the Olympics', *Daily Mail*, p. 26. June 17, 1975.

14

Sport and the Socialisation of the Secondary School boy*

Introduction

"The spirit of play is the source of fertile conventions that permit the evolution of culture. It stimulates ingenuity, refinement and invention. At the same time it teaches loyalty in the face of the adversary and illustrates competition in which rivalry does not survive the encounter. To the degree that he is influenced by play, man can check the monotony, determinism, and brutality of nature. He learns to construct order, conceive economy, and establish equity". (Caillois [6].)

"To say that the bulk of social activity consists of playing games does not necessarily mean that it is mostly 'fun' or that the parties are not seriously engaged in the relationship . . . 'playing' football and other athletic 'games' may not be fun at all, and the players may be intensely grim . . .. Play may be grimly serious or even fatally serious, but the total sanctions are serious only if the rules are broken". (Berne [3].)

These quotations, one by a French sociologist and the other by an American consultant in psychiatry, underline just two aspects of the relationship between society and sport. In the first the idea is put forward that play, including athletic play or 'sports', is part of both

* A revised version of a paper first published in the *Australian journal of physical education*, no. 50, pp. 5–12. October, 1970.

transmitting and evolving culture and, in the second, that sports are 'serious' in that they can involve risk to human life as well as serious social sanctions. Looking at recent interest in World Cup Soccer or the continuing controversy about international matches with South African teams, one can affirm that sport is very much the concern of many modern societies. This essay attempts to highlight the possible contribution that interest and participation in *school sport* can make to the socialisation of a boy of secondary school age.

Play, Games and Socialisation

The concepts involved in this discussion are all difficult. The word **play** has been widely and indiscriminately used to describe a whole range of human activities. A good conceptual analysis of 'play' is given by Dearden [12] and the term is obviously so misused that 'participation' is preferred here. Where the verb 'to play' is used in this essay, it is used only in an everyday sense to mean 'to participate in'.

Games are also a very wide category of human activities. When Berne [3] writes, "the bulk of social activity consists of playing games", he is thinking of a very wide variety of social interactions. This essay is concerned with organised *athletic* games, which constitute a great deal of what we call 'sport'. Sports in this category have much in common with activities described as play by Caillois [6].

They are *free*, participants choose to take part; they are *separate*, circumscribed within limits of space and time, defined and (often) fixed in advance; they are *uncertain*, the result and course of the play cannot be fixed beforehand; and, they are *governed by rules*, under conventions that suspend ordinary laws, and for the moment establish new legislation, which alone counts.

This latter point is only partially true. Although participants are rule governed, common law and normal social conventions still control their actions to a great extent – as has been proved, for example, by court judgements on incidents arising during sporting activities. Caillois [7] also says that "play is 'make-believe' and 'unproductive', creating neither goods, nor wealth, nor new elements of any kind . . . ending in a situation identical to that prevailing at the beginning of the game". These points are not applicable to participation in organised sport in educational situations and certainly not to spectator sports in society at large.

The third concept which needs careful examination is that of **socialisation.** This again is not a precise term but it is in increasing use in sociology. However, it is not used solely in sociology: socialisation is an area of interest for both the sociologist and the social psychologist. Parsons [28] writes, "The socialisation function may be summed up as the development in individuals of the commitments and capacities which are essential prerequisites of their future role performance". This is a life-long process and in Parsons' view it would seem to be a matter of 'moulding' the individual in two basic ways. The first by 'transmitting culture' and so passing on a commitment to the broad values of society; the second by preparing the individual to perform a particular role within the structure of society.

The broad values, norms and the traditional skills which are part of a society may be termed as its *culture*. The culture of different societies will place differing emphasis on the place in society of physical activities in general, and sports in particular. However, as sport is so embedded in most modern societies it is suggested that participation in sport *will* be an important factor in the transmission of culture in these societies.

Ward [34] raises a question about the nature of the socialisation process which at present remains unanswered. It is whether socialisation is a means of subjugating latent, possibly instinctive, drives or whether it is a learning process. The standpoint adopted has an important bearing on physical education, because it might be contended that "physical activity could have quite an important function in establishing social control over primitive imperatives". This view is supported by Lorenz [27], Leach [25], and Browne [5]. On the other hand learning theory could suggest that "aggressive physical activities will only teach a behaviour of a nature that is increasingly being disapproved of by society" [35].

Whatever the answer, *with the schoolboy* the process is not left purely to the chance effects of participation. It is interesting that Heaton [17] found that the moral and social education of the pupils was considered the first priority for the P.E. teacher. Participation in sport is not enough. Shaw [30] suggests that it is through the influence of physical educationists that sport (which has become degraded) may once again live up to the high expectations of Rene Maheu, Director-General of U.N.E.S.C.O., who sees it, "as the most explicit vehicle for the 'major ethical values of our modern civilisation'". If socialisation is a learning process, then the guiding presence of the P.E. teacher is very important in controlling which values are stressed in the sporting situation.

Socialisation and Adolescence

In this essay consideration of socialisation is somewhat arbitrarily limited to the years of attendance at secondary school. It has been said already that socialisation is a life-long process, so this artificial division of time focuses attention on only part of the process. The family is the first and the most important socialising agency but during the secondary school period the "adolescent role and peer group become important in determining physical activity interests and influencing behaviour and personality of the individual, whilst the importance of the family in transmitting culture is diminished" [36].

Wall [32] describes adolescence as "a psycho-social phenomenon", which means, "it is variable according to social pressures, educational action, and individual experience. It means that adolescent phenomena, in behaviour, value structures, attitudes, are modifiable if the appropriate means are found". Fleming [14], sees the most important social learning at this stage to be conducive to "the personal and social development of adolescents in relation to their contemporaries". She sees this in terms of four types of **acceptance.** Firstly, of *one's self* (appearance and capacities); then of *one's self in relation to a group* (with regard to status and leadership); thirdly, *of others* (their differences and unpredictability); and finally, *of others in relation to one's self* (friendship and making one's self acceptable to others).

These areas of social learning are aspects of socialisation which appear to be especially important at this stage in the life of a child. In Britain, and elsewhere, physical activities play a prominent part for most boys in this process because of their interest in sport. However, before examining the extent of this interest, it is necessary to consider some of the major agencies of socialisation likely to be functioning during the secondary school period.

Agencies of Socialisation

As emphasised previously, the family is the most important early socialising influence. "The child is exposed longer and during the most influential early years to the family influence. It is in those years that the basic structure of the personality is laid down" [37]. In a second period "(lasting from around eight at least through adolescence) the son tests new limits in which the focus of socialisation is not so much his within-home behaviour, as it is is his beyond-home behaviour", Strodtbeck [31].

At this stage, the influence of the peer group becomes of increasing importance to the adolescent. Hoyle [19] tells us that, "It supports his independence, meets his need for recognition, presents him with opportunities for achievement, and affords him the opportunity of playing a variety of quasi-adult roles". The possibilities for achievement in physical activities are noted constantly, for example, in the works of Coleman [8] and Hargreaves [16]. Hoyle points out that physical activities are only *one* possible category of activities but because of the great interest in sport amongst boys, it is likely that (in Coleman's terms) they will provide scope for prestigious achievements and consequently will act as avenues for 'outsiders' and help the talented performers to join 'a leading crowd'.

"The school is the first socialising agency in the child's experience which institutionalises a differentiation of status on non-biological bases" Parsons [29]. Within this situation one can look at the class itself (as Parsons does), at the total ethos of the school and its administration and rules, at contemporaries in class and other groups, such as, teams, houses, etc., and at the teacher as a socialising agent. In this latter case, for example, Hoyle [21] finds evidence of some conflict between the *instructional* role and the *socialising* role of the teacher. However, according to Waller [33], the good teacher, "lengthens and shortens the rubber band of social distance with consummate art", so that this conflict can be resolved. With some evidence (for example Crunden [11]) of increasing emphasis on the socialising role of the P.E. teacher, coupled with a formal commitment to sport on the school timetable in the form of 'organised games', plus representative sport involving class, house and school teams; it is obvious that sport is an interrelated part of the socialising force of the school as an institution.

In mentioning these socialising agencies, it is as well to note that some of them may be in conflict. Banks [2] notes that "the school itself is a socialising agency of some considerable importance, in which teachers and the peer group each play their part, a part which may reinforce or may conflict with the influence of the family". In a cross-cultural study by Dennis [13] of a Lebanese high school, it was found that American parents approved of sports more than the parents of Arab, Armenian and Jewish children. In this kind of situation where considerable emphasis is put on school sport, these activities would be supported by some parents more than others. This is also true with regard to class background differences in Britain. Looking at the sporting interests of secondary school boys, it seems that the interest and participation of children in sport is partially related to parental class background. Crunden [11] reports that amongst a sample of 281 13+ and 15+ year-old boys in a comprehensive school in Yorkshire, "the value a child places on sport will, in large measure, be culturally induced. For the sample group tested, children did not avail themselves equally of the opportunities which existed for participation in sport, and these differences could be stratified by relation to . . . social background". Children of middle class origin generally took more part in school sport (the other factor used in analysing this study was sex which is not dealt with here, although it should be noted that rather a different situation is found if one does look at the sport and socialisation of girls during adolescence).

The Sporting Interests of Adolescent Boys

Earlier the point was made that sporting interests are only *one* of the fields of activity which attract boys of secondary school age. One must be careful in making generalisations as there appear to be marked variations in interest and participation due to factors such as age, class background, geographic location, type of school attended, facilities available, etc. However, there *is* considerable supporting evidence for the statement that in this period boys are generally very interested in sport.

Coleman [8] reporting on the "General Interests and Activities of Teenagers" in nine public high schools in America, found that the majority of the boys like "to spend a great deal of their time in fairly active outdoor pursuits". One point, picked out as being of particular interest, was that only one of the categories of voluntary leisure activities – organised games – had any direct relation to school. Sport, it seems, "manages to run over into leisure time, breaking the barrier which separates work from leisure". This is supported by Lieberman [26] who showed that men between 15 and 24 years of age in a German city, mentioned sport as the leisure activity in which they engaged the most.

British studies are rather scarce. Crunden [11] found that, of his sample of 13+ year-old boys, approximately 71 per cent expressed medium or high interest in sport; whilst of 15+ year-old boys, 88.5 per cent expressed medium or high interest in sport. Although these figures are high, it is as well to remember the quite considerable percentages who were categorised as having 'low interest'. His research also showed that generally children from middle-class homes took more part in the sporting activities. Knapp [24] found that adolescent boys are more physically active than girls and that "a significantly greater number of boys say they will make an effort to take part in some kind of sport when they leave school". Ward, Hardman and Almond [39] investigated the pattern of participation and attitudes to physical activity of 11+ to 18+ year-old boys. They found a high interest in physical activities but that this decreased with increasing age, and this decrease was more apparent when total figures were broken down to pick out groups of poor performers. The interests of poor performers started to decline as early as the first year of the secondary school.

Another factor in this situation is the type of activity. In a Finnish study, Helanko [18] showed that gangs who played football reached a peak of participation at the age of twelve and then slowly began to break up. In Britain, Ward (et al.) concluded that "team games remain the biggest attraction, but there is increased interest in social games by the older age groups". They also found that team games remained of greater interest to sixth formers in grammar schools but no reason is suggested for this finding. In a study of adolescent activities in Glasgow, Jephcott [22] showed that informal 'scratch football' was the most popular sporting activity.

An attempt has been made to show some of the variation in interests that has been discovered in various researches. It is important to note that not all of these findings can be translated from one society to another. However, the findings of Coleman in America regarding sport are supported to a certain extent by the work of Hargreaves [16] in Britain. Having qualified the statement, one must return to the position that sport does occupy a dominant place in the interests of a large proportion of boys at secondary school age. With this in mind one can examine in more detail some of the effects that interest, participation and achievement in sport may have on the socialisation of adolescent boys.

Self Concept and Group Status

Fleming put 'knowing oneself' as an important aspect of social learning. Arnold [1] points out that physical education can make considerable contributions to the development of the 'self concept'. He deals with the possible contributions of games, outdoor pursuits and dance. He suggests that "the health of a society may be measured by the degree to which a person can distinguish himself from others". This is a rather different approach to socialisation from that of writers who see the socialising process as one of simply *moulding* an individual into a conformist position "patterned and programmed by culture" Ward [38]. Comer [10], talking of the relationship between sport and mental health, says, "Few would argue against the assumption that sport serves a useful purpose in promoting social interaction. It is suggested that sport, because of this character which it has affords the opportunity for making a direct contribution to mental health". It would seem this 'personal' level of socialisation *is* one at which sport and physical education has much to offer.

A number of studies [some examples 8; 16; 23], show that skill in sport is linked with status and prestige in an adolescent peer group. As noted earlier, this is not the only avenue into a 'leading group' but it is often mentioned in research findings. Coleman [9] reports, "The boy who was only an athlete won greatest recognition and respect from his fellows, in the sense of being named most often as a friend and on the elite criteria". This book describes an American situation and it may not be possible to translate its findings to other countries although, from personal experience, the findings with regard to the popularity of school sports 'stars' appear to hold good in Britain. An interesting example of the relationship between sporting ability and peer group, this time working in reverse, is given in Whyte's [40] account of Chicago street gangs. He showed that performers at the bowling alley were related to the position that the bowler had in the gang. One of the boys, Frank, "was accustomed to filling an inferior position" and even though he was good at bowls "was unable to star in his favourite sport when competing against members of his own group".

The possibility of assisting socialisation by giving special coaching is suggested by Fleming [15], "Where popularity and group prestige are directly related to any specific activity, an important service can be rendered by the adult who helps a backward adolescent to regain social confidence by an increase of physical or athletic skill". In 1956 Brailsford [4] looking at this aspect wrote, "It seems safe, however, to assume that a child's physical ability will do much to dictate his status in the eyes of his fellows and that the physical education teacher may thus, by careful direction and encouragement, be instrumental in making the unskilled child more acceptable to his fellows, and consequently, happier".

Conclusions

In an area as speculative as this it would be folly to attempt any *formal* conclusions. One might sum up some of the points of view expressed as follows:

1. Sport is an area of social interaction and as such is likely also to be an area of socialisation.

2. Games themselves can be seen as an expression of certain cultural values and highly organised games, such as found in schools and throughout modern Britain, are only supportable in a highly complex society.

3. Cultural norms and values can be learnt in sporting situations. In school sport this isn't, or shouldn't be, left to chance and the presence of the teacher as a socialising agent is important in this as in other situations in education.

4. Sporting activities can provide the individual with a series of experiences which will help him to take stock of his own capacities and to learn to accept and react to other people.

5. Skill in sport can assist social development at different levels, for example by helping those who are socially backward to attain acceptance or by providing an area of possible achievement for potential leaders which gives high prestige and status amongst peers.

6. In adolescence, boys appear to have strong general interest in sport but this needs closer examination before it is taken for granted in particular cases.

7. Although in adolescence the influence of the family is less strong it appears that parental backing and class background still play a considerable part in determining sporting interests.

These are by no means all the comments which are possible, even from this short treatment of the topic. Many questions remain. Hoyle [20] can have the last word. "Games have long been justified on the grounds of their (unproven) effect upon 'character'. Or the social influence of P.E. has been interpreted as a two-stage process: involvement in games being held to lead to a greater involvement in school which, in turn, leads to the internalisation of those values which are central to the culture of the school – ambition, self improvement, a pre-disposition to take a long-term view of things, constructive use of leisure, control of aggression, respect for authority, cultivation of courtesy, etc. But the social functions of physical education need not be strictly instrumental as this 'by-product' justification implies. It can be argued that where physical activities are engaged in for their own sake, an important social function is being met".

References

1. Arnold, P., 'Physical education, creativity and self concept', *Bulletin of physical education*, vol. 8, no. 1, 1970.
2. Banks, O., *The sociology of education*, Batsford, 1968.
3. Berne, E., *Games people play*, p. 19. Andre Deutsch, 1966.

4. Brailsford, D. W., 'Physical education and social psychology', *Physical education*, vol. 48, no. 144. P.E.A. July, 1956.
5. Browne, E., 'An ethological theory of play', *J.O.H.P.E.R.*, vol. 39, no. 7, pp. 36–39.
6. Caillois, R., *Man, play and games*, p. 58. Thames and Hudson, 1962.
7. *ibid.*, p. 9.
8. Coleman, J. S., *The adolescent society*, Collier-Macmillan, 1961.
9. *ibid.*, p. 232.
10. Comer, G., 'Relationship between sport and mental health', *Physical education*, vol. 60, no. 181. November, 1968.
11. Crunden, C., 'Sport and social background', *Bulletin of physical education*, vol. 8, no. 2, p. 40. April, 1970.
12. Dearden, R. F., *The philosophy of primary education*, pp. 95–105. Routledge & Kegan Paul, 1968.
13. Dennis, W., 'A cross-cultural study of the reinforcement of child behaviour', pp. 431–438, *Child Development*, no. 28.
14. Fleming, C. M., *Adolescence*, National Foundation for Education Research in England and Wales. Routledge & Kegan Paul, 1948.
15. *ibid.*, p. 123.
16. Hargreaves, D. H., *Social relationship in a secondary school*. Routledge & Kegan Paul, 1967.
17. Heaton, J., 'The role of the male teacher working with boys in the secondary school', *Bulletin of physical education*, vol. 8, no. 2, p. 33. B.A.O.L.P.E. April, 1970.
18. Helanko, R., 'Sport and socialisation', *Acta sociologica*, no. 2, pp. 229–241. 1957.
19. Hoyle, E., 'The role of the physical educationist in contemporary society', *Bulletin of physical education*, vol. 7, no. 6, p. 10. B.A.O.L.P.E. April, 1969.
20. *ibid.*, p. 9.
21. Hoyle, E., *The role of the teacher*, p. 109. Routledge & Kegan Paul, 1969.
22. Jephcott, P., *Time of one's own*, Oliver & Boyd, 1967.
23. Jones, M. C., 'A study of socialisation patterns at high school level', in Grinder, R. E. (ed.), *Studies in adolescence*, p. 363. Collier-Macmillan, 1963.
24. Knapp, B., 'Sex differences in the declared leisure interests of the 14–15 year age group', *Research in physical education*, vol. 1, no. 4. P.E.A. June, 1969.
25. Leach, E., *A runaway world*, B.B.C. 1967.
26. Lieberman, E., in Anderson, N. (ed.), *Work and leisure*, Routledge & Kegan Paul, 1961.
27. Lorenz, K., *Aggression*, Methuen, 1963.
28. Parsons, T., 'The school class as a social system', in Grinder, R. E. (ed.), *Studies in adolescence*, p. 29. Macmillan, 1963.
29. *ibid.*, p. 437.
30. Shaw, B., 'Physical education: can it rehumanize sport?' *Bulletin of physical education*, vol. 8, no. 1, p. 12. B.A.O.L.P.E. January, 1970.
31. Strodtbeck, F. C., 'Family, integration, values and achievement', in Halsey, A. H., Floud, J. and Anderson, C. A. (eds.), *Education, economy and society*, p. 345. Collier-Macmillan, 1961.
32. Wall, W. D., *Adolescents in school and society*, p. 67.
33. Waller, W., *The sociology of teaching*. Wiley, 1932.
34. Ward, E., 'Research in socialisation and physical activity', *British journal of physical education*, vol. 2. P.E.A. March, 1970.
35. *ibid.*, p. xii.

36. *ibid*., p. xiii.
37. *ibid*., p. xii.
38. *ibid*., p. xiii.
39. Ward, E., Hardman, K. and Almond, L., 'Investigation into the pattern of participation and attitudes, to physical activity of 11–18 year old boys', *Research in physical education*, vol. 1, no. 3. P.E.A. June, 1968.
40. Whyte, W. F., *Street corner society*, Chicago University Press. 1943.

15

Tchouk-ball *†

An International Sport-for-All

with Michel Favre

Historical Background

For many years Dr. Hermann Brandt, an eminent Swiss biologist from Geneva, studied and experimented with the practical application of scientific knowledge in the sphere of physical activities. As early as 1928 he formed in Switzerland, within the Fédération de Gymnastique, the Contrôle Medico-Sportif which, through his perseverance, was firstly extended to the Canton of Geneva and finally to the whole of the country. Furthermore he introduced the game of volleyball and basketball for women into Switzerland. In France in 1938 he was awarded

* A revised version of a paper written with Michel Favre, of Switzerland, and first published in the B.A.A.L.P.E. *Bulletin of physical education*, vol. 9, no. 5, pp. 51–66. January, 1973.

†The name 'Tchouk-ball' was chosen as one likely to be adopted internationally without translation. It is an onomatopoeic representation of the sound of a ball rebounding from a highly tensioned net.

the title of Advisory Member of Honour of the Société Française de Cinésiologie 'in recognition of his services', and in 1960, the French Government made him Officier du Mérite Sportif [1].

His studies and experiments led to the publication of a book entitled, *From Physical Education to Sport through Biology* [2]. The formal conclusion of his work was that sporting activities can only satisfactorily be justified through their educational potential. Starting from this point, Dr. Brandt presented *A Scientific Criticism of Team Games* as his entry for the 1st International Literary Concourse on the Theory of Physical Education, organised by the Fédération Internationale d'Éducation Physique, with the "Thulin Prize" for the winner. On August 16, 1970, he was presented with this famous world prize at the University of Lisbon. The practical expression of his ideas, arising out of his critical study of existing games, is tchouk-ball, a new team game combining elements of Basque pelota and hand-ball, to create a game which is designed to meet the needs of physical educationists, and which is primarily non-aggressive whilst retaining an atmosphere of healthy competition.

Following a sudden illness and a period of ill-health through which he worked to ensure the future of his game, Dr. Brandt died in November, 1972, but he could already see something of his high hopes becoming reality. The first national Tchouk-ball Association was formed in France on February 27, 1971, at Mundolsheim, Bas-Rhin, closely followed by a Swiss Association on April 18 in the same year. Finally an International Tchouk-ball Federation came into being on June 5, 1971 at Gunzgen in Switzerland [4].

The first international match, organised by the Swiss Federation under the aegis of the Fédération Internationale de Tchouk-ball (F.I.T.B.), took place on October 31, 1971 at Geneva. In this match the Swiss met the French and victory went to France by 53 points to 49. On that day the game of Tchouk-ball came of age.

International development has continued and the game has been received with interest in countries as widely apart as Australia and Mexico. The Fédération Internationale d'Éducation Physique has played a great part in spreading knowledge of the game through its international *Bulletin*, and via its delegates in seventy-seven countries around the world.

In Britain the game has made steady progress. It received television coverage on the famous B.B.C. Blue Peter programme, which led to the rapid growth of knowledge of the new game. In 1975 and 1976 it was featured at Butlin's children's weeks. The British Tchouk-ball Association was formed in Cheltenham on December 9, 1972 and is now affiliated to the International Federation.

Basic Principles and Advantages of Tchouk-ball

This game is based on a fundamental ideal; to realise the educational potential in sport for the greatest number of individuals. Thus tchouk-ball is conceived to be played as a school activity, as a family game, as a leisure time relaxation, and also as a competitive sport.

Its major advantages include:

1. That it is primarily a non-aggressive game, designed to allow enjoyable matches as much between individuals as between nations.

2. That the rules oblige players to respect their opponents, who cannot be prevented from playing by man-to-man covering and tackling which so often nowadays involves, or results in, real aggression. (In any case it is felt that this form of play demands relatively little intelligence and is often used to compensate for, or cover up, technical inferiority.) By comparison, whilst allowing an opponent freedom of play, allowing him to move, pass or throw at the frame without hindrance, the tchouk-ball player must seek to anticipate the actions and reactions of his opponents as well as regulating his own movements and opportunities to pass and shoot. As play develops, movements and thought become more complex and the educational potential of the game is increased.

3. That tchouk-ball avoids the tense competitiveness which afflicts many of our national team games at present. The game allows each player to express himself within his own physical and intellectual capabilities, and players of different capabilities can play together without a weaker (or even handicapped) player being played out of, or left out of, the game.

4. That the dimensions of the playing area can be varied to obtain different physiological effects, and also to ensure the effective organisation of teaching. In cases where space is limited, the game makes a high density use of the space available.

5. That, as the ball should not touch the ground, the game can be played on virtually any reasonably smooth surface; from the gymnasium or sports hall floor to the beach, and including grass, tarmac or beaten earth surfaces.

6. Finally, that as the rules are simple and can be understood and assimilated rapidly without difficulty – they are accessible to everyone.

Simple Tactics

One of the advantages of introducing a new game is that tactics have not reached a highly developed form. Tchouk-ball awaits the development of advanced tactics, 'set plays', etc. by the players and teachers of the future. However, beginners must start with a few essential tactical points in mind.

1. *To score* a point, the ball must rebound from the net to fall into unoccupied ground within the limits of the field of play. This means that a team in attack (unless the player receiving the ball is well positioned) must interpass to send the ball to that team member who is best placed to make such a shot. This involves a rapid assessment of the positions of team members and opponents, and also of the variations of rebound trajectory which can result from shots made using different techniques. Similarly, assessment of these possibilities and appropriate covering will be the role of the defending team.

2. The rules allow a player to stand still but not to obstruct an opponent in any way. Obstruction is a contravention of the essential spirit of the game. Any move into a particular shooting or covering position must therefore be made before an opponent occupies that position. To move and obstruct a player about to take a pass, a rebound, or about to shoot, is a deliberate fault.

3. In breaking down the covering of rebounds, it is useful tactically to remember that balls returning with quite a range of trajectory differences height-wise (for example, balls which can be caught below knee height or caught jumping to full stretch height) can be covered with relatively little displacement of the catcher, but that shots which cause the defending players to move rapidly sideways are most likely to unbalance territorial coverage by the opposition and open up unoccupied areas in the field of play. Passing to and shooting from wide angles, away from the central positions immediately in front of the rebound net, will result in a more active game and many more opportunities to out-manoeuvre the opposition.

Basic Techniques

For the purpose of this discussion (and possibly for useful emphasis within teaching/coaching – learning/practising sessions) one can consider five aspects of the game; each one involving very basic techniques. These are:

Shooting, catching, moving, passing, positioning.

Shooting

The purpose of a shot is to reach, via the rebound net, a particular part of the field of play which is seen to be unoccupied. To achieve this a player must have at least two basic shots at his disposal.

1. A shot from above downwards with considerable force, the net sending the ball back to ground quite close to the semi-circular line of the 'forbidden zone'. This shot will quite often be made in mid-air.
2. An underhand shot, the ball swinging through about knee height, to rebound high into empty space towards the parts of the field of play farthest from the net.

These two basic shots should be supplemented with a number of other shots:

3. A horizontal shot with sideways displacement. A central player may use this to widen the angle of the rebound, or possibly to move across the face of the net to achieve a reversal of the game's axis. That is, where a ball has gone into the net slightly right of centre and rebounded slightly left, the player may be able to move back to right of centre in making his shot so that the rebound is again left of centre – so breaking the normal rebound sequence of in right – out left, in left – out right.) Players should be capable of this shot with either hand.
4. A shot in mid-air from a catch in mid-air – without returning to the ground (forwards).
5. A diving shot, parallel with the ground, particularly useful from the wings, in order to make the ball rebound wide and low almost parallel with the base line.
6. A shot performed in mid-air moving forwards, either from above downwards or from below upwards, i.e. forward moving mid-air variations of (1), (2) and (3) (backs).

Catching

Catching is important for the handling of passes but even more so as the main method of defence. Every time a ball rebounding from a shot at net is dropped, a point is scored by the opposing team.

1. *Taking a pass*: the player should reach towards the ball with two hands which close onto the ball on contact and which will normally bring it back into a control position, generally in front of the body at about chest height.

2. *Catching in defence*: long ball rebounding from the net should be taken in the same way as described for the pass above. Closer to the net it may be necessary to attempt diving catches to the left or right and particularly with low rebounds near the edge of the semi-circular 'forbidden zone' it will be necessary to pick up the ball with both hands stretched forward and flat. If a catch is not possible, a player may scoop or hit the ball up (as in 'digging' in volleyball) for a clean catch to be made by a team mate. This counts as a pass between team members.

Moving

1. *Movements without the ball:* all movement around the field of play, however rapid, should be controlled to avoid obstruction and barging which are offences and contrary to the essential idea of the game. The speed and timing of moves to take up attacking positions must be balanced between the necessity of arriving before an opponent can take that position, and delay in taking up a shooting position to delay the opposition's cover for the shots which might be made from that position. As players move they must be ready to receive a pass at any moment.

2. *Movements with the ball:* the rules allow three contacts with the ground. Players must therefore be made aware of three possibilities open to them:
   i. Receiving the ball with both feet in contact with the ground. Only one more step is permitted.
   ii. Receiving the ball with one foot on the ground. Two steps may then be taken.
   iii. Receiving the ball in mid-air, three steps can then be taken.

In all three cases further progress can be made by jumping forward on the final step provided that the player has passed or shot before making contact with the ground the next time.

In early attempts at the game, beginners will probably tend to be very static, but if in learning they are encouraged to at least lift one foot before catching the ball, and later to take the ball on the move – jumping just prior to the arrival of the ball to make the most of the three paces allowed – a very fluid and active game will ensue.

Passing

The essentials of passing in tchouk-ball are speed and accuracy. As no interference with the pass is allowed, elaborate attempts at deception including disguised passes (which as often as not deceive team mates as well as opponents) are best avoided in favour of quick clean ball handling.

The oft quoted phrase, "look where you are passing and pass where you are looking" is very applicable in this game. Speed of pass should be as fast as possible, provided that control is not sacrificed; one-handed passing with both the left and the right hand, as well as two-handed passing, should be practised. Passing to a player on the move should be particularly stressed in teaching, with emphasis on the ball being delivered in front of the moving player at sufficient height for a jump to be made to make maximum use of the three step ruling.

Anticipation is important in giving (and taking) passes. A pass to a particular area of the field of play may be timed and weighted to arrive at the same time as a player arriving to make a shot for which the rebound area is at that moment unmarked. Hand signals may be used by the receiver, for example, to indicate to the passer whether the ball should be delivered straight to the receiver, or to one side or the other, or into a part of the field of play towards which the receiver is moving.

Positioning

1. In general the stance of players during the game should be that adopted as a 'ready position' at times in most team games; weight forward on the balls of the feet, legs slightly bent, upper body slightly leaning forward. This position allows rapid changes in position to be made.
2. In defence, depending on the system of marking adopted – either area defence or individual marking – the positioning of players on the field of play will differ.

Area Defence

In covering an area a defensive player will 'float' in his zone ('floating' being a broad semi-circular movement from side to side) according to the position of the ball. He should thus be moving every time the ball changes place in relation to the net. An immobile player is one who is not fully following the game.

Individual Marking

In contrast to the usual idea of individual marking (which generally involves two players playing close together) the wider the game moves, the wider towards different sidelines the attacker and the defender move, the defender continually trying to judge how best to position himself to catch the various shots 'his man' could make if he received the ball.

References

1. Revue Éducative Physique et Médecine, no. 13, October, 1938.
2. Brandt, H. *De l'education physique aux sports par la biologie*. Editions Médecine et Hygiène, Geneva, 1967.
3. Brandt, H. *Étude critique scientifique des sports d'equipe; le tchoukball, le sport de demain*, Editions Roulet, 1227 Carouge-Geneva, 1970.
4. Werey, T. 'Introducing tchouk-ball', *Bulletin of physical education*, vol. 9, no. 2., pp. 55–58. B.A.O.L.P.E. April, 1972.

16

Fédération Internationale* d'Éducation Physique World Manifesto on Physical Education

Preamble

The F.I.E.P., founded in 1923, is the oldest international organisation concerned with physical education. It includes both individual and collective members (Associations, Schools and Advanced Institutions for Sport and Physical Education, Research Institutes, Professional Groups of Physical Educationists, etc.) from the eighty countries in which it is officially represented by a delegate. Members of F.I.E.P. are specialists in the sciences of anatomy, physiology, psychology, sociology and pedagogy, or are engaged in physical education or in social work. The *FIEP Bulletin*, edited in four languages, has appeared regularly since 1931 and offers its readers information on the physical

* A revised translation of an official document of the Fedération Internationale d'Éducation Physique first published in English in the B.A.O.L.P.E. *Bulletin of physical education*, vol. 8, no. 5, pp. 10–20. January, 1971.

education activities in various countries in articles of high scientific and pedogogic standard.

The constant aim of the F.I.E.P. is to contribute, at world level, to the educational process by means of physical activities. It is universally acknowledged that, among these activities, sport must have an important place. In its ideal concept – which is that of a game, an intense struggle, a proving of oneself against an obstacle (time, space, material elements, etc.) or against an adversary (an individual or group) – sport has distinct educational values which are universally recognised. The F.I.E.P. approves in general of the fine study made on this subject by the International Council for Sport and Physical Education in its *Manifesto on Sport* (1965).

However, educationists, those with social associations, are worried about the evolution of sport. In fact the concept of 'sport' covers extremely diverse activities; from the quiet walk to the extreme commitment of the great winter climbs; from the game played solely for pleasure and self-appraisal to the publicity train of the cycle races, to the clownish (and ignoble) spectacle of female wrestling or four part wrestling; from 'spectator sport' (in the stadium or on TV.) to the solitary unskilled holidaymaker out in a canoe. The physiological effects of sport vary, therefore, from bodily activity so slight as to be inadequate, to total exhaustion, occasionally even death; there being, fortunately, positive states of well-being between these extremes. Social manifestations may be anything from loyal friendship to brutal opposition between individuals or groups. We are sometimes a long way from our educational aims and, in certain places, there appears to be sad separation, if not, opposition, between physical education (or education for physical activities) and sport.

For better sport, for sport really integrated with the educational system, it becomes necessary for educationists to see more clearly what is good and what is bad in the many aspects of sporting activities, in order not to serve, perhaps unwittingly, a wrong cause.

Let us list in evidence certain essential facts:

1. Modern sport is a social phenomenon of considerable importance, expressed mainly in the forms of 'selective competitive sport' and 'spectacular sport'. It is mainly these forms of sport which retain attention and get the help of public bodies, of the public, of the mass-media (press, radio and TV.) and of certain commercial enterprises.
2. These forms are characterised by: permanent, strong competition in order to determine the champion; rigorous training which can demand several hours a day and become a real burden; financial obligations which lead it towards the spectacular, the sensational, and enslavement to commercial interests; a primitive concern for 'victory

over another' and the use of all means for this purpose. Chauvinism, disloyalty, cheating (doping for example) even hatred, appear all too frequently in this context.

3. This state of affairs has the following consequences in too many countries: undervaluation, if not ignorance, of basic physical education (which must include, however, certain forms of sport) which should become a reality in schools if one wishes to build the sound man – the true sportsman – of tomorrow; insufficient funds, personnel and necessary facilities being available for this fundamental sector of education; the tendency, apparently logical but unfortunate (especially for physical education in schools) to replace university lecturers (who have as a rule a solid cultural base plus a firm concept of their educational mission) by specialised coaches, trained more quickly and cheaply, whose principal role will be to 'make champions'; indifference towards 'sport for all' and non-competitive, leisure-time physical activities which, from the individual and social points of view, are a necessity in modern times and have high educational value.

4. However, educational and recreational sport still exists. In numerous countries there are young people and adults who take part in sport for personal enjoyment, effort and progress (even at the highest level – but, alas, this is increasingly rare). It is essentially this concept of sport which must be safeguarded and developed.

5. Finally, a problem of choice of priorities confronts educationists and others with social responsibilities. On one side there is professional sport and highly competitive (more or less professionalised) sport which can only involve a minority of exceptionally talented individuals. We must accept this professionalism or semi-professionalism as an inescapable reality – the logical pattern in a world dominated by the spirit of competition, concern for national glory or by commercial interests – but above all as a phenomenon which can acquire certain human and social values. It can be an honest career and, like any occupation, have its usefulness, its joys and its greatness. But its intentions must be more clearly defined, its organisation better structured. It should serve not to debase the specialist but to promote his social and humane aspects. On the other side there is sport which serves the purposes of education, health and recreation, which is necessarily 'sport for all' and which falls naturally into the general system of physical education.

Between these two sides, whose mutual ties are becoming increasingly slight, we must choose, or more precisely, must establish what proportion of aid, whether political, administrative, technical or pedagogical, should go to each side.

For educationists the choice would seem obvious.

The first option is scarcely justifiable from the social point of view unless there was actual proof that the example of the champions actually leads to longer lasting, more extensive practice of formative and educational physical activities. In spite of all the assertions, all the so-called 'evidence', such proof remains to be established by scientific sociological enquiry. Moreover, it becomes more and more obvious that the development of mass sport is essentially dependent on economic, social and educational factors, and far less on the number and popularity of champions.

The second option is justified through human social activities which are almost certainly of value, and the strong probability of eventually finding champions among a much larger number of participants.

It is then a question of reversing the priorities; to such purpose that tomorrow those socially responsible – governments and associations – instead of directing the bulk of their support, their energy, their time, often their generosity, to the glory and interests of a few champions (a new social aristocracy sometimes more cherished than learned benefactors of humanity), should undertake with vigour and perseverance to make a much more marked effort in favour of the community's health; in favour of healthy, recreational and educational activities available for everyone.

This will not be easy! For we will need to bring about a veritable revolution of attitudes and realities, against forces (political and financial interests, local and national passions, customs and habits) which are considerable. This then is the true aim to be attained.

It can and must be reached.

The first condition for success is to create, or recreate, a clear, healthy concept of physical education in order, finally, to develop another social trend. Such is the purpose of this World Manifesto.

World Manifesto on Physical Education

A General Concept of Physical Education

Physical education is the element in education which uses, in a systematic way, both physical activities and the influences of natural agents — air, sunshine, water, etc., — as specific means. *Physical* action is regarded nowadays as a favoured means of education, for it involves the whole of one's being. It is universally recognised that **oneness** is a characteristic of this form of education. We shall, however, separate the following distinct aims, to facilitate theoretical analysis.

A well-balanced, healthy body

Able to resist attacks from both the physical and social environments; this implies the systematic training of adaptive functions, to attain a quality of health which is more than simply the absence of disease. This is the hygienic aim; a fundamental aim (pursued by both hygiene and medicine, by means which differ in some respects), an aim of which we should never lose sight.

Physical aptitudes

Physical aptitudes can be categorised in the following three ways:

1. Qualities of perception – acuteness of internal perception (knowledge of one's own body), speed and accuracy of external perception (sensory acuity).
2. Motor qualities – optimum mobility, speed, strength, skill, endurance, ability to relax, giving each action efficiency and maximum effectiveness.
3. Qualities of self-control and judgement – intelligent appraisal of a situation and the ability to find the right solution quickly. The sum of these psycho-motor qualities – which are often interdependent – should facilitate the adaptation to activities in everyday life, in professional life as much as in leisure-time activities.

Moral values

Physical education should be 'morals in action'. Here the determining factors are the moral climate of teaching sessions and the active social environment (in the separate group activities) which can be created by the teachers. In the real world – and even more in tomorrow's world – we should have this constantly in mind when concerned with children's education; these aims of P.E. have considerable social importance.

We must obviously take into account the particular social environment in each country: concepts and means of education always depend on a political, economic and human framework. But, bearing in mind the probable evolution of societies where physical education can really operate, certain common trends can be determined.

More and more the task will be one of preparing the child and helping adults and elderly people to operate efficiently, to preserve their psycho-physiological balance amidst the unfortunate effects of mechanisation, sedentary life, pollution, and nervous exhaustion brought on by the increased tempo and tensions of civilisation.

It will be increasingly a question of creating and preserving a liking for physical effort and appreciation of healthy living to combat such great evils as alcoholism, drugs, physical laziness, lack of enthusiasm, etc.

The Means of Physical Education

The specific means of physical education is physical exercise, that is, planned physical activity, devised in order to educate, to exercise (to train, to perfect). The nature of the exercise is by no means the determining factor here, but the intention which promotes the action; for this intention decides the general direction and particular forms which the action takes, and determines its results on the individual. All psycho-motor activity conceived primarily for educational purposes forms part of physical education. The latter is characterised far more by a state of mind than by the choice of this or that technique. Techniques are only the 'tools' – infinitely various and always evolving – to serve in execution of clear educational objectives.

At this higher level of intent, the unity of physical education can be realised, and fundamentally different techniques can work together in harmony towards a common aim.

Attempts at classification of physical exercises are numerous. Any classification of things concerning life where the 'frontiers' are always indefinite, is necessarily artificial but convenient. In regard to the main intention which promotes the action, we propose a definition which seems at the same time the broadest and the simplest.

1. Exercises properly called educational

The forms of exercises and situations are chosen or created solely to serve those formative and educational aims which are considered fundamental: acquisition and maintenance of optimum mobility, development of strength and endurance, self-knowledge and self-control, etc.

1. Practical activities, games and sports

—in which the prime objective is to achieve a concrete and immediate goal such as enjoyment, beating an opponent or a record. To remain in the sphere of physical education, these exercises must also be, at least in the teacher's mind, infused with an educational intent.

The formal character of exercises in the first category results in lack of incentive, at any rate for the majority of pupils. However, they should not be neglected because they are essential in the early formative periods. Teaching skill plays its part in making them interesting for all pupils.

The second group covers, generally speaking, highly motivated activities. But these must be used with care because they are the battlefield between practical or sporting interests and educational interests; between passion and reason.

Very often in practical teaching these two categories of exercise can, and should, be merged under a single general form of motivation towards self-control and self-affirmation. This liaison should become established, particularly in the sphere of sports activities.

The Place of Sports Activities in Physical Education

Sports activities consist of:

1. *Sports competitions* – systematically organised – usually by sports federations. This is the best-known and most characteristic form of present-day sport. It operates mainly by a process of elimination and selection. It is strictly codified in its technical forms, numbers, duration, etc.
2. *Sports training* – which covers all preparatory activities for sports competitions, seeking firstly 'general conditioning' then 'peaks' and 'top form'. In the first stage it naturally pursues the same objectives as physical education: improvement of fundamental qualities (suppleness, skill, strength, resistance, bodily control, training of the will, etc.).
3. *Sport-games* – competition freely adapted in order to satisfy the needs of recreation and education, such as friends playing basketball with improvised teams.

This form of sport does not eliminate the weaker players. It does without spectators or expensive equipment. It is solely the responsibility of educationists or of the participants themselves who can, if they wish, change the rules so that they are better suited to everyone's needs and the possibilities.

It is conceivable that sports training and sport-games can easily be integrated into the general system of physical education. In the modern world, it would pay to give them an important place, because they fulfil a very great need for both leisure time and the formative period in schools, and these are subject to very powerful motivation.

The use of classical sports competitions is a much more delicate matter. The actions of teachers, club organisers, even doctors and journalists, now become the determining factor. Every precaution must be taken to ensure that all competition retains a definite formative and educational value. It must, therefore, be used with care.

In any case we must consider that this sector of activity is limited in the number of participants, and also in the length of time of actual participation (about ten years on average).

The greatest possibilities of success – and the most worthwhile human action – will result from a movement in favour of sport for all. This would mean sport-games first and foremost and then classical sports competitions, these being conceived primarily for purposes of education and recreation.

In fact this cannot be founded mainly on the existing structure of sports associations, on selective competition, for this would lead inevitably to all the dangers already pointed out. It will be primarily sport for school children and students, organised by educationists, freed from the inclination to win at any price, as financially independent as possible, organised so that even the weakest can join in, taking place at regular intervals which can be continually adapted to the possibilities of pupils and the requirements of their studies (so as to enhance, and not detract from, these studies).

This will be family sport and leisure-time corporate sport. The sports clubs will eventually rediscover the friendly match, which needs no fixed rules about the length of the game, substitution of players, etc. because it remains at the level of playing for pleasure. This will be participant sport and not simply spectator sport.

From these 'game-like sports', 'leisure-sports' and 'true mass sport' – there will emerge naturally from among the young, an elite which, as now, will prove itself at the highest levels, but one hopes with a different spirit, in "A purer, more chivalrous sport, more transparent and calm" as was envisaged by Pierre de Coubertin.

Techniques and Teaching Methods

Physical education is relatively new in its scientific bases. It can scarcely be dogmatic or rigid about certain of its techniques or teaching methods. To ensure its correct evolution, to determine the best techniques and most effective teaching methods, scientific research in physical education must be better organised and developed.

It is regrettable that, until now, research centres have directed their work too exclusively towards knowledge of extreme exertion, and organic and psychological adaptation to difficult conditions (altitude, deep-sea diving, etc.), and not enough towards the fundamental problems of physical education in schools and 'sport for all'.

Scientific research should be in the hands of proven experts, grouped in working-parties, in regional or national research centres (in touch with each other through the international organisations, and close contact with other biological, psychological, sociological and pedagogical research centres). Here we must never forget that we are necessarily experimenting on groups of children. This 'experimental material' cannot be sacrificed in any way, and the experiments must therefore be conducted with competence, and a deep sense of human values.

Elsewhere, physical education should establish itself as a major applied science, having its own sphere and specific methods. It can also play its part towards progress in other human sciences, by mutual contribution. However, present empirical knowledge and certain data scientifically established already allow a valuable part to be played by physical activities in the realm of education. A few fundamental principles can guide the actions of educationists.

Biological degree of exertion

Effort is not educational – not transformed into progress – until it exceeds a certain level of intensity and sufficient repetition. This is the principle of over-load, scientifically established both in biology and psychology.

Dosage of effort (adaptation to individual potential)

The effort must be intense enough to come into the positive sector of biological effect, but excess leading to over-exertion must be avoided.

In physical education it is exceptional to reach over-exertion (whether in school sessions or in adult voluntary gymnastics). Too often we fail to reach the necessary intensity or quantity (through insufficient allocation of time). In sports training and especially in sports competitions, the physiological limits are quite frequently reached. While intense effort is beneficial to the young (as much physiologically as psychologically), it can become dangerous for adults and elderly people. And, for all, if repeated, it could lead to over-exertion. Here prudence and regular medical checks are essential. It is up to biology and pedagogy to resolve the delicate problem of individual dosage during group instruction.

The prime importance of general training

During the essential physical, mental and emotional growth period of childhood and adolescence, educative action must revolve around the development of the availability of learning-ability and the fundamental qualities (health, mobility, strength and endurance, judgement, self-control, etc.).

This entails general physical training, comprising the most varied exercises in equally diverse situations. This, then, is the best preparation for future activities in everyday life, in professional life and in specialised sports. In the field of educational sport it is better to avoid all premature specialisation. We must never imprison a child too soon in a single activity, where his body and soul can be moulded by a closed environment and narrow conditioning, which could prevent certain other potentialities from establishing themselves. As in other spheres of education, we must progressively put the child and then the adolescent in a position to choose, freely and judiciously, one or more sports activities which he will practise thereafter for as long as possible. It is sensible to prepare particularly for those adult physical activities which are fundamental, for it is in the adult period (the period of family and social responsibility) that a man needs to be in good health and physically able.

The importance of outdoor activities

In the modern world, which inclines more and more towards urban civilisation, an important place must be given, in school as in adult leisure, to outdoor physical activities. These activities have an important formative, liberating and balancing function.

Motivation of exercises

There is no true education without voluntary commitment on the part of the subject; that is, his active participation. The important thing from the teaching point of view is therefore to find the motivation which will lead the subject to act usefully for his own progress. Modern psychology has established that most interests are created by education and the environment (family, social group, propaganda). But there is a universal, fundamental interest, specific to the human being: the desire to test and surpass himself in the 'search for success'. This need to affirm and enlarge oneself, through the medium of any activity finds natural expression in games and sports. Thus man is fundamentally a sports-loving being in the broadest sense of the term. This is one of our fundamental differences from animals.

Motivation through games and sports must therefore have a large place in physical education. But it must be used with care and, above all, it must not be the only sort to be brought into play. Apart from the first school years (ages 4 to 8 years, approximately), an educational system could not be based solely on games. It is necessary too, in preparation for life, that the notion of work should become clearly evident and that the child should finally develop a liking for work.

The usual sports motivation (connected with competition) is much more complex. It is formed – and often distorted – by the influence of social surroundings. It corresponds to a very pronounced characteristic of the modern world, 'the struggle for life, with elimination of the opponent': a characteristic which it is desirable to replace for the world tomorrow, by a joint effort for mutual progress. To remain of value, sports motivation must be separated from a social context which is sometimes dangerous to education, by surpassing it.

We must enlarge the concept of sports motivation and consider that all situations, all exercises that lead children to know, to prove and declare themselves better, are interesting for them and are sports activities.

There is also 'sporting activity' in the sense of self-discovery and self-proving in truly educational exercises (fully conscious, methodical efforts for the systematic development of basic qualities), in activities directed towards people helping each other, and in making intense efforts in natural surroundings (away from the enclosed field of competitive sport and the influence of spectators, etc.). An educationist aware of his important mission could not neglect these higher motives, which indeed form the true sporting spirit.

Educational activity through groups, and the influence of social environment

In the modern world, education is necessarily collective. The relationship 'teacher-pupil-group' is, at school and club level, considered a fundamental factor in the educational process. Physical education must call more and more on psycho-sociology in deciding on its teaching methods, and must always take into consideration the favourable or unfavourable influence of the social environment.

The Educationists

Techniques, pedagogical forms, and material possibilities themselves, are only tools whose efficient use depends ultimately on those who use them. Those in positions of political and administrative responsibility in the various countries must be thoroughly aware that the viability of their efforts on behalf of physical education, is primarily determined by the provision of a sufficient number of educationists and by their quality.

The task of education through physical activities demands a sound knowledge of biology, psychology and sociology, and a solid grounding in teaching. Particularly during the delicate period of childhood and adolescence, this task must only be entrusted to teachers who have been thoroughly prepared at graduate level.

In the preparation of these teachers the accent must be on general culture, scientific knowledge and fundamental techniques (all of which have a permanent general value), on educational aims and the development of the scientific mind. The deeper study of sports techniques – which are many and constantly changing – should be seen as chosen specialisation during and after general studies.

But we must also prepare the minds of the teachers: create faith and enthusiasm for the task ahead, develop the essential pedagogic qualities, which are love of the pupils, devotion, respect for human values, etc. Physical educationists should be – and remain as long as possible – examples of good physical condition and sporting spirit. This advanced level of preparation is just as desirable for teachers operating in other sectors of a school or in sports clubs, in the army and in adult physical education. This should be possible in many countries as soon as governments make available the necessary funds.

But to satisfy this multiplicity of needs, especially for mass sport and voluntary adult gymnastics – we must think in terms of training a large number of instructors and organisers who, either voluntary, or paid on a full or part-time basis, can undertake the direction of these activities. Here a simple, precise technical training, commonsense, devotion, teaching skill, and a healthy concept of the role of physical activities in the service of humanity, are the essential attributes.

Administrative and Material Conditions

To ensure the effectiveness of physical education, it is essential that public bodies and the administrators directly responsible:

1. Make a special effort in the organisation of physical education in primary schools (7 to 11 years) and even in the infant schools. This is the true starting point and it is, alas, the most neglected in the majority of countries.

Educational action is indeed imperative and decisive during this time of great organic and psychological malleability. What comes later . . . comes too late!

Children's rights, confirmed in the United Nations General Assembly declaration of November 20, 1956, cannot be safeguarded unless schools, parents and the social group provide for the child a physical education designed with regard to his needs and his potential. Children's physical education must have positive, formative and educational value, and cannot limit itself to simple recreation.

2. Arrange sufficient time-tabling of compulsory P.E. in schools, and see that this time-table is not purely theoretical. A minimum of 5 hours a week is essential. This time-table should be supplemented by optional physical activities, outside school, in the form of specialised training, sports, and outdoor activities.

3. Undertake a widespread advertising campaign (particularly in the press and on TV.) and give effective aid to promote healthy physical education and recreation for adults. ('Voluntary gymnastics' and 'sport

for all'.) Leisure-time activities must not be left entirely to commercial enterprises for whom educational aims, if they exist, must necessarily come second.

In tomorrow's world we hope that political and economic conditions will permit every individual to have sufficient time for healthy leisure pursuits.

4. Increase the number of facilities so as to enable the needs for physical activity of the great mass of children, adolescents and adults to be satisfied; needs which are increasing in a mechanised world where physical effort tends to be suppressed. In this indispensable effort over sports equipment, absolute priority must be given:

(a) to simple, practical physical education halls, swimming pools and sports fields in sufficient numbers and in, or in the immediate vicinity of, schools and university institutions; (b) to similar facilities in all large population centres and all town districts: public stadia and public physical education centres (not commercial), open to everyone, at all times, for training by individuals or groups; these facilities would be simple and inexpensive, supplied with sufficient personnel for maintenance, supervision and advice (paid by the State, municipalities and clubs); (c) to large playing fields, without stands but with suitable changing rooms and showers, built at least on the outskirts of each big city; (d) to simple, but sufficiently large and comfortable installations to facilitate participation in the great outdoor activities: sailing, mountaineering, rambling, canoeing, etc.

The viability of educational effort should be the prime concern of educationists and public bodies. To ensure this viability it is indispensable to use the most effective techniques and pedagogical forms. This necessity again underlines the importance of sound preparation for educationists, and for scientific research. P.E. cannot, any more than other subjects, be left to just anybody. We must use fully, and in the best possible way, the time allowed for P.E. We must never lose sight of the fact that the two essentials for the efficacy of an educative activity are intensity and frequency (adapted to the potential of the subjects). Three one hour sessions a week, at suitable intervals, are much more effective than one three-hour session, bearing in mind the actual time given to physical activity. We must accept the necessity for lasting education, from childhood to old-age. The effects of training are only temporary, and it is not sufficient to have indulged in sport between the ages of 15 and 20 years, for instance, if physical activity is neglected afterwards. We must make a special effort for the weak, those physically handicapped or deficient. In other words, those most in need of help from society.

The return of physical education is not defined in terms of victories won by top specialists, but rather is measured by the improvement – more difficult to judge, certainly – it can bring to physical, intellectual and moral values by its social effectiveness, and, finally, the chance of well-being which it offers each individual.

SECTION 4

Teacher Education and Professional Training

17

B.Ed. – Boon or Bombshell?*

Physical education is still a young subject and like any child it is growing and developing. The increasing use of the 'movement' approach to gymnastics, more dance and dance-drama in men's training, and the widespread introduction of outdoor pursuits into the P.E. programme of schools, are only three of the growing points in our work. These developments are well established alongside the more traditional elements of P.E. What will be the major factors in shaping progress over the next ten years?

One might speculate that the first will be an increasing accent on preparation for leisure activities in the post-school period and a further change in the concept of the physical educationist away from that of a person concerned only with work in schools. Progress will be most easily seen in terms of the wider range of activities through which we will interpret our aims for physical education; but behind these moves lies a better understanding of the needs of the individual and the community.

The difficulties of defining a physical education specialist have been highlighted in correspondence in *The Leaflet* a few years ago [1]. Although one can appreciate the practical problems and the need for greater clarity in certifying the competence of teachers to undertake certain potentially dangerous activities with children, this discussion could have some unfortunate results. Firstly, above technical com-

* A revised version of a paper first published in *Physical education*, vol. 60. pp. 39–43. July, 1968, the official publication of the Physical Education Association of Great Britain and Northern Ireland.

petence should be placed the man's commonsense and sense of responsibility; this may not be easy to examine but it must be taken into account. It will be a sad day, for example, if coaching awards in canoeing became obligatory rather than highly desirable, and one feels there is a move in this direction in a number of activities.

Secondly, there appears to be a danger of defining physical education as a series of activities. Physical education should be discernible as an academic discipline. Henry [6] defines such a discipline as "an organised body of knowledge collectively embraced in a formal course of learning". The student studying this discipline also needs training and experience in a variety of physical activities. To be a *teacher* of physical education one also needs considerable professional training, but teaching should not be the only avenue open to the physical educationist. When we have more men who can speak with authority amongst the town planners, public health authorities, and at the higher levels in industrial management and politics, then we will have outgrown the present situation where matters to which we could contribute greatly are passing us by because of our general lack of status and lack of wider experience.

In bringing physical education in Great Britain to the status of a widespread university study, B.Ed. may be the first step in changing this situation. Certainly there has been considerable discussion between colleges of education and universities and attempts to define the theoretical basis of our subject. Whether P.E. emerges as a widely accepted academic discipline now depends very much on its progress in the B.Ed. degree. Most observers see B.Ed. as a means of progress, but it creates problems as it sets out to solve others.

The award will be a degree in Education with P.E. as a component. In some ways this could narrow the scope of the study but with the increasing interest in leisure and the role of sport in society, study is not likely to be confined to the school situation. On the other hand there are those who see these developments as endangering the roots of our work in schools. This is unnecessarily fearful, as the degree will grow out of and embody the present Certificate in Education course which is heavily orientated to the professional training of teachers of physical education. One may speculate that with the wider and deeper knowledge that the extra year's study should develop, these students will be even better teachers. Above all they should have the ability to stand back from a situation and analyse its requirements, and it is perhaps to these students that we must look for the constructive criticism and new ideas which will keep the subject forward looking and continue its development.

Another aspect of the final year of B.Ed. study which seems to worry some college lecturers, is the apparent lack of emphasis in some courses on personal practical performance. As with the professional training aspect this becomes less of a problem if one looks at the balance of the four year course as a whole. Within all our P.E. training courses, personal practical performance weighs quite heavily in the assessment of the student. Taking the overall view, practical work will still be a major component of the degree and if there are to be practical investigations carried out by the students in the fourth year then many of these will require students to continue with some personal practical work.

The mention of investigations leads one to consider another aspect of B.Ed. studies which, properly handled, could produce progress. J. N. Oliver in 1961 [8] put forward a sound approach to the subject of research in P.E., and perhaps in studying for B.Ed. more students will be able to spend time developing the necessary techniques and using them in limited projects. However, there is a possibility of over-estimating the amount of beneficial research that will come as a direct result of students studying for B.Ed. What is more likely is that they will develop an enquiring mind and that they will be introduced to the many areas in P.E. where research is badly needed. Cratty's [4] outline text on the social dimensions of physical activity, for example, is a pointer to just one area. In addition, the possession of a first degree will presumably lead to more P.E. students going on to higher degrees where further reasearch may be undertaken.

If this research can be related to the wider problems of P.E. so much the better, although this may be prejudging the value of highly specialised investigations which may be easier to design but be of considerably less value at this stage in the development of the subject. The development of what Cratty [3] calls 'basic research'; the improved status of the subject with its acceptance as worthy of degree study by most universities; the increased status of P.E. staff in colleges and eventually in schools; the increased prospects for further study and higher qualifications, including B.Ed. for teachers already in schools; all these points make the introduction of B.Ed. an event of paramount importance.

Some of the dangers of this innovation cannot be overlooked. Already mentioned is the possibility of over-theorising in what is essentially a practical based subject. Taking an overall view again, this is not seen as a major problem. In P.E. in particular we have the safeguard that it is personal enjoyment of physical activity that attracts most physical educationists to their career in the first case.

Another danger is that of distorting the three year certificate course. This should be avoided in as far as it is a bad thing, but great good may come to all students, whether degree candidates or not, from a re-appraisal of the content of our present three year course. If one accepts Evans' statement [5] that, "a P.E. teacher is first and foremost a teacher of children which requires that the child's interests, abilities and aptitudes are key considerations" and adds to this a view that one of the most useful things a student can take from college, is a grounding on which to form his own philosophy of physical education, then perhaps we should ask again if we have our priorities right in the three year courses? Also, we must decide whether there really is, or needs to be, the distinction quoted by Brooke [2], who suggests the existence of two related disciplines in P.E.; one the academic study of human movement, the other this study applied to the educational process.

The view has also been widely expressed that the introduction of B.Ed. will cause a further rift in the profession. Amongst those courses accepted there is already the problem that degrees of different status have been set up. In some institutes the award will be at pass level only, while in others students will be eligible for places in honours classes. This will mean considerable financial advantage throughout their working life for students gaining a good honours classification.

Again, there is the problem of relating B.Ed. to the present pattern of training in physical education. Anthony [1] has already written of these difficulties and suggested a conference to sort out the situation. One could assume, with reservations, that the men's Wing courses should be taking the majority of the main aspirants to the profession and that they have advantages in time allowance for the subject, money available, facilities and staffing. This is arguable, and one accepts Anthony's point that, in fact, there is overlap between the men who do well in Main courses and some Wing course students. However, anomalies will arise where B.Ed. is only seen as suitable for a certain percentage of a college intake. Despite the idea of establishing universal standards, for example within a particular institute, it must be accepted that marks are quite considerably group orientated. The result may be that only a percentage with top marks will go forward from the Wing course, and the same will happen from Main courses elsewhere. Within the Wing course, men of equal calibre to top Main course students may be excluded because they are up against stronger opposition and perhaps higher standards. It could be said that the final examination will sort this situation out but this is not necessarily so unless four years' work is examined on a common syllabus. Also, the non-degree Wing course men will not even be competing at this stage.

Some Wing colleges may attempt to get round this by recruiting only potential B.Ed. candidates so that they become effectively four year colleges and the certificate is only given to failures in the B.Ed. course at the end of the third or fourth year. This would seem an unsatisfactory situation to say the least!

The problem of failure has other practical effects. If, as is true in some institutes, progress to the fourth year is ultimately decided by the performance of the student in the certificate course, even if this is only the last barrier, then he will be at considerable disadvantage if he fails at this stage. In seeking his first appointment he will be competing with other non-degree candidates who may have been applying for posts and attending interviews since February. Not only does he become something of a failure when he is being interviewed but he may be forced to accept any job which is available; not an ideal start to a career.

A final problem, concerned particularly with the mounting of B.Ed. courses in the early stages, is the staffing of the courses in the colleges of education and the acceptance of the existing staffs as competent to lecture in B.Ed. by the universities concerned. Looking at the problem nationally one sees the diversity so typical of British education. Some college staffs have been accepted en bloc; in other places it has been decided that the majority of the work will be undertaken by university lecturers; in other cases individuals have been asked to apply for recognition as university lecturers and some have been accepted and others of similar or greater experience have not. In most cases the acceptance where it has been in question, seems to have been on the grounds of initial qualification and certainly with our more experienced college staffs this is of relatively minor importance. Evidence of further professional study is of value but above all the best indicator is to examine the course mounted by the college and the men who are contributing. In the majority of cases the lecturer will learn more than he can give in contributing to any course. In physical education, given time, we have men who will grow with their roles as lecturers for the B.Ed.

One method of filling the gap whilst we demonstrate our competence to deal with B.Ed. studies as a profession, is the employment of lecturers with specialised qualifications in other disciplines related to P.E. These men can make an outstanding contribution, but as a method of staffing there is a danger that it may be overplayed. This is partly due to the fact that it is relatively easy to validate a qualification in, for example, physiology, whilst most universities have difficulty in assessing a lecturer's qualification in physical education, particularly where much of this may be in terms of lecturing experience in a college of education. There is hope that by their employment in departments of physical education and their full integration into activities of the department, these psychologists, physiologists, etc., will develop something of the philosophy of a physical educationist. The physical educationist has need of their specialised knowledge and it is his ability to draw together information from other quite different disciplines which gives him his unique point of view. As B.Ed. develops there will be an increasing need for men with special interest in areas such as psychology and sociology, but these men must identify themselves as physical educationists, however they arrive at that point. In fact, the amount of overlap is not as great as one might imagine from the casual reading of names of related disciplines. Very often the parts of a related discipline which we would consider central to the study of physical education are given scanty, if any, coverage by a student concentrating on that discipline. Despite the problems outlined, B.Ed. is with us and one can generally feel optimistic about the changes it is bound to bring.

To sum up: Cratty asks [3], "Should prospective physical education teachers be interested in the teaching of sports, dance, or individual activities as ends in themselves, or should they take a more basic approach? And if so, where shall one look for knowledge – to the psychologist, the physiologist or the therapist? Or should principles be derived unique to the field of physical education?" The progress of B.Ed. in the next decade should give some, if not all, of the answers to these questions.

References

1. Anthony, D. W. J., 'A letter', *The leaflet*, January/February, 1968.
2. Brooke, J. D., 'A taxonomy for human movement', *The leaflet*, August/September, 1967.
3. Cratty, B. J., *Movement behavior and motor learning*, 1st edn., Lea and Febiger, U.S.A., 1964.
4. Cratty, B. J., *Social dimensions of physical activity*, Prentice Hall, 1967.
5. Evans, J. C., 'A letter: reply to P. C. McIntosh', *The leaflet*, P.E.A. April, 1968.
6. Henry, F. M., 'Physical education – an academic discipline', *The leaflet*. Reprint from J.O.H.P.E.R. vol. 35, no. 7. January 1965.
7. McIntosh, P. C., 'A letter', *The leaflet*, P.E.A. June, 1967.
8. Oliver, J. N., 'Research in physical education', *Physical education*, vol. 53, no.160, P.E.A. November, 1961.
9. P.E.A., Executive committee statement of policy on professional qualifications, *The leaflet*, December 1967 (Later withdrawn).

18

Problems of Width and Depth in the Initial Training of Physical Education Specialists*

Introduction

To examine the problems of specialisation during the initial training of 'physical education specialists' is to attempt to lay bare a grey area of compromise. Even to try to show how some of the problems of specialisation have been resolved in England is nearly impossible, due to the great diversity of institution, course structure and programme content which exist side by side in our decentralised educational system. However, there is the possibility of examining *some* of the pressures which are exerted on teacher training institutions and how one college, St. Paul's College, Cheltenham, is responding to these demands. The programme is, of course, almost constantly evolving. Very few years pass where exactly the same course is received by a succeeding generation of students.

* A revised version of a paper first presented at the International Congress on Physical Education held at the National Institute of Physical Education and Sport, Madrid, Spain in June, 1977 and first published in the *FIEP Bulletin* vol. 47, no. 4. October-December, 1977.

Teacher Training in England

For those less familiar with the British educational system it is perhaps necessary to point out that in recent years there has been a tremendous upheaval in the teacher education sector of higher education. There have been moves towards merging many formerly monotechnic teacher training institutions, called colleges of education, with polytechnics and universities. Moreover a falling national birthrate and the consequent falling demand for newly trained teachers have also meant there have been college closures and severe cutbacks in the numbers involved in teacher training.

Some colleges of education, formerly linked regionally with traditional universities, have in a number of cases turned to a new national body, called the Council for National Academic Awards, to validate new degree proposals. In the future, most college trained teachers, including physical educationists, will graduate at the end of three or four years, training with an ordinary or honours Bachelor of Education Degree.

Whilst many are pleased with the increasing academic acceptance of physical education which many of these mergers and new course proposals have entailed (a trend which started with a fourth year 'B.Ed.' qualification being added onto 3-year Teaching Certificates seven or eight years ago), there are also many who fear that in the struggle for 'academic respectability' the practical, technical aspects of physical education, and teaching skills, have been devalued in comparison with the associated theoretical aspects of teacher education.

In a period where there have been increasing demands on physical education teachers for greater technical competence and specialisation, colleges have been under great pressure to increase and deepen the academic and theoretical content of their courses. Inevitably something must lose in the battle for the limited time available. Time available has *not* increased with recent changes. University courses have a tradition (at least in England) of requiring *less* student–staff teaching contact time than that used in former times during college of education training of P.E. specialists.

Initial and In-Service Training

Perhaps a more encouraging sign over the past few years has been the apparent acceptance at both professional and governmental levels that a student completing a three or four year period of initial training is not then 'trained' for the remainder of his or her working life. There has been a steady growth of in-service training courses for more advanced qualifications such as Post Graduate Diplomas and Master's Degrees, although there are still very few institutions in Britain where the study of physical education, in its own right, can be carried through to Doctoral level.

By comparison there has been in the past a good choice of one and two weeks' holiday time P.E. courses in Britain but students applying for grant aid for these, like those wishing to follow one year in-service study-leave courses, have been feeling the effects of the drastic economies made in our educational expenditure due to Britain's recent difficult financial state. In theory it is possible for teachers to go on after initial training and specialise through in-service courses, but at present the financial support to do so is severely limited.

Amongst the many specialised in-service courses, there are many organised and/or staffed by the various national governing bodies of sport, that is, the national sports federations, such as the Football Association or the Amateur Swimming Association.

Despite financial problems at present, many P.E. teachers attend such short in-service training courses to widen and deepen their specialised knowledge in particular sports activities – even though they do not necessarily get further promotion or additional pay for holding these qualifications, as happens in some other countries.

Relations Between Teacher Training Institutions and Sports Federations

It is probably fair to say that relations between national governing bodies of sport and teacher training institutions have not always been easy. In a number of activities, especially some of the more potentially hazardous ones like swimming, trampolining and outdoor pursuits such as canoeing, mountaineering and sailing, employing authorities (Local Education Authorities which are more or less autonomous) have demanded that teachers have a national governing body of sport award at an appropriate level before being allowed to engage in the activity with children. Training institutions have naturally resented this tendency, seeing it as casting doubt on the adequacy of their own training and passing the power of ultimate qualification into non-educational hands in the sports federations.

In recent years there has been increasing dialogue between physical educationists and the sports federations, who now tend to see their roles as *complementary* rather than in *conflict*. For example, at St. Paul's College, students are exempt from initial parts of national mountaineering qualifications by successfully following the college course. In a number of sports disciplines, especially where high ranking coaches are working in teacher training institutions, national governing body of sport awards are integrated into, or done alongside, the normal teacher training courses.

Demands for Specialisation on Training Institutions

It is inevitable that sports federations, and all agencies – including governments – interested in sporting success at top international level, look to physical education in schools and the trained teachers working at this level, to supply a stream of technically well-taught youngsters who will move through to become members of successful representative sports teams – some of them whilst they are still schoolchildren. Obviously to push such talented children to the limits of their abilities needs a degree of specialisation not often achieved in an initial training course and hence the course can come under criticism.

Perhaps in Britain we are fortunate in not being subject to direct external pressures but there is no doubt the opinion exists that quite a large part of the role of physical education should be to find, nurture and produce such latent sports talent. Only recently after comparitively mediocre 1976 Olympic performances, one can read of the Olympic Committee once again turning its attention to physical education in schools. When England's football team puts on a particularly forgettable performance, one finds the manager questioning the teaching of soccer at school level. Periodically one reads or hears an executive of one of the sports federations bemoaning how little or how badly his particular sport is taught in schools.

Even without these pressures there is certainly a problem of *programme width* in modern school physical education programmes, which is to a certain extent transferred to the institutions trying to prepare the teachers to staff such programmes.

For example, in a report published in 1970, Newman [4] stated that in Gloucestershire, "There are 65 different physical activities in secondary schools in the County, ranging from major games to skiing, cycling, roller skating, dance and rock climbing. The problem is deciding what should and what should not be included". The report goes on to ask, "Which *must* form part of the basic programme and be taught in time-table time? Which must be attempted out of time-table time but still have a place in the child's physical education career? And which can be offered on a purely recreational basis?'" One might add the question, "And how can the training institutions adequately prepare teachers to teach *all* or at least *some* of these many activities in the relatively short training available?' "

This widening of P.E. programmes in schools has brought many new and interesting activities within the grasp of children, but, although certain traditional 'national games' and sports have retained their place, the new width of programme has brought many problems to the training institutions in the last two decades.

Finally, in this brief look at the various demands on physical education, one can not overlook the increasing importance of the national sport-for-all movement and the increasing integration of schools and their staff into local community physical recreation and sports provision. The specialisms needed to work in these fields, even as a practical teacher/leader, are again different from those of the secondary school teacher or the high level track and field coach.

Differences Between Teaching and Coaching

Where the demand for higher specialisation comes from a particular sport, the pressure is often to try to move the teacher into the role of 'coach'. In some countries 'teachers' and 'coaches' are not differentiated, and/or are trained alongside each other. There are advantages to this latter approach and this is starting in certain centres in Britain. There remain, however, some potential problems if differences between teaching and coaching become too blurred, or it is assumed that there are *no* differences.

A colleague, John Heaton [3], in a guest editorial to the January, 1974 *Bulletin of Physical Education* (by whose kind permission the copyright material is reproduced) set out some of these differences as follows:

The Teacher

"The Teacher is usually involved in dealing with a relatively large number of pupils, often thirty or more at one time. He must group them and teach them with the ideal in mind of giving each child some individual attention. He is heavily loaded with class organisation in order to make best use of time and facilities. He is there to improve performance and he must also stimulate and maintain interest. He is continually introducing new ideas, teaching fundamentals and should be fostering ideas and attitudes.

"In this work he will find himself concerned with the underlying principles of a wide range of activities. He must try to satisfy children with varied backgrounds, aptitudes and abilities, seeking out their interests and encouraging them, as well as introducing his own. Above all, he must know when to 'hold back' and when to 'step in' in order to short-cut the learner's experience in the light of his own. The good teacher realises that pupil satisfaction will come primarily from 'doing' rather than being 'done to'. The standard by which a pupil's progress is measured and judged will be particular to him and only very secondary importance will be given to external criteria, national norms, awards, etc. The most important things about a successful teacher and his teaching are his concern for the individuals, his ability to retain this concern and yet deal with a class, and his broad knowledge of children, built up by a combination of study and experience. Finally, he must be consciously part of the total educational process. Thus the teacher of physical education can not be prepared by a short, narrowly conceived, mainly technical course.

The Coach

"By contrast the coach is usually concerned with smaller numbers of interested, often dedicated, specialist performers. He is searching for the talented performer and, in collecting together a selected group of individuals, or a team interested and able in his chosen sport, his primary aim is to improve performance. Success in terms of winning performances under competitive conditions is the main criterion by which the coach is judged, although this has been obscured somewhat in Britain because of the large amount of 'wide base' recruiting and general 'missionary' work done by particular sports through their national coaching schemes.

"For the coach, novelty comes into his work through the introduction of new techniques and training methods and not from a change to totally new activities. The coach deals with the higher and highest levels of performance within the group with which he is engaged, and as an enthusiast and specialist in a relatively narrow field he can gain a depth of knowledge to enable him to work effectively at these levels. The total education of the performer is not his prime concern. If the learner does not respond or, perhaps, conform to the coach's method, or if he fails to achieve in terms of external standards, he may well be treated as 'a failure' or become another 'drop out' from the coaching programme. Such 'pruning' allows the coach to concentrate on the most talented, on whose success his own will ultimately be judged. In contrast the teacher can only be properly judged on his degree of success with all the children who are directed to him for part of their education. Selection of and concentration on the talented few, as a coach, for the teacher would be totally indefensible."

Of course there are many similarities in the training and roles of the teacher and coach. As Heaton points out, "differences are often of emphasis, of degree, and in attitude to the learner". If on the other hand, one is still unconvinced that differences exist and about the adverse effects which can result from them, then Dr. Paul Governali's [2] article 'The Physical Educator as Coach', which deals with the role of the coach in the United States collegiate system, should spell out clearly the dangers as they can arise in practice.

The 'Specialist' Training Course

So how *do* training institutions cope with the multitude of demands made upon them?

John Evans [1], Director of the Carnegie School of Physical Education, Leeds, addressing a national conference in 1969 said this, "There is therefore a real need for teachers with highly specialised knowledge and expertise particularly in the traditional activities of athletics, games, gymnastics, swimming and outdoor pursuits. It is also true that the production of a teacher with specialist abilities in all these fields – a 'poly-athlete', is an impossible task . . .. I believe there is a very strong case today for what have been called 'specialist' colleges, but to be realistic their purpose should be to train *semi-specialists*. These colleges should be producing teachers who through natural endowment and developed abilities are capable of challenging and developing the abilities of the average child, capable of stretching the gifted child in one or two particular fields. These teachers will be the organisers of physical education departments or group schemes."

Working towards this, various English colleges have solved their problems in quite different ways, as is shown in a survey published in 1976 by Whitehead and Hendry [5]. The amount of time given to physical education in total, the split time between theorethical and practical work – and the time given to particular sporting activities, varies tremendously from college to college. This reflects the variety of outside pressures on the different institutions, their own ideological and traditional thinking, and the internal constraints of course time, facilities, and staff expertise operating differently on each. In a number, course programmes aim to give a basic coverage of the traditional sports activities mentioned by Evans, plus a series of options through which specialisation can be built up in a limited number of activities. (Although this chapter is looking particularly at the various sports disciplines, this kind of option system is also used to give some depth and specialisation on the theoretical side as well.)

To give an example, the programme of practical studies offered for men at St. Paul's College is shown in Figure 18.1.

St. Paul's College, Cheltenham
3 Year Course leading to B.Ed. Ordinary Degree.
(Followed by Honours Year)

PHYSICAL EDUCATION PRACTICAL STUDIES (MEN)

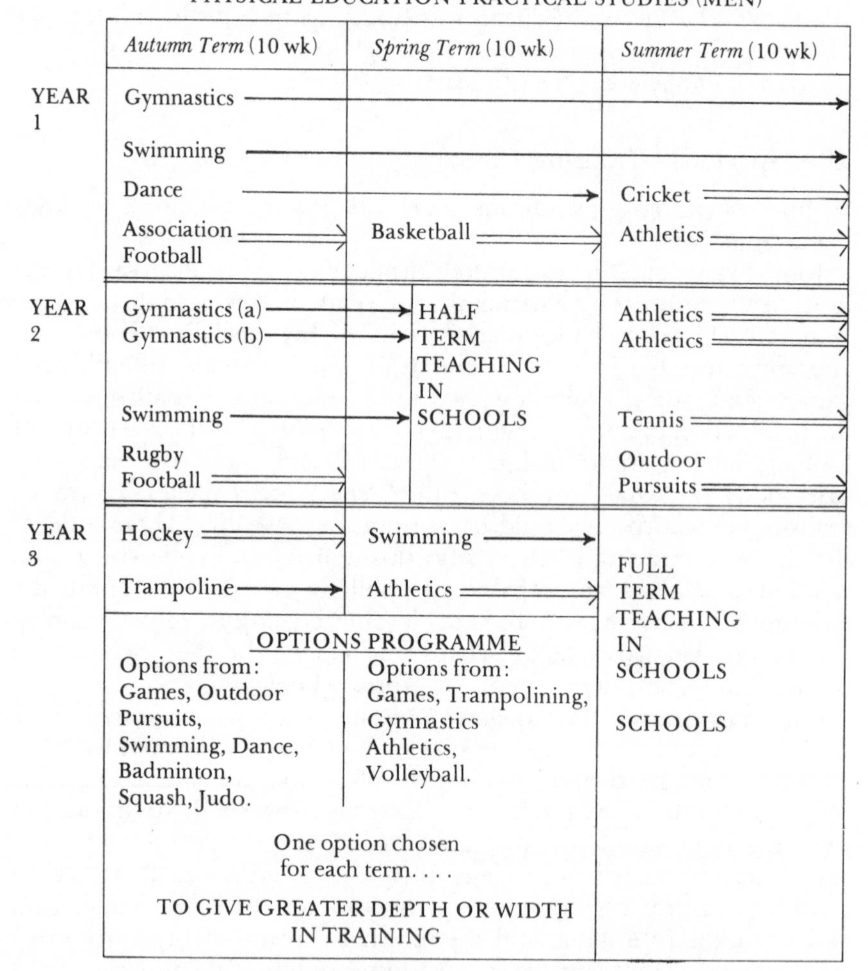

Additional 'Outdoor Pursuits' Courses during the three years:

Year 1 (1 week full-time) Basic Campcraft and Orienteering.

Year 2 (1 week full-time) Canoeing and Lightweight Camping;
and (1 week full-time) Mountain walking and Camping.

Year 3 (1 week full-time) Ski-ing (in France)
and/or (1 week full-time) Sailing and Cruising (inland waters).

Fig. 18.1

These programmes are for students taking the highest level specialist training offered. In addition there are five one-week off-campus courses – devoted to aspects of outdoor education. In Year 1, Basic Campcraft and Orienteering; in Year 2, Canoeing and Lightweight Camping and Mountain Walking and Camping; in Year 3, Ski-ing and/or Sailing. Students *must* do one course in Year 3; they *can* do both (they have to make an additional financial contribution to the Year 3 course).

Concluding Comments

In conclusion, it is worthy of note that despite a somewhat gloomy atmosphere which is always created by looking at problems, there are many reasons to celebrate the successes achieved through current specialist training. Of course we will continue to be critical of results as others are, but one must not overlook points in its favour.

One advantage in England, not always open to all colleagues in other countries, is that *pre-selection* of students is possible and so despite the short periods allowed within initial training courses, it is possible to find students who are already highly specialised and experienced in certain fields before they even come to college. Secondly, despite constraints on the time which can be given to specific activities, ex-students have demonstrated many times that a soundly based training in physical education is, with effort, *transferable* to many specialised and associated fields. The theoretical study of physical activity, organising ability and experience, discipline, motivation, and teaching-learning interaction with others, can all transfer to more specialised situations where specific technical matters may be evolving at such a rapid pace as to need constant revision even by those specifically trained in that activity some years before. In such circumstances the well motivated but more generally trained physical educationist need be at no disadvantage.

Finally, by retaining a broad-based system of what Evans [1] has described as 'semi-specialist training', we may avoid losing a place within the broad stream of general education. There is a very real danger in too much specialisation that physical educationists may disappear from schools to be replaced by teams of part time specific activity sports coaches with little or no place or status, and hence contribution, in the education of future generations. Would that be progress?

References

1. Evans, J. C. 'The physical education teacher – his training and future prospects', *Bulletin of physical education*, vol. 9 no. 3, pp. 29–32, B.A.O.L.P.E. July, 1972.
2. Governali, P. 'The physical educator as coach', first published in *Quest* VII, December, 1966, also in *Bulletin of physical education*, vol. 9 no. 3. B.A.O.L.P.E. July, 1972.
3. Heaton, J. 'Differences between teaching and coaching', *Bulletin of physical education*, vol. 10, no. 1, pp. 6–7. B.A.O.L.P.E. January, 1974.
4. Newman, D. C., 'Timetable, method and content', *Secondary physical education in the seventies*, p. 16. Report on conference for Gloucestershire secondary men teachers.
5. Whitehead, N. and Hendry, L. B., *Teaching physical education in England*, pp. 43–71. Lepus Books, London, 1976.

19

Student-Tutor Interaction During Supervised Teaching Practice*

with Edward Ravenhill

Introduction

In the British system of teacher education, students spend periods of time of varying lengths teaching in schools but still under college guidance and assessment. These teaching practices are spread throughout the three or four year full-time courses of teacher education.

This school experience, especially in its later stages, can be seen as part of a student's training during which it is possible to observe the degree of success achieved by individual students in integrating all other parts of their courses. The school experience phase may also expose the effectiveness of the opportunities provided by colleges to facilitate such integration. As yet, and despite many years of experience, one cannot escape the impression that colleges are still in the relatively early stages of knowing exactly what to look for and how to assess a student's potential as a teacher.

* A revised version of a paper first presented by Edward Ravenhill at the International Congress on Physical Education, Liege, Belgium in April 1977 and first published in the *FIEP Bulletin*, vol. 47, no. 1, pp. 41–46. January-March, 1977.

Such problems are partly inherent in the process of assessment itself, and partly in the practicalities of providing school experience. In such a complicated enterprise there have obviously been shortcomings.

The whole system of teacher education has been under review in recent years: the government established a Committee of Inquiry under the chairmanship of Lord James in November, 1970. Teaching practice came in for heavy criticism; for example Lord James [4] noted, "Many students are vehement in asserting that teaching practice is one of the most valuable and one of the worst conducted parts of their training".

This is a student viewpoint and it introduces another source of confusion about school experience. The student can be seen to be 'the consumer' but the practice is established and controlled jointly by schools and colleges. An examination of the values attached by the different interested parties shows that whilst the students, teachers and college tutors are all operating within the same system, significant differences of outlook and perceptions of what is most important, exist between the different groups.

Of course the school experience phase of teacher education is complex. Each student is developing and there are recognisable differences between practices organised at different stages in the total course. Also many training tasks are pursued within these periods. Activities include 'micro teaching', students observing college staff teaching, group teaching in schools with tutors in constant attendance, and longer periods in schools with only occasional visits by tutors during which times students are exposed, as nearly as possible, to the full teaching situation.

At the organisational level, there are many administrative problems to be faced in establishing a programme of school experiences. The number of schools available within reasonable reach of colleges will also limit the variety which can be offered and their frequency of use.

Due to decreasing demand for teachers now in Britain, with the resultant decrease of students under training, this problem of excessive demand on schools may be reduced in the foreseeable future.

Although one could go on to discuss many aspects of teaching practice, the remainder of this essay concentrates on the preconceptions and reactions of students and, in particular, on student-college tutor interaction.

Student Preconceptions and Reactions

No student enters a school for teaching practice with an 'open mind'. He will have preconceptions as the result of his own experience as a pupil; these experiences may be helpful or otherwise. It is fascinating to observe how often students *do* refer back and imitate both the ways in which they were taught and also some of the material learnt in their own school days; even where this is in opposition to work they have done more recently in college.

The college course should provide a suitable background on which the student can build. Each school will have its own strengths and weaknesses and will make its demands on the student's knowledge, skills and attitudes.

The school will also be visited by the student prior to the start of an extended period of practice and again this leads to certain preconceptions following initial contacts with staff and a superficial look at the school.

Finally, information and second-hand experience are handed on from student to student. In extreme cases this has led to a student asking *not* to be placed at a certain school for teaching practice, even before he has had direct contact with that school! In any consideration of teaching practice it would be difficult to ignore these preconceptions. To think that a college course is the sole preparation for a practice would be unwise indeed.

The Artificiality of School Experience

Students, school teachers and college tutors alike *are* aware of the artificiality of the teaching practice situation, but it is as well to note that a student does not, and can not enjoy the same status as permanent members of school staff.

This is bound to make important differences to his work. For example, in relatively short periods there is little chance to develop either personal relationships with children or on-going units of work, from one year to another. **Content** may be restricted by safety and insurance considerations and even where students are encouraged to be adventurous and to try new ideas and approaches, there is always the dilemma of 'playing safe' and getting a good assessment versus trying something different and failing – with perhaps less credit being obtained in the final assessment. There is also the very real problem of having a more experienced teacher watching the student.

The school physical education staff may need to be present to fulfil safety and law requirements, and the college tutor's presence, however unobtrusive, must affect the student. Singer [9] tells us, "Social presence may be distracting as well as motivating but (it) inevitably produces some effect on behaviour". Whether the presence of other adults stimulates, supports, or adds to the worries of the student will depend largely on that individual, but it is certain that the situation is significantly different; (a) when the student is on his own with a class of children; and (b) especially later when he becomes known and accepted as a full-time member of a school staff. Accepting that there are possible disrupting and damaging elements in teaching practice, the sensitive tutor will work towards minimising them.

Tutor-School Relationships

Clearly the school's physical education specialists can contribute a vast range of valuable experience and they have, certainly during extended practice periods, more day-to-day contacts with the student than do the college staff. There are often no exact guidelines established between colleges and schools, so it is very much left to the visiting tutor to establish and maintain the working relationship with the school staff, including the headteacher. The ideal arrangement is one of 'partnership between school and college' but this has not always been achieved.

Cope [1] tested the view that "teachers are in partnership with college supervisors in the assessment of students" and found that whilst some 67 per cent of college staff agreed with the statement, only 35 per cent of teachers agreed. This suggests that teachers may not always feel that they are adequately consulted by college supervisors.

In a study of teaching practice at St. Paul's College, Cheltenham, done in 1976 (Ravenhill [7]), observation of physical education tutors showed that they *did* spend a considerable time in consultation with the staff of schools, not only on assessment but to ensure that the total experience was as beneficial as possible for the student.

Lesson Evaluation

As well as facilatory and guiding functions, the supervising tutor (in consultation with school reports and other colleagues) has the difficult task of assessing the student.

Perhaps in matters as complex as the teaching-learning interaction it is not really surprising that a general consensus of opinion about evaluative criteria should be so elusive. A great deal of time and energy have been spent on criteria for judging performance and potential. Yet over the years emphases in assessment have changed, just as attitudes to and styles of teaching have also changed. In the final analysis, whatever the complexity of the assessment process, all that can be really conveyed is an impression of a student at a certain stage of training. Some assessments given to new teachers on leaving college may well be misleading. Robertson [8] for example, commented that there is "little correlation between college assessment and the various criteria of success in the profession".

Morrison and McIntyre [6] concluded, "that teaching marks as currently given are of little value as predictors of teaching ability". A modern tendency seems to be to avoid sophisticated systems of grades by simply according 'pass' or 'fail' status to students on completion of school practice. Students seem to favour this. However, where such a simple system of final assessment is adopted, this is often linked with an appeal for more detail in tutors' written observations. The call for standardisation versus the need to avoid undue limitations in giving as full information as possible, is one of the unresolved problems associated with school experience.

At present, in addition to lack of clarity about the *criteria* which are being used for assessment, there are also marked differences in *what* is actually being assessed. For example, some tutors direct their attention almost exclusively to lesson content, technical detail and class control, and evaluate very much on the basis of the children's work and response rather than looking more directly at the student. Others look more to the student's personal development, his growing confidence and teaching style, taking account of the transience and artificiality of the situation.

In practice, assessment of teaching practice will probably continue much as it has done for many years: individual tutors making in the end, as Heath [3] points out, "a subjective assessment or value judgement". Given well qualified and experienced tutors this may yet be the best and most practical system.

Tutor Guidance and Communication With the Student

The study of teaching practice supervision at St. Paul's College included observation of tutors, who were in turn supervising students teaching physical education lessons. In addition, recorded comments on more than 150 different lessons were received in an attempt to pick out some related pattern of guidance which was common to many lessons. The studies revealed the great variety of comments made on teaching skills and all aspects of school life directly affecting students during their school experiences. The most useful outcome was the recognition of the 'professional philosophy' which seemed to permeate all these lesson comments. There did not seem to be a useful classification of the wide range of guidance given. To classify would have risked masking the breadth, depth and richness of the comments included.

In another part of the study, the agreement in observation between two experienced tutors was compared as well as their individual manner in communicating observations to students. For example, one student was observed by two tutors working independently. Strengths and weakness of the lesson were noted and it was interesting to find that there was almost complete agreement between tutors at this stage in the process. However, there were subtle but essential differences noted in the approaches employed in conveying these comments to the student.

Whereas the first tutor adopted a fairly narrow view of the lesson, the second tutor seemed more aware of the overall conditions under which the lesson had been conducted. He was thus able to appreciate and align himself much more closely with the student's point of view. Whereas the first tutor was rather too blunt, the second tutor's criticisms were so presented that each was specific and in sequence with the general development of the lesson. Throughout the discussion, this tutor had the ability to counter-balance comments on the student's weakness with praise and encouragement. In fact the guidance and communication skills of the second tutor were close to the ideal of a 'helpful supervisor' applying 'constructive criticism'.

There would appear to be a vital lesson in this simple piece of observation. The *manner of communication* between tutor and student is at least as important as the information the tutor wishes to communicate. Sensitive tutors have appreciated this fact for years, but it has not yet received wide enough acceptance or detailed research study.

Concluding Comments

In conclusion one can reaffirm the importance of school experience in teacher education. Furthermore, "the relations between colleges of education and the schools are a factor which decisively affects the quality of the training given to intending teachers, the reception of the students in the schools and their first experience as members of the profession" [2].

It may be that the balance of control within the partnership may swing more into the hands of the schools of the future. The National Association of Headteachers [5] has stressed that, "The art of teaching will be learnt by the student in the school itself". The extension of teaching practice to one term out of three in each college year, and the appointment of 'teaching tutors' to the staff of schools, are also major recommendations of this association.

Whether the tutor is school- or college-based, experience should continue to develop the student's self-sufficiency and freedom to act – based on enquiry, analysis, and self evaluation. This development will be facilitated and supported by the tutor's personal and professional abilities.

Suitably tutored, the student should appreciate the help which he is being offered, but also he should realise that whilst experiences during school practices are of value, in no way can such practice establish a 'set of rules for teaching', to be rigidly applied in all other schools.

During school practice, there is great pressure on the student to demonstrate high standards of technical knowledge and teaching skills, but this must not make tutors unaware of the personal adjustment needed to take on the role of student-teacher. During this time the student needs to enable his personal sets of values about education to grow into a 'professional outlook', "mature enough to accept, without denigration, the existence of differing views" [10].

Above all the student will need encouragement to come alive to his own personal qualities, and how best to express them in his teaching. A great contribution towards this should come from exposure to a professional philosophy that can be shared, at a very personal level, between tutor and student.

References

1. Cope, E., *A study of school supervised practice*, p. 109. School of Education, Bristol University.
2. Department of Education and Science, 'Relations between colleges of education and schools', *Teaching practice*, Circular 24/66.
3. Heath, J. E., 'Assessing the student teacher', in Archer, R. G. (ed), *The school and the student teacher,* Professional Association of Teachers, 1975.
4. James of Rusholme, Lord, *Teacher education and training*, p. 20. Report of Committee of Inquiry, H.M.S.O., 1972.
5. *ibid.*, comment issued by the National Association of Headteachers.
6. Morrison, A. and McIntyre, D., *Teachers and teaching*, Harmondsworth, Penguin, 1967.
7. Ravenhill, E., 'Values and problems of a college of education programme in physical education and the assessment of P.E. lessons' – with particular reference to the new C.N.A.A. B.Ed. Degree Course at St. Paul's College, Cheltenham. Unpublished dissertation Dip. Ed., University of Bristol, 1976.
8. Robertson, J., 'Innovations in teaching practice', *The mess in education*, no. 19, p. 9. School of Education, University of Exeter, 1965.

9. Singer, R. N., *Motor learning and human performance*, 2nd ed. p. 54, Macmillan, New York, 1975.
10. Working Party Report, *Themes in education*, no. 35, p. 12. School of Education, University of Exeter, 1973.

20

Training The Future Leaders of Physical Education and Sport in Developing Countries*

Introduction

"The Conference **Recommends** that member states establish coherent national policies for the development of programmes and activities in physical education and sport, both in school and out of school, the objectives of which should be . . . to promote the development of training schools for physical education instructors, trainers and sports technicians of a calibre corresponding to the educational development possibilities and needs of each country" [31]. So reads part of 'Recommendation 2' of the First International Conference of Ministers and Senior Officials Responsible for Physical Education and Sport, held at UNESCO House in Paris, in April, 1976.

Investment in Education

From this it would seem obvious that now, perhaps more than ever before, the climate of world opinion is right to obtain governmental

* A revised edition of a paper first presented at the 1st Scientific Congress of the Arab Union of High Schools and Institutes of Sport, King Abdul Aziz University, Jeddah, Saudi Arabia. March, 1978.

support for developments in physical education and sport. Many countries would seem to have great possibilities for large scale and rapid developments: they can learn from the experiences, successful and otherwise, of the so-called 'developed countries'; they can note the progress and directions taken in other developing countries; and they can also make their own valuable contributions to the world-wide movement in favour of physical education and sport.

Great opportunities exist to profit from other countries' experiences; to tap the pools of knowledge and expertise in the international field; to take short cuts, avoid mistakes and make rapid and relatively economical progress. But the way forward is not clear of pitfalls!

Economic wealth is one of the major factors in all such progress. In the past 'aid to developing countries' had often been thought of primarily in terms of *financial* aid, but in the future as Kirsch [21] has reported (with respect to West German sport science development promotion), "In many cases, the primary assistance expected will not be financial aid, but the 'know-how' to go along with these countries' own financial resources."

Those developing countries enjoying great wealth at present – especially where this wealth is based on natural resources which are not limitless – must take a long term view.

As Vaisey and Debeauvais [33] have pointed out, "education in itself is a fundamental economic fact . . . the highest productivity is in the human capital. Education is investment in mankind".

It is generally accepted that developments in physical education and sport can only be planned and implemented against the total background of national development. Sometimes changes in the whole political, economic or cultural structure must precede or accompany the developments in physical education and sport which more directly concern this congress. Unrelated, *piecemeal* redevelopments can lead to wastage, or only limited progress, and eventually to frustration and dissipation of wealth, human energy and goodwill.

Change is virtually inevitable. "We live in a time when knowledge is exploding. More knowledge, new techniques, and new abilities have to be given to more and more people because of this fact. Knowledge and techniques are changing the world, and education must change with it." [32] So must physical education and sport.

The **rate of change** is often a crucial consideration and developments in parts of social systems often have to keep pace with changes in other parts. Where, for example, high priority and expenditure is given to education and school building, it is obvious that if these schools are to be effectively staffed short term interim measures may be necessary to match the rapid building programme. For these and other reasons the problems of preparing leadership are considered in this essay under three approximate time scales: those of *short term, medium term* and *long term measures.* Of course, all these measures may need to be initiated simultaneously but their results will 'mature' at different stages and at different levels of eventual effectiveness. Generally, short term measures are seen as those which could produce results within a year or so of initiation; medium term measures should 'mature' within 5–10 years, whilst long term measures may take 10–15 years to become established and from then on show the high degree of relative stability and gradual change one associates with any well established system of education and training. However, before examining these measures there are certain questions which need to be asked and answered.

Preliminary Research

Preliminary research is so often overlooked, yet this is quite vital in directing efforts from the very earliest stages. For example, one may ask; Does factual information exist on; (a) the current stage of development of physical education and sport in the country under consideration with particular reference to numbers of leaders, their qualifications and experience? (b) existing facilities and equipment? (c) the administrative and organisational channels controlling physical education and sports? (d) the particular problems, prejudices, etc., affecting developments in the country? (e) the best strategies to employ in developing physical education and sport – whether it be within a particular institution or nationally?

As Schmidt [30] has reported, "Unfortunately much of sport and physical education in developing countries and the concepts and strategies to improve structural deficiencies are virtually unstudied, lacking serious work of research". Until such basic preliminary research has been carried out, the selection of priorities and the search for the most effective strategies cannot be much more than a 'hit or miss' affair.

Occupational Analysis

Another approach to the more detailed planning of course structure, duration and content, is to consider the eventual role of the trained leader. Dr. Fadali [17] briefly mentioned 'a job analysis' in his paper to the I.C.H.P.E.R. Congress in 1969 and this would seem to be a piece of preliminary research of great value in all developing countries. Development cannot be a simple matter of transferring the roles and expectations of a physical educationist, for example, in Britain to very different working situations elsewhere in the world.

Varstala [34] presented an interesting paper on the subject of 'Occupational Analysis' at the 1977 A.I.E.S.E.P.-F.I.E.P. Congress in Madrid, some aspects of which are summarised, in codified form, in Figure 20.1.

An Occupational Analysis of the Work of Physical Educationists

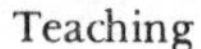

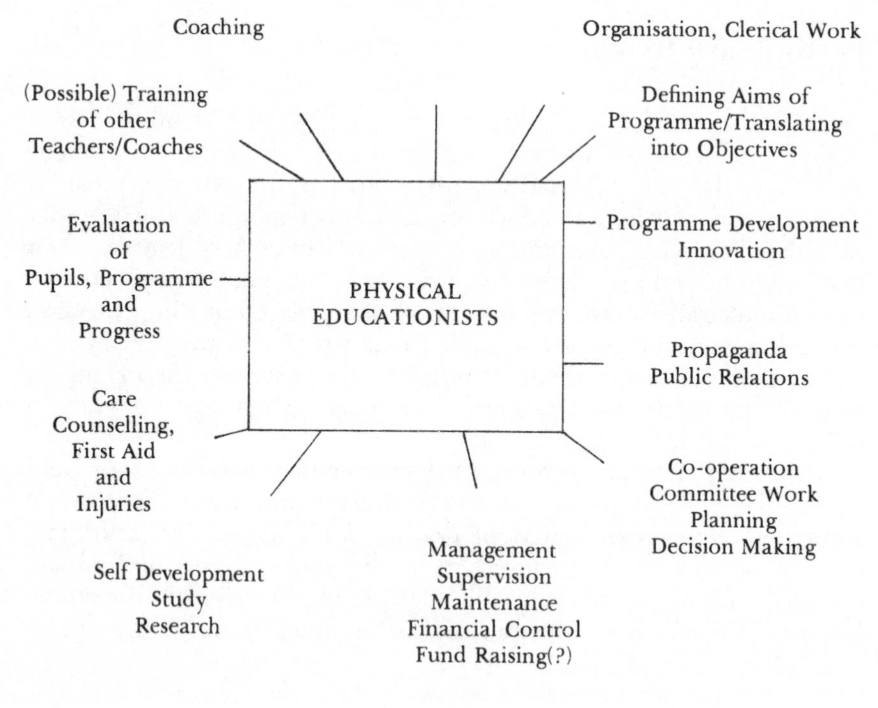

Fig. 20.1

One needs to ask, "What combination of these occupational aspects are particularly needed for any new generation of leaders in physical education and sport?". There may even be other aspects, not mentioned, which are equally, if not more, important in some countries.

The real point is that until such an analysis is made training curricular developments are less likely to lead to actual needs being met.

A fundamental problem concerning the roles of physical education and sport in a developing country is that, on one hand, they are often welcomed as agents of **socialisation** – setting up and maintaining social integration; whilst on the other hand they may also be seen as agents of **change and social development** which put them in conflict with social and cultural norms operating at any particular time. [10,9] Decisions on how far the new leaders should be trained to support and maintain the existing social order and how far they will be expected to act as agents of innovation and change, can lead to marked differences in the selection of students, the courses given, the roles awaiting them, and the status which they will have in their working life.

Such searching questions need to be the subject of considerable preliminary discussion, and research where possible, in any overall, planned development process.

Different Spheres of Leadership

It may well be decided that the various occupational functions already outlined show such diversity as to make it necessary to sub-divide training into different spheres. This means that either one sphere or another will be chosen as a 'career', but after training and experience in one sphere, a conscious decision and perhaps further training may be taken to move into another. Some of these 'spheres' are broadly outlined in Figure 20.2.

Even within spheres there are marked differences, especially where specialisation is needed, as, for example, in the Support Services sphere where completely different training is needed to become a recreation facility manager, a sports medicine expert, or perhaps a research worker in the field of motor learning.

Mosston and Mueller [25] have been quite outspoken against the tendency to make the physical educationist's role too diffuse. They said, "Physical educators are not physicians, psychiatrists, psychologists, sociologists, biologists, physiologists, or para-medical people, even though we should and do utilise their knowledge... Further, physical educators are not athletic coaches, athletic trainers, recreational leaders, or athletic (sports) officials. Athletic (sports) competition and recreation are separate fields from physical education, with their own objectives and principles."

In some countries, there appears to have been a decision to disregard fundamental differences between 'physical education' and

Spheres of Leadership

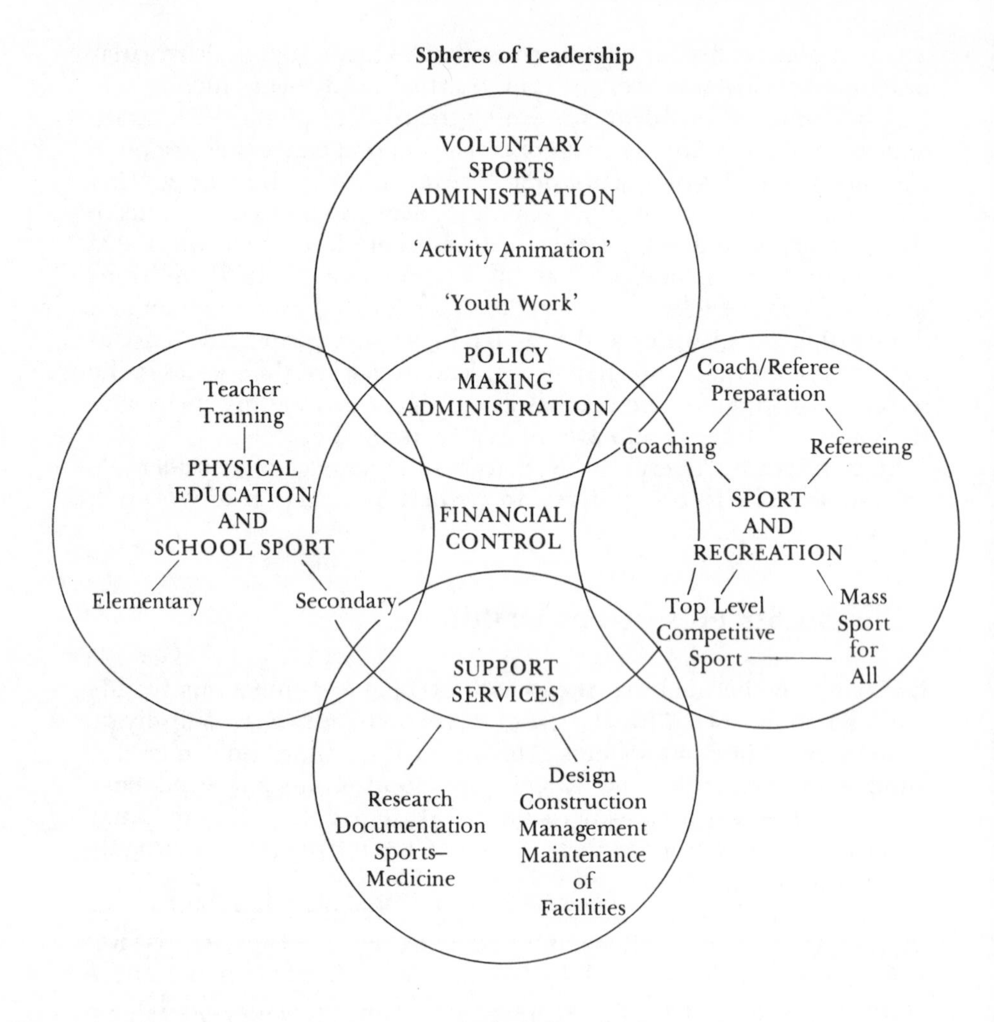

Fig. 20.2

'sport' which has in turn led to problems of role definition, conflicting influences on teachers and coaches, and difficulties in training programme construction. Whilst P. E. teachers and sports coaches may profitably be trained alongside each other, and movement is possible between the spheres, this is not to say that their roles are the same – or that the training should be the same – although it may have some overlapping elements*. This discussion has obvious implications for

*For a closer look at this problem readers may refer to a discussion of the differences between teaching and coaching by Heaton [20].

the model of curriculum building selected to underlie initial training of teachers and coaches and will be returned to in the discussion of setting up institute curricula. However, pressures may be so strong that short term measures must be taken while new institutes are set up.

Short Term Measures

No doubt many countries and institutions represented here are only too aware of the short term measures possible and their advantages and disadvantages.

In many situations the short term problem is one of *quantity;* of filling staff vacancies as quickly as possible, without too much attention to the *quality* of the staff so trained and employed.

'Crisis' Measures

A very short term measure – but one where there may be still some advantage to be found – is in what in Britain was once called 'the monitorial system' – in which older children in a school helped with the teaching of the younger ones.

This can never replace an adequate supply of properly trained teachers, but the idea of older children sharing their skills with others, especially in sporting situations, is not completely untenable. As Burgess [13] has commented, "The system was cheap, and it meant that the absence of teachers did not entirely mean an absence of education. It lasted for a generation because there was nothing better to be done" Except in real crises, there *are* many better solutions, but this spirit of **voluntary aid,** given by the more talented to the less able, may yet be an important attitude to re-establish, especially in face of a growing demand from some of the most talented that their gifts mean that society should give even more to them. Certainly the tradition of **voluntary leadership** is still of major importance in Britain. Many youth and adult sports would not exist without it.

Emergency Training Schemes

Britain, after the Second World War, also introduced an *emergency training scheme* for teachers, including physical educationists. Entrants took a one year 'crash course' before taking up the empty places in the sadly depleted ranks of the teaching profession. One of the problems of this largely successful short term measure was that these emergency trained teachers then remained in the education system for many years, sometimes actually being, or just feeling, at a disadvantage throughout their careers in comparison with other more highly qualified (at least on paper) younger, 2 year, then 3 year, then 4 year trained entrants to the profession. Certainly where such a scheme is introduced – and it has many good points in its favour as a short term measure – it must be remembered that its products may remain in the system for a long time after the 'crisis' period is over and they may even form a 'generation' of leaders unduly influenced by the way in which they themselves were trained. Therefore in all such cases, and *in any rapidly developing system,* it is important to establish on-going in-service training for those already in the system, so that the whole profession updates its qualifications and not simply its newer entrants. In certain cases this may need to be *an obligatory aspect of professional life* if stagnation of those who have passed through initial training is to be avoided. Colleges and institutes have their part to play in such in-service training.

Imported Expertise

In many developing countries there is a great deal of quite legitimate reliance on imported expertise. It has the advantages of open market selection of talents, speed, and the chance that parity of standards and a healthy mix of international expertise will be achieved.

On the other hand its disadvantages are that it can delay the appointment of home trained staff, so robbing them of vital experience, growing responsibility and status. Also many of the 'real experts' in the world, successful in their own systems, may not wish or have the time to work in other countries for long periods – despite financial and other inducements.

A major problem is likely to be the general one of *transfer* in that some overseas experts may be so bound up in their own cultures, concepts and traditions as to be unable or unwilling to rethink and apply their expertise to the new situation in which they find themselves. In some ways the more apparently similar the two situations, the more the imported 'expert' is likely to be lulled into a false sense of security and think that little or no application is needed.

Where real experts *are* willing and able to work in foreign systems it is generally more economical to employ them as teacher and coach trainers rather than in direct contact with a class or even school of children. In this way their expertise should be more widely used, but this does mean some of the already limited number of 'top'jobs are denied to home nationals; a problem which needs careful planning if unnecessary tensions are not to be created.

Short Visits, Seminars and Workshops

Short term visits and seminars are measures of a rather different type which nevertheless may have long term value. Fact finding tours to other countries, the making of personal contacts on the international scene, workshops, congresses and courses on specific topics, can all provide great help in a relatively short amount of time. Of course their effects are limited and it is possible to get wrong impressions. Note, for example, that it is easy to be impressed by buildings, whereas ideas and processes are more difficult to evaluate quickly. 'Transfer' in such situations is the main responsibility of the 'home nationals' who must take from the visits or visitors that which they deem useful. Such meetings need to be a regular and increasing feature of physical education and sport at the international level.

To pinpoint some of the problems of short term, and in this case *shortsighted* aid, here is an actual example from South America.

As part of a national foreign aid programme, a four year trained 'specialist' was sent out to work alongside the local staff of a University Department of Physical Education. Some local members of staff had been trained to the best of that country's national system – which, nevertheless, involved, a much shorter and lower level of preparation – and their sessions were boycotted by students, whose ranks they had not long left, because they claimed the local staff were unqualified, by comparison with the visiting expert. After a student strike the University authorities eventually gave way and the locally trained staff effectively lost their jobs. This seems a complete negation of the benefits of 'foreign aid' but it happened only recently.

Medium Term Measures

Medium term measures are considered here under two headings: firstly **Initial Qualifications,** and secondly **In-Service Training.**

Generally the discussion here is centred on the **curricula of training institutes.** It is too easy to fall into the trap of listing the material needs of training in terms of sports halls, swimming pools, pitches and stadia. Of course these *are* necessary and architects, designers and construction companies will be quick to provide multi-million pound services. Getting what goes on in such facilities *right* is an equally, if not more complex problem, although it is less tangible.

Initial Qualifications

Duration of Training

There are many differences in the amount of time given to the initial training of physical education teachers and sports leaders throughout the world. Bennett, Howell and Simri [6] in a comparative study of the preparation of teachers of physical education, reported, "a physical education specialist must have at least two years of preparation to teach, and he may need up to six years. The usual time is three or four years, which will qualify him or her to receive one of a variety of degrees or titles. He is then ready to go out into the world on his own as a professional physical educator in the schools of his country".

At St. Paul's College in Cheltenham, a Bachelor of Education Degree is awarded at Ordinary Degree level after 3 years, and a fourth 'Honours' year is taken by a percentage of the more able students. This is a so-called 'concurrent training' course, in which the professional aspects of education studies, the teaching of P.E. and in-school teaching practices are all included alongside academic and practical studies in physical education.

Level of Study

In the past ten years physical education has become increasingly accepted in Britain as an area of study *at University level,* especially as part of Bachelor of Education Degrees. "However, the facts do indicate that in the majority of countries physical education is still waging an uphill battle for academic recognition and respectability. It is something of a stepchild in the educational family" [5]. This search for 'academic respectability' has partly been the reason for some of the changes which have been made in the basic theoretical structures used for designing university level courses.

Higher Institute Curricula – Physical Education

The St. Paul's course is based on the following, perhaps traditional, idea of 'Background studies appropriate for the preparation of a physical education teacher's. Figure 20.3.

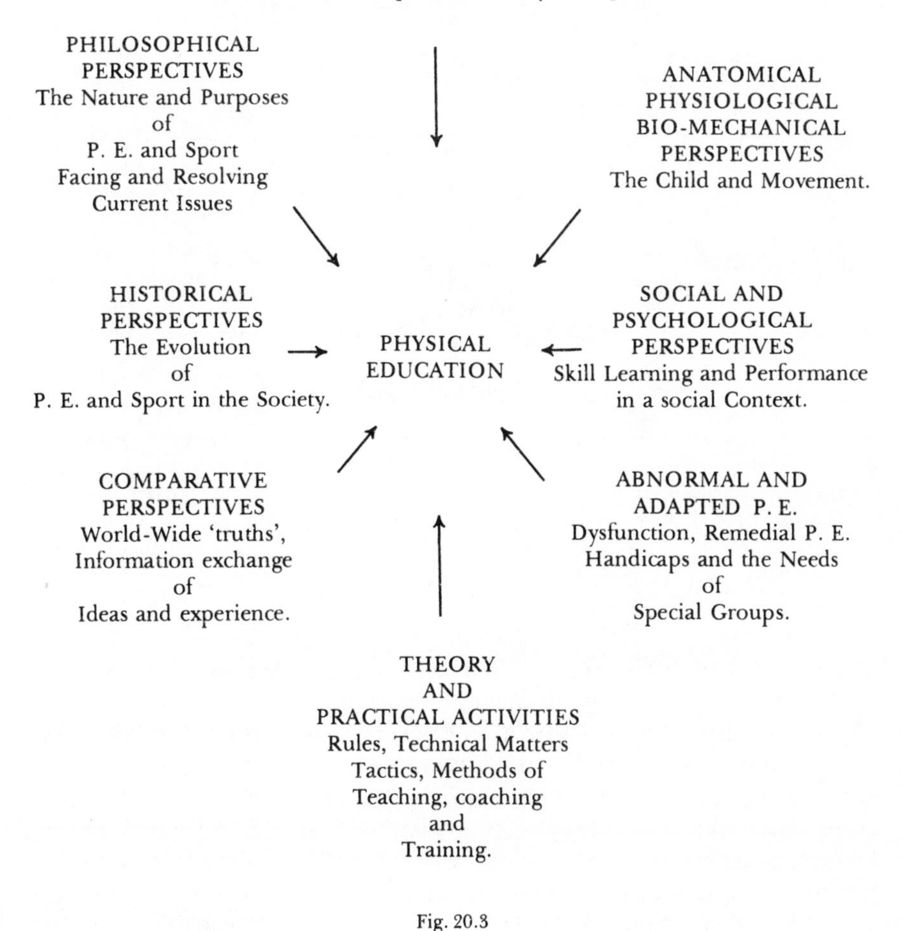

Fig. 20.3

Human Movement Studies

In parts of North America, and in certain British institutions, the study of *human movement* has gained ground as an appropriate 'free standing' academic study, and in such places physical education is seen simply as one work outlet and application of a far more general body of knowledge.*

*For further details see Ref. 12 and Figure 20.4.

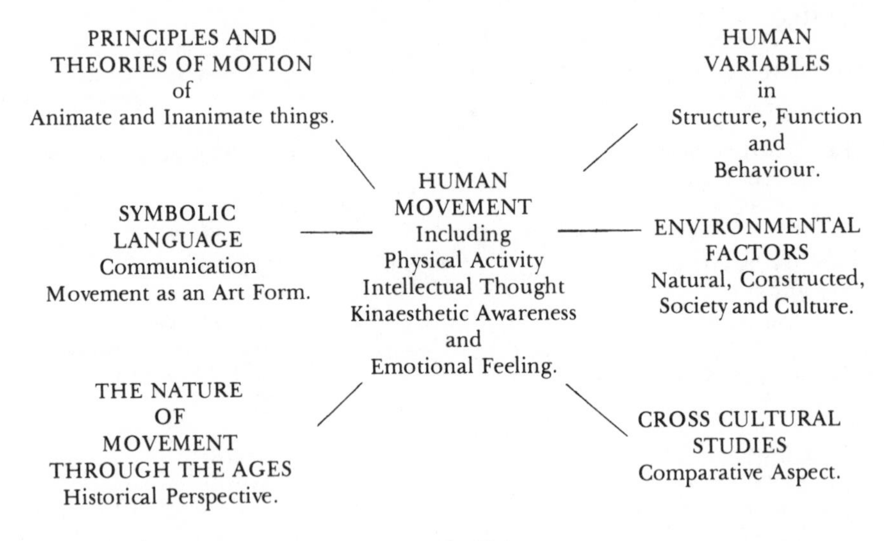

Fig. 20.4

Curl [15] has attempted to justify human movement as a field of study, and he points out important differences between this and the study of physical education: "Physical education theory, like educational theory, serves to determine what ought to be done in educational processes in which motor activity predominates; it consists of an assemblage of different forms of knowledge which are used in the formulation of principles for practice. Human movement as a study, on the other hand, is not tied to any practical functions, it is free to develop its own standards of relevance which are intrinsic to it. . . those who pursue human movement as a field of knowledge will do so for its own sake irrespective of any immediate field of application".

Whilst acknowledging the interest such a field of study can have for physical educationists *it is not,* it seems, *the most applicable and direct field on which to base professional training.*

Sports Science

Many will be aware of the increasing influence of the trend reported by Diem [16] whereby the term 'physical education' is being replaced by 'sports and sports science'. Many countries have been influenced in this way and the change has already been made.

The reasons for, mechanisms, and results of this change are of considerable interest. Bernett [8] for example, tracing the changes says that, "in the middle of the 60's this specific branch of science undergoes a dynamic movement. Following the international trend it extends to the biomechanical, psychological, and sociological aspects. The term of 'physical-education-science' starts to assert itself." It is interesting, to note, however, that the word *sport* had already replaced 'physical education'; in Bernett's original German text, he called it – 'sportwissenschaft'.

Preising [28], discussing the 'scientification' of the education of physical education teachers, gives as one of the background reasons for the change that, "We are living in a time of 'scientific civilisation', this means that all our actions are mediated by reflection, we are no longer living in a direct way, our actions are not only based on traditional ideas, norms and values". One is bound to ask, "Is he right?". Is the only world the scientific world? Are not many of the traditional ideas, norms and values worth preserving? Are there no times when man can still 'live in a direct way' – perhaps this may still be possible at times in physical education and sport? What has happened to the arts, the other traditional branch of knowledge: not as in science, 'ascertained' by observation and experiment, critically tested, systematised and brought under general principles, [24] but arts based on human skill and endeavour, applied perhaps to the creation of beauty and the use of imagination, involving craftmanship and linked with emotion?

Of course, this is not to deny the value and contributions of science to physical education and sport, but simply to warn that in making everything *scientific*, one could be in great danger of missing the essential balance necessary in life – and in physical education and sport.

Perhaps in subsuming all under the title of *sports science* these aspects have not been completely forgotten. Indeed Haag [19] lists the following sports sciences:

Sport medicine	Sport pedagogy
Sport biomechanics	Sport history
Sport psychology	Sport philosophy
Sport sociology	

If the definition of 'science' is to be stretched so widely, then it should not be too long before *sport aesthetics* [23] will also be added to his list, whatever nonsense this may make of the English language. Surely the most effective background study for physical education teachers must be in the relevant parts of both the sciences *and* the arts?

Similarly there are difficulties in simply replacing 'physical education' with the word 'sport'. There is no time to explore fully the debate which could arise; let it suffice to say that for those intending to take up leadership roles in the *educational* sphere; in this view their orientation should be more towards education and to the children in their charge, than to the demands of sport, especially commercial, professional and spectator sport.*

On the other hand those going into sports coaching and administration as careers do need a theoretical background in *sports studies* (this term is preferred to the possible over-emphasis on science entailed in the term *Sports Science*. As Bennett, Howell and Simri [7] have written, "The demands of modern high level competition seem to dictate a different kind of preparation and background for the coaches than can be obtained through the physical education curriculum". (See Figure 20.5.).

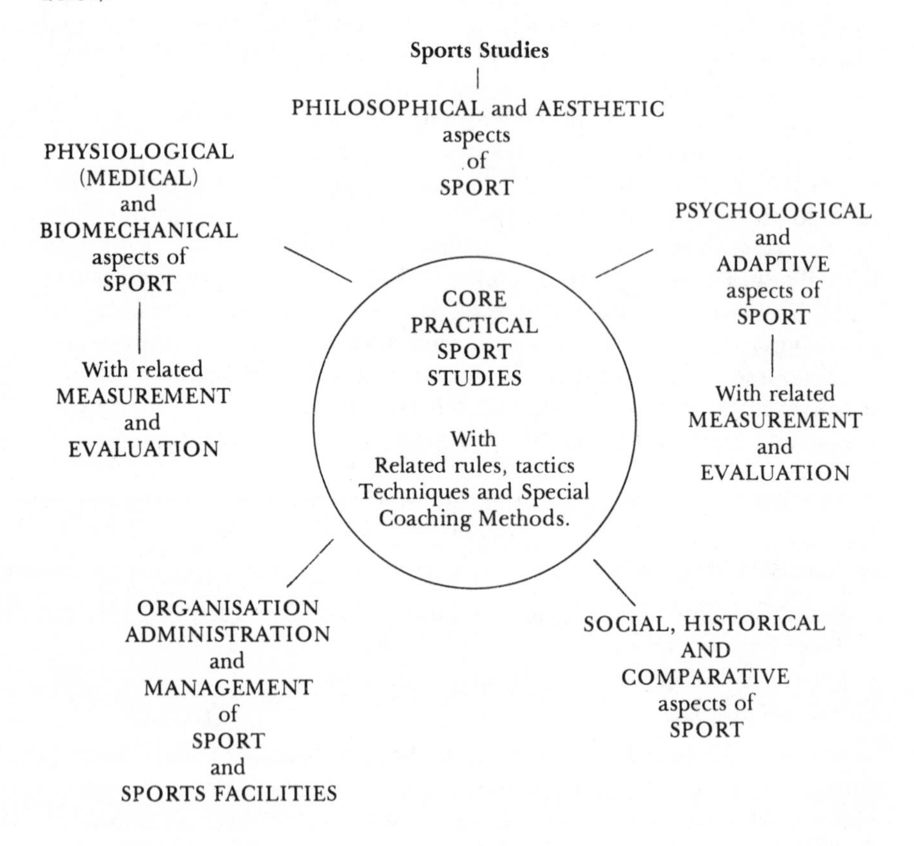

Fig. 20.5

*See essay 12 in this volume for a further discussion of this subject.

In-Service Training

To move rapidly on in this coverage of some of the basic problems concerned with medium term measures, it is necessary to stress again the importance of in-service training as an essential and effective means. **Day release** of relatively quickly trained and inexperienced staff can be supported by a strong *on-the-job advisory service, peripatetic teachers, short courses* as near as possible to places of work, and *co-operative local curriculum development groups* with expert outside leadership; these are all examples of really active on-going in-service work which, in the medium-term scale, will do much to ameliorate particular staffing problems and raise the general level of staff qualification.

Long Term Development

The Ideal Solution

The ideal, aimed at by most developing countries, is to establish a system of nationally based training, integrated into the social system in which it operates, recruiting its students and training staff mainly from its own ranks, and, above all, really serving the needs of the nation – evolving as the national situation changes.

Such a system is not established overnight, however much money is available. The build up of a nucleus of trained staff takes time and sudden realisation of training needs and rapid provision of facilities can, more often than not, lead to an over-dependence on outside help.

In establishing national systems great responsibility lies with the present leaders in physical education and sport who will be setting the pattern for at least the next twenty to thirty years, if not longer.

There are dangers in indiscriminate copying of foreign systems. Obviously, many of tomorrow's leaders are being trained outside Arab countries at the present time and there is nothing wrong in this provided the students are of sufficient calibre and realise the importance of not simply chasing 'paper qualifications' solely to give themselves high positions and increased status when they return to their home country. More than ever before, they should be looking for worthwhile courses which have genuine applications to their own rapidly developing situations. Too many courses which accept foreign students simply give a straightforward (or even 'watered down') version of the same training given to students entering from their own system, with little or no attempt made to meet the different and individual needs of foreign students.

Comparative Studies

One answer to this problem is that offered in the *International and Comparative Course* mounted at St. Paul's College, Cheltenham, which is under the patronage of the four major international federations concerned with physical education and sport. This course attempts to give a small number of qualified and experienced overseas students the chance to follow a programme of studies designed to encourage individual interests and to stimulate comparative study with a specific concern for the applicability of such projects in the student's home country. **Courses like this are needed in many countries.**

Comparative studies are increasingly valuable in the long term and will remain so throughout the future of physical education and sport if knowledge is to be systematically exchanged on a world-wide basis. Exchanges, international meetings and particularly comparative studies of other systems, are essential safeguards against any system becoming too inward-looking and parochial.

Long Term Problems

Perhaps one of the major dangers in any developments involving wholesale use of imported ideas and expertise is in what might be called the 'package deal philosophy'. It is relatively neat and easy to 'buy' a complete package of philosophy, concepts, facilities, materials and 'experts' to match, but the danger is that the package may result in a situation like that, for instance, of the man who buys a unique model of a machine, only to find that the only place he can get spares, maintenance and the rest of after-sales service is from the same manufacturer who then retains a controlling influence. Moreover, the greater the financial outlay in the first place, the less the tendency will be to throw the model away if it doesn't prove capable of doing the work expected of it, in the situation in which it is needed. The hybrid mix, whilst more difficult to construct, is usually a more flexible, robust product.

Many governments see *sports aid* as an aspect of foreign policy, and this is not necessarily dangerous, especially if this aspect is fully recognised. One can not dissociate sport and politics in the modern world [26,29], but it is interesting to reflect, for example, that the professional aid offered by F.I.E.P., A.I.E.S.E.P. and other international organisations is most unlikely to have any political 'strings' attached but to be motivated by genuine professional concern for colleagues working in other situations around the world.

Having said that, one can not deny the great benefits of national schemes of foreign aid and the complete professional integrity of, for example, West German colleagues who have made tremendous systematic contributions to developments all over the world: or the value of the work done by the British Council [11] in sending experts abroad and providing other services. As the *1971–2 Report* stated, "educational and cultural relationships are – or should be – long term in their effects; they can keep the channels of friendship and influence continuously open through all the ups and downs caused by political and economic events. . .".

Long Term Priorities

Finally, in considering the long term, one can not avoid mentioning the all-pervading effects of **channelling of available finance**: whether this be towards training leaders – or training top performers; whether to huge prestigious facilities – or to more widespread basic facilities for schools and the community at large. Concentration of facilities into central training institutes can lead to students, trained in ideal facilities, not wishing (and perhaps not being able) to work in less palatial surroundings in the towns and villages they are being trained to serve. Physical education and sport are essentially to do with **people** and not with buildings and other inanimate things. This realisation is all important.

For F.I.E.P. the policy in the past has been to strongly recommend that priority be given to training teachers and sports leaders, and to constructing widespread facilities for school and community use. All too often governments, and even some of our professional colleagues, have reversed the priorities. As Pooley and Webster [27] record, "Undoubtedly, a most prevalent aim of governments is to produce superior athletes for international competition".

Where good facilities are built for training (and one can cite the National Institute of Physical Education and Sport in Madrid as a superb example) it is important that sufficient staffing and *support sphere* leaders are available as well. Library facilities, documentation and research facilities, technicians, clerical and administrative staff, grounds, buildings and maintenance engineers; **all** need high levels of competence which in turn requires specialised training. Too often one hears of highly qualified teachers, coaches or research workers being unable to work effectively due to lack of support services and equipment; of marvellous facilities not used through lack of overall organisations, supervision and management; and one sees them starting to deteriorate and fall apart through lack of simple maintenance.

In the long term, a whole set of new socio-cultural attitudes to physical education, sport and recreation may be needed and these may take a long time to build up. A recent *Policy for Youth and Sport*, published in Ireland [2], reported, "Figures quoted in a recent publication by the French Olympic Committee showed that 94.5 per cent of the French people considered sport to be useful and even indispensable to the search for a sound physical equilibrium. Yet the same survey disclosed that only 8 per cent of the people actually took part in sport". The statement went on to say, "the problem in Ireland as well as France is to turn a passive assent into active commitment".

Although in many developing countries rural dwellers may not yet be needing the remedial effects of physical education and sport, there is no doubt that they *will* soon be needed for the many city dwellers for whom the motor car is the main means of locomotion and the television set has pride of place in every living room. *The development of new attitudes needs to start as soon as possible.*

Professional Status of Leaders in Physical Education and Sport

Without going into the arguments as to whether teaching is truly a profession [29], it is obviously of importance that recruits into any of the occupational spheres outlined previously must be rewarded with salaries and conditions of service in keeping with their length and level of training and the very real social importance of the services which they provide. Dr. Fadali [18], speaking in Olympia in 1975, noted an urgent need for "well prepared sports and physical education leaders who must be placed on the same level and status as personnel in other professions". Talking of certain African and Arab countries, he reported that in many countries, "key and critical positions are in the hands of untrained administrators or non-specialists". This is a situation which can and must change.

As education, sport and recreation are largely in the hands of central governments, it is perhaps easier for at least the financial rewards to be regulated. The harder struggle may be to convince the government and general public of the social status and respect due to our work.

Some of the ways towards greater *professional* status are under the direct control of the institutes and colleges of physical education and sport. Kob [22] has written, "the development of professional consciousness is . . . strongly affected by the problem of teachers' social position related, for instance, to *motives of professional choice, problems of training, problems of professional policy, and social prestige*".

Other support will come through the formation of professional associations at local and national levels. As Bell and Grant [4] have pointed out, "Teachers' organisations are not merely concerned with salaries. They are concerned also with the more intangible 'badges' of true professional status. Those badges, which have been widely regarded as characteristic of true high professionalism, include: widespread university graduation (with the high social status that it brings); control of entry, training and discipline by the profession itself; professional autonomy in decision making at work; and more recently, the building up of a respectable body of academic work and research related to the profession's needs".

Before leaving these few words on status, one can return to the U.N.E.S.C.O. *Final Report* [31] mentioned at the opening of this paper. What a pity that the **Recommendation** used the term *physical education instructors, trainers* and *sports technicians*. Higher status will not be achieved if this is the level of qualification governments deem appropriate to meet "the educational development possibilities and needs of each country." Later, though, the same report recommends that, "teachers of physical education and sport should have the same professional status, remuneration and prestige as other teachers who have similar responsibilities and equivalent qualifications . . ." and charges governments that, "Where necessary, action should be taken to assure that these conditions are accomplished."

Sources of Aid for Developing Countries

International Federations

The various resources of the major federations: F.I.E.P. (Fédération Internationale d'Éducation Physique); A.I.E.S.E.P. (Association International des Institutes et Écoles Supérieurs d'Éducation Physique); I.C.H.P.E.R. (International Council on Health, Physical Education and Recreation); I.C.S.P.E. (International Council of Sport and Physical Education, are well known and their services are outlined in various documents to be presented to this Congress. These services are available to the developing countries and it is hoped that in a steadily increasing manner, these countries will both *draw from* and *contribute to* the pool of expertise which is available at international levels. The major federations are also co-operating with each other to a greater degree than ever before to meet the growing needs of physical education and sport all over the world.

National Schemes of Foreign Aid

National opportunities for foreign aid are well known in many instances. Here, three quite recent developments are cited: The new A.C.I.S. [1] (American Council on International Sports) brochure states: "A.C.I.S. provides American expertise in assisting foreign governments in the planning of sports facilities and establishing physical education programs to aid the individual development of all citizens. The generation of goodwill toward our nation is one of our government's principal foreign policy objectives; and in a world of competing ideas and ideals, A.C.I.S. seeks to further the U.S. viewpoint".

In Britain another recent initiative has led to the setting up of the Centre for International Sports Studies, with its new journal, *Sports Exchange World* [14]. The first issue proclaimed that, "C.I.S.S. can promote links, exchanges, conferences, seminars, basic studies, research, training, coaching, development, study visits, advice, information, contacts, news service, intensive courses, topping-up courses, language of sport, equipment courses, videosport, etc. Through its International Sport Development Service it is accessible to coaches, teachers, management, volunteers, advisers and organisers worldwide,"

As well as operating at international level and setting up **international groups of consultants,** F.I.E.P. National Committees may act in a consultative capacity and through F.I.E.P. delegates at the national level, **advisory groups** may be made available to work in other countries. It is generally possible to arrange – either completely or in conjunction with other agencies such as the various national physical education associations and sports federations – visits courses and contacts in many countries.

Lastly, a vast storehouse of varied, individual expertise is always available on a world-wide basis and this can be contacted either through international or national networks of contacts. Experts might well even be provided with some form of financial aid from their own governmental resources.

Contacts and Exchanges Between Institutes of Physical Education and Sport

Another form of aid to developing countries, as well as something of great benefit to all institutions, is the setting up of special links between colleges and institutes in different countries. For example, at St. Paul's there are already regular exchanges of students and staff with colleges in West Germany and Norway, and students from many different countries attend both initial and advanced courses. This increasing international element in the student population is in part due to the reduced demands for teachers in the British systems, and partly due to a growing awareness of how interested many countries are in the sport and physical education in British schools and in society at large. There remains great potential for the development of still more contacts with institutes in Britain, *and between many institutes and colleges around the world.*

References

1. A.C.I.S., *American council on international sports brochure*, 817, 23rd Street N.W., Washington D.C., 20052, U.S.A.
2. An Roinn Oideachais, *A policy for youth and sport*, p. 25. Stationery Office, Dublin, Ireland, 1977.
3. Andrews, J. C., *Essays in physical education and sport.* Stanley Thornes, Cheltenham, 1979.
4. Bell, R. and Grant, N., *Patterns of education in the British Isles*, p. 170. Allen and Unwin, London, 1977.
5. Bennett, B., Howell, M. L. and Simri, U., *Comparative physical education and sport*, p. 91. Lea & Febiger, Philadelphia, 1975.
6. Bennett, B., Howell, M. L. and Simri, U., *Ibid*, p. 93.
7. Bennett, B., Howell, M. L. and Simri, U., *Ibid*, p. 257.
8. Bernett, H., 'The development of the curricula of the universities in the F.A.G.', in Cagigal, J. M. and Pieron, M. (eds.) *Teaching the teacher in physical education*, p. 85. A.I.E.S.E.P. Year Book vol. 1, Madrid, 1976.
9. Bloss, H., 'Sport development assistance under educational and political aspect' (part 1), *International journal of physical education*, pp. 21–23, vol. XIV issue 3. Fall, 1977.
10. Bloss, H., *Ibid*, (part 2), p. 11, vol. XIV issue 4. Winter, 1977.
11. British Council, *Annual report 1971–2*, p. 13. H.M.S.O. England, 1972.
12. Brooke, J. D. and Whiting, H. T. A. (eds.), *Human movement – a field of study.* Henry Kimpton, London, 1973.
13. Burgess, T., 'Teacher training within higher education', in Bell, R., Fowler, G. and Little, K. (eds.), *Education in Great Britain and Ireland*, p. 267. Routledge/Open University Press, 1973.
14. C.I.S.S., 'Aims and objects', *Sports exchange world*, no. 1, p. 4. Winter 1977.
15. Curl, G. F., 'An attempt to justify human movement as a field of study', in Brooke, J. D. and Whiting, H. T. A. (eds.), *Human movement – a field of study*, p. 13. Henry Kimpton, London, 1973.
16. Diem, L., 'The teaching staff in physical education colleges'. Paper presented at the International congress of A.I.E.S.E.P.-F.I.E.P. in Madrid, June, 1977, p. 1.
17. Fadali, M. M., 'Issues and problems of H.P.E. and R. in recreation and professional preparation', pp. 56–60. *I.C.H.P.E.R.* 12, Congress Report, July, 1969.
18. Fadali, M. M., 'Physical education and olympism through the thoughts and

achievements of African and Arab countries', pp. 62–63. *FIEP Bulletin*, vol. 45, no. 4, 1975.

19. Haag, H., 'Principles of paedogogical aspects', in Sie, Swanpo and Sie, Mary W. (eds.), *Concepts of sports sciences*, p. 25. Indonesian Sports Science Centre, Jakarta, 1975.
20. Heaton, J., in Andrews, J. C. 'Problems of width and depth in initial training of physical education specialists'. *FIEP Bulletin,* vol. 47, no. 4, 1977.
21. Kirsch, A., 'Sport science and development assistance', *International journal of physical education*, vol. XIV, issue 3. pp. 8–13, p. 12. Fall, 1977.
22. Kob, J., 'Definition of the teacher's role', in Halsey, A. H., Floud, J. and Anderson, C. A. (eds.), *Education, economy and society*, p. 575. Collier-Macmillan, London, 1961.
23. Lowe, B., *The beauty of sport*, p. 22. Prentice Hall, 1977.
24. Macdonald, A. M., *Chambers twentieth century dictionary*, -. 1210. Chambers, 1972.
25. Mosston M. and Mueller, R., 'Mission, omission and submission in physical education', in McGlynn, G. H. (ed.), *Issues in physical education and sports*, p. 98. National Press Books, U.S.A., 1974.
26. Petrie, B. M., 'Sport and politics' in Ball, D. W. and Loy, J. W. (eds.) *Sport and social order*, pp. 185–237. Addison-Wesley, U.S.A., i975.
27. Pooley, J. C. and Webster, A. V., 'Sport and politics: power play', in Yiannakis, A., McIntyre, T. D., Melnick, M. J., and Hart D. P., *Sport sociology: contemporary themes*, pp. 35–42, p. 37. Kendall/Hunt, Iowa, 1976.
28. Preising, W., 'The 'scientification' of the education of physical education teachers', *FIEP Bulletin*, vol. 47, no. 3, p. 15. 1977.
29. Singer, R. N. (ed.), *Physical education: foundations*, p. 19. Holt, Rinehart and Winston, New York, 1976.
30. Schmidt, B., 'Towards the promotion of sport in developing countries', *International journal of physical education*, I.C.H.P.E.R. vol. XIV, no. 4. p. 20. Winter, 1977.
31. U.N.E.S.C.O. *Final report* of First international conference of ministers and senior officials responsible for physical education and sport, pp. 14–15. Paris, April, 1976.
32. Vaisey, J. and Debeauvais, M., 'Economic aspects of educational development', in Halsey, A. H., Floud, J. and Anderson, C. A. (eds.), *Education economy and society,* p. 37. Collier-Macmillan, London, 1961.
33. Vaisey, J. and Debeauvais, M., *Ibid*, p. 40.
34. Varstala, V., 'Occupational analysis of the field of physical education with special reference to the P.E. teaching'. Paper presented at the international P.E. and sport congress, Madrid, June 1977.

SECTION 5

Outdoor Pursuits and Outdoor Education

21

Outdoor Pursuits in Schools*

The Scope of Outdoor Pursuits

One of the problems which has beset numerous writers on outdoor pursuits, has been how to define the scope of this aspect of physical education. A glance at the bibliography at the end of this essay will reveal three terms; 'outdoor pursuits', 'outdoor activities' and 'outdoor education'. The first two seem largely a matter of personal preference and are used interchangeably; 'outdoor education', on the other hand, is a newer concept, and implies perhaps a wider range of activity and an integration of physical activities with other aspects of education.

The Department of Education and Science publication, *Safety in Outdoor Pursuits* [6], lays down recommendations concerning Safety on Land: on mountains, caving, ski-ing and riding; Safety Afloat: dealing with swimming, sailing, canoeing, expeditions, off-shore cruising and underwater swimming; and Safety in the Air: covering powered flight and gliding. To these many physical educationists would add camping, caving, cycling, rowing, skating (though not normally done 'outdoors' in Britain) orienteering, water ski-ing and youth hostelling (in conjunction with one or more of these other activities). At the same time not many would consider 'powered flight' to be part of physical educa-

* A re-edited version of a paper first prepared for the Outdoor Pursuits Course, at St. Paul's College, Cheltenham, in September, 1976.

tion, and activities such as archery, fishing, and rowing and skating find a place in education, and support from physical educationists without being generally included under the title of 'outdoor pursuits'. The precise range of activities dealt with in college courses in outdoor pursuits and taught in the many Outdoor Pursuits Centres, varies partly according to differing philosophies, and partly according to differing environments, facilities, staff interests and expertise.

In 1972 John Passmore [9] made a survey of developments in outdoor education and environmental studies in Canada and he too found difficulties in defining his chosen field of enquiry. He quotes a number of definitions which he encountered, including, "Outdoor education is learning in and for the out-doors"; a statement which found quite wide support.

Many subject areas are spreading their work from the classroom into the outdoors, and physical activities such as hiking, canoeing, camping, caving, etc. are being pursued within an integrated approach to education – alongside such subjects as history, geography, or field studies, environmental studies, etc. This 'blurring of the edges' of the recognised subject areas and new thinking and timetabling which has set up 'activity afternoons' or 'project days' on a regular basis, has been linked with the development of outdoor pursuits centres and the rather different ethos surrounding such centres. Those which came first in Britain tended to take their early example from the Outward Bound Schools but today the local education authorities own and staff many centres which are more concerned with the teaching of the various outdoor activities in their own right and as part of a wider 'outdoor education'. For many children a period of at least one week's residence in such a centre is an accepted part of their curriculum. [2]

The Value of Outdoor Pursuits

Whilst accepting outdoor pursuits can also play their part in outdoor education the fact remains that activities such as hill walking, rock climbing, ski-ing and sailing are of great value in themselves. Some of them figure amongst the most popular forms of general community recreation, and their popularity appears to be increasing in relation to other forms of physical recreation. They have the advantage of permitting a long period of active participation throughout life.

Participation in these outdoor pursuits can bring great benefits, though such benefits are not an automatic result of participation. Terry Parker, for example, author of *An Approach to Outdoor Activities* [8], has written "One of the immense values of the activities is that all experiences mean one thing to one person and, for example, the technically incompetent can gain the most satisfying experiences especially those perhaps of tranquillity, beauty and companionship".

Chris Bonington, author and well known mountaineer, addressed a national physical education conference on the topic of 'Adventure, Risk and Education' [5] and tried to give some insight into the benefits of outdoor pursuits as he saw them. "Mountaineers can enjoy the actual splendour and beauty of the environment in which the activity is carried out. I think that this stimulation by the natural environment is experienced in practically all outdoor pursuits . . .. In fact the very tension of the situations that you get into heightens your perception to a tremendous degree."

In brief, outdoor pursuits are a particularly rich group of activities for the consideration of the physical educationist. They involve the use of knowledge and merge with other subjects through life's possibilities; they make differing demands in terms of skills and physical capabilities; they provide opportunities for social education; and finally, for some at least, they may be the source of aesthetic experience.

Safety

"The element of risk is a fundamental theme running through all outdoor activities. In fact it is their mainspring. It is present even in the most controlled situations" [7]. This statement by E. Langmuir is quoted from the introduction of the official handbook of the Mountain Leadership Training Boards of Great Britain and it puts its finger straight onto the major problem of the place of outdoor pursuits in the curriculum, especially with younger children who (presumably) are less able to be self-responsible. Risk is an integral part of many activities, if it is removed completely (even if this is possible to do) then the activity has quite probably lost much of its point.

A first step for the teacher to realise is that what is important is not so much the *actual* risk involved, but how far the child *feels* at risk. To give a simple example, a child on a first climb can be tightly secured by a rope from above and yet be very diffident about committing himself to the next difficult move. Actual risk here is minimal; the feeling of being at risk – tremendous. With this in mind the teacher can do much to make activities safe without removing the sense of exploration of the unknown (to the child) and adventure. Feeling 'at risk' is a form of stress on the child and it is part of the teacher's task to assess the different reactions to stress of different children. In what is apparently the same situation, one child will be under little stress and his reactions will be casual and disinterested; others will seize the challenge in the situation and succeed, so getting satisfaction; others will be overstressed and may try to avoid the situation or get to a stage where they can go no further. It is for the teacher to watch for these differences; challenging, praising, encouraging and reassuring as necessary.

Each activity has its own safety rules and in Britain a Department of Education and Science booklet [6] summarises many of these. Additional guide lines are generally available from the national governing body of the sport, the Royal Society for the Prevention of Accidents, and local education authorities. There is considerable concern at present following some very highly publicised accidents involving children, and articles appear from time to time in the national press and in professional journals. In 1973, for example, the British Association of Caving Instructors, on behalf of the National Caving Association, published a leaflet entitled *The Organisation of Novice Caving Trips,* which is packed with useful advice [4]. All teachers intending to organise aspects of outdoor pursuits should make sure they have studied such relevant material. It may come as something of a surprise to teachers 'escaping' from the classroom into the 'freedom' of the outdoors to find that they are still expected to study the 'rules' of the different activities; but rules there are, and the penalties for lack of study or non-observance can be very severe!

There is a stage, perhaps even with quite young children (depending on the particular activity, just how young) when they must be allowed, for example, to be in a boat by themselves, to paddle their own canoe, to move in a group through open country without a teacher in the party, or to set off for the first free ski-ing descent. This is a worrying time for the teacher but it is also an important stage in the teaching of outdoor pursuits where self-reliance and possibly teamwork amongst children, are important aspects of learning performance.

At times such as these the teacher retains his responsibility for the children but has to do this at different distances according to the activity. In teaching climbing, for example, he may be able to stand close by and fight the urge to give too much advice. He may be in another canoe on the water or watching the young helmsman from the safety boat. Perhaps the most difficult situation is encountered where children are out of contact with the teacher on some form of expedition, not necessarily in difficult country nor on foot. The essay 'Long Range Responsibility' [1] following, was written to provide some pointers to the safe organisation of unaccompanied summertime open country expeditions.

This is only a very brief coverage of safety considerations involved but these points, and more particularly the clues they provide to the necessary thought and organisation, should help a teacher to become aware of the background knowledge of organisation which is necessary to keep actual risks to an acceptable minimum.

Teaching Outdoor Pursuits

Because of the varying nature of the range of activities termed 'outdoor pursuits' it is not possible in a short essay to attempt to give recommended content of sailing, canoeing, camping, etc., instruction. However, a few general points can be made for the newcomer to this aspect of physical education.

1. Don't over-teach. Exploration is not always a matter of going to distant places; one can explore locally, and even within oneself, when one is placed in challenging situations.
2. Remember the limitations of the human voice out-of-doors. Too many 'words of wisdom' are lost against the background noise of a stream or tossed against the breeze when the class is up-wind in a gale.
3. Pupils straining to see against the sun, so warm and comfortable on the teacher's back, may find difficulty in picking out even the broad outline of an excellent demonstration.
4. Because outdoor pursuits are performed in natural surroundings, changes in environment will often cause quite drastic changes in performance; the sudden extra strong gust of wind, the snow icing as the shadow falls in the evening, the 'safe hold' that comes off in the climber's hand, the sunny day which finishes with a thunderstorm and downpour.

Teaching Competence

There have been increasing pressures brought to bear to restrict the numbers of teachers permitted to take children for outdoor pursuits. In Britain the final decision as to whether a teacher is qualified or not rests with the local education authority, although individuals are more likely to deal, in the first case anyway, with the head teacher of the schools. In April, 1973, the British Association of Organisers and Lecturers in Physical Education published a Policy Statement [3] on *Competence to Lead Expeditions of a Potentially Hazardous Nature*. Although particularly concerned with expeditions in this publication, the questions which the B.A.O.L.P.E. recommended should be asked, give a clear picture of the range of considerations upon which a decision about competence will (or should) be made. They examine the teacher's:

1. Reasons for wanting to do the activity?
2. Teaching qualification?
3. Sense of responsibility?
4. Organising ability?
5. Personal level of skill in the activity and present state of fitness?
6. Experience – with children of the age involved? – in the activity? – in the situation and area proposed?
7. Relevant certificates or coaching awards of national governing bodies concerned with the activities, such as The British Canoe Union, National Ski Federation of Great Britain, Mountain Leadership Training Board, etc.?

As should be apparent from this essay, the introduction of outdoor pursuits into schools is not simply a question of being convinced of their values and then deciding to include them into the curriculum.

References

1. Andrews, J. C., 'Long range responsibility' (also in this volume). First published in *Bulletin of physical education* B.A.O.L.P.E. vol. 9, no. 1, pp. 53–60, January, 1972.
2. B.A.A.L.P.E., 'Outdoor pursuits centres in Great Britain', Outdoor Pursuits Working Party Report. *Bulletin of physical education,* B.A.O.L.P.E. (Now B.A.A.L.P.E.) vol. 8, no. 1, pp. 29–45, January, 1970.
3. B.A.A.L.P.E., 'Competence to lead expeditions of a potentially hazardous nature', Policy statement, *Bulletin of physical education,* B.A.O.L.P.E. vol. 9, no. 6, p. 13, April, 1973.
4. B.A.C.I., *The organisation of novice caving trips,* British Association of Caving Instructors, on behalf of National Caving Association, 1973.
5. Bonington, C., 'Adventure, risk and education' *Bulletin of physical education,* B.A.O.L.P.E. vol. 8, no. 4, pp. 71–79. October 1970.
6. Department of education and science, *Safety in outdoor pursuits,* D.E.S. Safety Series no. 1. H.M.S.O., 1st edition 1972.
7. Langmuir, E., *Mountain leadership.* Official Handbook of the Mountain Leadership Training Boards of Great Britain. Published by S.C.P.R., 1969.
8. Parker, T. (ed.) *An approach to outdoor activities.* Pelham Books, 1970.
9. Passmore, J., *Outdoor education in Canada – 1972.* Canadian Education Association, 1972.

22

Junior Exploration*

"Young people . . . can show intense curiosity about differing ways of life and an admirable persistence in ferreting out information."

This simple statement from the Albemarle Report [1] points the way to many worthwhile activities. Despite the steady increase in exploration each year, there is ample room and great opportunity for the formation of many more 'Exploration' and 'Expedition' groups for young people. There is no fixed pattern to which all such groups must conform. Indeed the flexibility of their aims and methods is a great attraction. Each expedition will have its own difficulties and demand new methods, but there are certain basics underlying *all* projects.

Adventure

A spirit of adventure must surround each activity. If the project is so attractive that too many people want to participate, the right atmosphere is engendered from the start. Each member feels excited at the prospect and proud to be part of the team. An attitude of casual participation will break down at the first task.

*A revised version of a paper first published in *Youth service*, vol. 2, no. 8, 1 June 1962.

Group Effort

For success, each expedition must contain individuals working together as a team. Each member accepts part or complete responsibility for some aspect of the work, and, wherever possible, this corresponds to his natural ability or special knowledge: for example the person who is keen on photography will take charge of that department. In this way self-confidence is increased and each member can claim a real place in the team. He can appreciate at once his own contribution; equally, however, individual weaknesses are forgotten. Everybody is encouraged to raise general standards in all the expedition's activities and must be ready to turn a hand to any job. The quality of the group's personal relationships colours every other aspect of the expedition.

Increased Knowledge and Experience

Each venture should offer opportunities to increase the participant's knowledge and offer a new and stimulating experience. Travelling is an excellent way of achieving this, provided an attempt is made to understand the country through which the expedition passes. Because of the great value in visiting new and contrasting regions, local expeditions, although they can be highly successful, best may be thought of as training runs for journeys to more distant and unknown areas. In the months before departure a full training scheme can be carried out, its exact content varying with the project.

As well as physical preparation (fitness is too often overlooked), subjects which may be covered include campcraft, map reading and navigation, hill walking, surveying, recording results, photography and so on. This work is tied closely to the needs of the project. For instance, first aid or a course on emergencies in the mountains would be preparation for a hill walking expedition. In this way the whole training programme will have the appeal of knowledge suitable for direct application in the near future, and necessary but unexciting aspects can be covered in the enthusiasm raised by the whole expedition.

Adult Participation

This is perhaps the most controversial of the underlying ideas. The presence of suitable adults in a junior exploration team has many advantages. It brings the young people in contact with adults having a real enthusiasm for the activities involved. Where such men and women are available, more ambitious and adventurous projects can be undertaken. Within a youth group there is the chance that the 'youth leader' may be accepted as a true leader of the group for the first time. This will depend largely on personalities, but being away from a normal youth club atmosphere, working together towards a common aim, and sometimes dependent upon the superior experience and judgement of the adult in difficult or dangerous situations, can have a helpful effect.

Types of Expedition

There are several distinguishable types of expedition work and a hint of some of them may help to guide the prospective youth leader in search of a challenging project.

One can 'explore' simply by visiting an area new to the group and finding out as much as possible about its physical and human geography. If the area is wild and virtually uninhabited (and these areas still exist even in Britain) the party will have also to learn how to move and exist in difficult country. Other expeditions may be specifically intent on physical conquest, like attempts to climb certain mountains, or cover particular routes by land, sea or air. One can draw inspiration for junior expeditions from the many published accounts of recent senior expeditions of this type.

Field studies on an expedition can be very fruitful. They can be linked with preparatory work done in the club and can offer the practical application of techniques, like map-making previously learnt in theory. This type of work can be developed to serve the community. Many national authorities are pleased to accept help from serious expeditions prepared to study subjects in the field on their behalf. The work will generally be non-technical so there is every chance of producing successful results.

A group's own ideas and equipment can be tested in the field. They might discuss for example, why an area has been depopulated and then visit the place to see how far the theories produced match the facts. Each expedition needs some special equipment and it is great fun to try out items made or adapted by members of the group. Often a call to solve a particular problem will produce many ideas. What better than to put these ideas to the test in the field?

The Challenge

As the Albemarle Report [1] said, "Some of the most arousing challenges to individual achievement come from enterprises which have to be corporately met, as in exploration or mountaineering, for then the individual satisfies his own longing to achieve something worthwhile by contributing to the group effort. In this way he often secures a better feeling of his worth as an individual than in competition with other members of the group".

Reference

1. Ministry of Education, *The youth service in England and Wales*, Report of a committee under the chairmanship of the Countess of Albemarle. H.M.S.O., 1960.

23

Hill Walking Technique*

INTRODUCTION

The popularity of lightweight camping tours through mountainous country as a school activity is increasing year by year. Here are some notes on a few of the physical problems worth considering if you intend to introduce this activity for the first time.

Hillwalking, particularly when carrying a rucksack, demands sustained physical effort and yet at the end of each day on expedition you will need the energy to pitch camp and prepare a meal before you relax completely. For this reason, as well as in case of an emergency, it is as well to try to save some energy for the evening as you plan and follow your route for the day. It has been said that real hill walkers are *born* and not *taught*, but you can increase your skill and enjoyment by giving your attention to a few details.

General Well-Being

This has a direct effect on your performance. Firstly you should be properly equipped. It is assumed that excess weight has been cut from your load by limiting equipment and clothing to essential items. Much of what you take will depend on personal preference and expense and

* A revised version of a paper first published in *The camper*,

the final balance between comfort and the weight you will carry will only be found by experience. As a rule it is better to start with as light a pack as possible; the novice generally takes too much.

In mountainous country wearing unsuitable footwear can lead to a serious accident and, even if this is avoided, fatigue will be increased by lack of support for the ankles, frequent slipping, and tension arising from a feeling of insecurity.

It is important to effect some temperature control by wearing suitable warm and windproof clothing and varying the amount worn according to the conditions. Extremes of heat and cold both impair the efficient performance of the body. Furthermore, although a healthy person can withstand change in routine, sufficient food and sleep are needed if the holiday is to be truly recreative.

Above all there is a strong mental factor in this type of extended physical exercise and although sometimes conditions may be difficult, *peace of mind* and *good companionship* will carry you on in face of minor physical discomforts and fatigue.

Economy of Effort

This is one of the main features of skilled performance in any sport and is well shown in the seemingly effortless gait and balanced footwork of the experienced hill walker. Let's make a closer examination of what is involved.

Each pace represents the outlay of a certain amount of energy and this amount should remain almost constant throughout the day. Making this rhythmic, even-paced effort *does not* mean that the length of stride, and hence the speed over the ground, must remain the same whatever the terrain. Generally on level ground your stride can be lengthened, while on steeper slopes it will be shortened so that upward progress will be slower. It is helpful to begin by consciously relaxing the leg which is swinging forward for the next step. After a while this relaxation becomes automatic and the saving, although small, adds up during a full day's walking.

Having adopted an even pace it is as well to interrupt it as little as possible. Your body will be warm and your heart and circulatory system will have settled to a pattern adjusted to the demands being made upon them. Certain stops will be necessary, however, and it is best to restart slowly. Your legs may be cold although you put on an extra sweater immediately to keep the upper body warm. For this reason an exposed summit is seldom a good place to break for a meal.

It is better to move around and enjoy the views if it is clear and then wait for a more sheltered spot in which to rest and eat.

Good balance and neat footwork will also help to delay the onset of fatigue. It is important to plan your next few steps in advance when walking over rough ground. Feet should be placed rather than stamped down and always try to find support for as much of your foot as possible. Avoid walking straight up steep slopes as it is very tiring to step upwards from the toes only. It is better to attack a really steep slope in a series of zig-zags so that with each pace at least one side of the whole foot is in contact with the ground. The direction of climb can then be changed to suit the lie of the land and, where there is little to choose between two routes, a change can be made to rest the ankles. Even if this is not possible much of the strain from a long traverse in one direction can be avoided by the careful placing of each foot to get maximum support.

Nevertheless, occasional slips do happen, usually as one foot is swinging forward for the next step. The novice jumps forward from the slipping foot making an effort out of all proportion to the height gained. In these circumstances it is better to rest back on the slipping foot until it stops and then take a normal forward step. This is much less tiring and dangerous than moving over loose material in a series of despairing leaps.

Route-Finding

So far conservation of energy has been considered in terms of improved walking technique, but all the careful saving made in this way can be squandered by a poor choice of route. Firstly, the chosen destination, if you have one, should be related closely to the intervening country. Trying to cover too much ground in one day of a tour usually has the effect of reducing the next day's distance and, anyway, much of the pleasure and purpose of a mountain expedition is lost if it becomes a race to cover a fixed amount of ground, come what may. Also, trying to walk too far in one day, particularly in the early days of your trek, may lead to foot troubles which could curtail your journey or, at least, add an undertone of discomfort to the remaining days.

In the first place the route to be followed can be decided from a map and then, provided the weather is clear, the exact line to be followed should be picked out well ahead. Contour walking can be used to avoid unnecessary switchbacking, and difficult ground such as bogs or steep scree climbs should be by-passed wherever possible. Correct use of a map and compass to avoid getting lost will make sure that no effort is wasted on aimless wandering.

Descending

Much of the advice given so far refers to walking uphill or on level ground. It is unfortunate, however, that time spent descending is not as relaxing as might be expected, particularly if the slopes are steep. It is here that the need for a well fitting boot becomes really apparent as the foot is pressed forward into the toe cap. Toe nails which are too long cause additional discomfort.

Considerable effort is needed to control descent. It is very tiring and dangerous to keep your legs straight as this practice jars the whole body and your balance is seriously affected. The answer is to flex the knees to absorb the shocks and compensate for uneven footing but this is also tiring, particularly if the descent comes at the close of a long day's walking. It is better to descend in a series of fairly steep zig-zags, changing the direction of the attack to rest the knees and ankles and to suit the lie of the slope.

Your rucksack should be firmly fixed, perhaps by a waist strap, to avoid it swinging around your body and upsetting your balance. I have deliberately omitted any reference to the technique of 'scree-running' as it is best to avoid this form of descent altogether when carrying a loaded rucksack (and/or with an organised school party).

The Rucksack

I have assumed that for this expedition you will take your camping gear with you and although nothing unnecessary will be carried, you will need a rucksack in which to carry your equipment. There are many different designs to be purchased but perhaps a few general remarks may help you to choose a suitable type.

When carrying full gear a 'frame rucksack' or 'pack frame' will be found most useful. This should be of a strong but lightweight construction and it should be waterproof. If this is not the case then a large polythene bag can be used inside the sack. Carrying straps need to be at least 60–80 mm wide and a third tummy strap is most useful for stopping your load swinging when descending. Heavy articles should be packed close to the frame and you should avoid having one side of the load appreciably heavier than the other.

The principle of load carrying is to keep weight high and close to the body so that its downward thrust is taken through the spine. The frame holds the pack slightly clear of your back, allowing free passage of air. This cuts out the formation of an uncomfortable damp patch of perspiration. The frame also stops any oddly shaped or hard items from rubbing your back. The very high carrying positions used by native porters are not readily suitable for our use; moreover, if the load is too high the problem of balance becomes increasingly difficult on rough or steep ground.

Finally there is one item I thoroughly recommend you to add to your load. Its presence will cause no serious increase in weight and it is something no one setting out on their first mountain expedition should be without. I refer to the excellent booklet *Safety on Mountains* [1] which contains a great deal of useful information and very sound advice.

Reference

1. John Jackson and members of the staff of Plas y Brenin National Mountaineering Centre. *Safety on mountains*, British Mountaineering Council, Revised edn., 1975.

24

Mountaineering Safety*

Much that needs saying about mountaineering safety is common sense and has been said elsewhere, but I repeat some of it in the hope that it may stimulate you to ask the right questions at the right time *when a mountain expedition is first planned.*

'Mountaineering' is a term which can embrace the whole art of moving through mountainous country. This sport is largely free of rules, indeed one of the greatest attractions of mountaineering is that it has such a variety of rewards to offer. Of these perhaps the greatest thing about the sport is the freedom of *why, where, how, when* and *with whom* one goes mountaineering. Having emphasised this freedom it must be added immediately that a code of accepted practices has been built up during the last century. These are unwritten rules prompted by common-sense and experience; if they are followed they will protect the novice from the dangers of his own inexperience. Unfortunately each year there are far too many people who go onto the hills with no preparation and no knowledge of this code whatever.

It often amazes me to encounter adults shivering their way along a mountain ridge in shorts, summer skirts and thin pullovers. No doubt this is how they were dressed as they stepped from their cars onto the lower slopes earlier that day. Many have no map, and the majority no

* A revised version of a paper first published in *Physical education*, vol. 54, no. 161, pp. 1–4. March, 1968, official publication of the Physical Education Association of Great Britain and Northern Ireland.

compass. Often those who carry these aids do not appear to be sure of their exact use. Most are quite hopelessly lost if caught by low cloud (for, once this happens, visibility drops to a few yards in a matter of minutes). Consequently they are left groping their way over hillside, muscles aching with the unfamiliar exercise, their inadequate footwear exposing them to injury and at worst, death. If these people have young children with them, equally tired and ill-equipped to meet such conditions, then the dangers are still greater.

Whilst many mountain rescue incidents involve casual climbers, it is a distressing fact that a large number of accidents, fortunately many of them not serious, do occur in organised parties. The man or woman who is prepared to give up a weekend or part of a holiday to lead, for example, a school hill walking expedition deserves the thanks of both the children and their parents. At the same time there must be a full realisation of the responsibilities and risks involved. The leader must do everything to ensure that there is as little *real danger* as possible. This need not affect the adventurous nature of the project.

A good method of introduction to mountaineering is in the care of an established club, or of a local education authority centre, which employ experienced mountaineers. However, in addition, many well intentioned but completely inexperienced individuals organise hill walking expeditions. Where some of these parties fall foul of other mountaineers is in their obvious ignorance of the accepted practices of mountaineering and their general abuse of the countryside through which they move. This latter point is not the failing of novices alone and many climbers will feel somewhat ashamed of the litter-strewn camp sites used by the regular rock-climbing fraternity.

Despite the publicity given to serious accidents there is little public appreciation of the time, energy and expense involved in a search over mountainous country. The missing person must first be located and then if injured, be carried to safety. This may take many men, many hours' hard work in appalling weather conditions. There is an understanding that brother looks after brother in the climbing world and this extends to novices and members of organised parties who get lost or have an accident in the hills. In most cases all the help given will be on a purely voluntary basis. If, however, these helpers are called upon too frequently then good relations may become rather strained.

I am sure that many who venture into the hills do not realise how far they are removing themselves from the medical services which they have come to take for granted. Even when all reasonable precautions have been taken, accidents can still happen. For example, one of the party may sprain an ankle, break a leg or receive a fractured skull from a stone carelessly dislodged by another climber many hundred feet above. At home, or on the roadside, an injured person would receive first-aid almost immediately and expert medical attention within the hour. On a mountainside first-aid, unless prepared for, is more difficult, and depending on the exact place the accident occurs, medical attention may not be available for a number of hours. If the accident happens late in the evening, as is often the case when climbers are tired and making hurried descents, then it may be dawn before a rescue party can even start to search. In that time the effects of shock and exposure can easily turn a minor injury into a fatality.

What must be done when there has been an accident? Help should be sought at once. Some pain and perhaps aggravation of the injury is almost unavoidable if the injured person has fallen into a difficult position on a rock face, or needs to be moved over very rough ground. Without drugs, expert handling and specialised equipment, attempts at rescue could be abortive. The obvious source of assistance is the nearest mountain rescue post; this should be contacted directly or through the police. At this post will be found a stretcher and first-aid equipment. The supervisor of the post will usually supervise the rescue if he is available. He will at least know the best course of action and be able to advise on sources of volunteers to make up the stretcher party. Again I must stress that these men are voluntary workers although there could be a charge to cover the expense of medical stores, etc.

Where there are not enough civilian helpers available, the assistance of the Royal Air Force Mountain Rescue Teams may be requested, again via the police. These teams are established primarily to search for and rescue the crews of crashed aircraft but they are well qualified to deal with most accidents in the hills.

A fact not widely known is that these men, with the exception of a small permanent staff, are all volunteers, working full time in other R.A.F. trades and that they devote their evenings, week-ends and sports afternoons to this valuable service. This means, therefore, that during a midweek search these men, as well as the local inhabitants, are missing from their everyday work. In addition they will almost certainly be joined in the search by other mountaineers who will be giving up part of their own climbing holiday. I do not mean to imply that assistance is given grudgingly – far from it – but many of the accidents to which these men are called need never have happened.

My aim here is not to produce a comprehensive list of 'do's' and 'don'ts' for those intending to organise their first hill walking expedition. Rather, may I underline the need for self-appraisal and full preparation on the part of the leader. Nevertheless I would suggest in the case of an organised holiday with adult supervision that whoever is ultimately responsible for the party should ask questions along the following lines.

1. Knowing what is to be attempted, is the leader experienced enough and is the ratio of experienced leaders to novices high enough? This could be as low as 2 or 3 to 1 on difficult ground and *never* higher than 10–1.

2. Are the aims of the leader reasonable considering: the composition of the party, the time of year and possible weather conditions, the amount of daylight available, the distances to be covered and the nature of the terrain, and, finally, the strength and fitness of the weakest member of the party?

3. Is the necessary equipment available, including maps, compasses, whistles, windproof clothing, reserve clothing and particularly suitable footwear?

4. Is the leader prepared for accidents? Will someone not with the party know the proposed route each day? Is there a first-aid kit and someone with the knowledge to use it? Does everyone in the party know where the nearest mountain rescue post is? (One might stress here the need to send a *coherent* message requesting help, written if possible.)

5. Finally, does the party realise its duties to the countryside through which it will pass? A trail of litter and damage will reflect no credit on anyone connected with the party and may well affect the welcome for others who will pass that way.

25

Long Range Responsibility*

Some Pointers to the Safe Organisation of Expeditions

Each summer there are many open country expeditions made by groups of young people unaccompanied by adults. These groups come from schools, youth clubs, voluntary organisations, or from the many training courses offered at outdoor pursuits centres throughout the country. All candidates for the Duke of Edinburgh Awards must take part in such an expedition. Indeed it is an important stage in the development of these activities with young people that eventually they are allowed to set out without an adult in the party. Parental consent is essential but this does not relieve the organisers of their responsibility and this responsibility must be exercised at long range, without removing the need for responsible thought and action from the young people themselves.

Throughout this discussion the word 'organisers' is used because, although one person should be in charge overall, there ought to be one person in the staff party for every separate group involved, es-

* A revised version of a paper first published in the B.A.A.L.P.E. *Bulletin of physical education*, vol. 9, no. 1, pp. 53–60. January, 1972.

pecially in rugged open country. So far, recognition of the need for a high staff-pupil ratio has not always gone hand in hand with the widespread recognition of the educational value of these activities. If all parties are using the same route it may be possible to have less staff, but this should not be reduced below the ratio, one organiser for every eight young people.

Many expeditions will run smoothly but changes of plan and accidents must be anticipated. Even experienced mountaineers have been known to misjudge distance when hill walking in dense cloud. Illness and minor disabilities such as blisters slow a party down so that it is faced with the choice of spending a night out or attempting to complete a long walk, and perhaps a descent, made more difficult by darkness. Sudden changes in weather, often very local and unmentioned in general weather forecasts, can change an easy fair-weather route into a hazardous undertaking. These events are worrying when an adult is leading the party, they are even more worrying and difficult to deal with at long range. Moreover, it is often the case that a number of groups are involved in similar expeditions at the same time, and it is seldom that all difficulties are confined to one group, particularly if the problem is that of a sudden deterioration in the weather.

In considering methods of organisation which could be used to prepare for some of the situations mentioned, points are gathered under five headings:

1. Preliminaries.
2. Normal Procedure for the Expedition Party.
3. Normal Procedure for Organisers.
4. Emergency Action by the Expedition Party.
5. Emergency Action by the Organisers.

Preliminaries

General Reconnaissance

It is very desirable that the organisers should visit the expedition areas before the main party arrives and a vehicle is essential if this visit is to be really effective. One still hears of local education authorities which are prepared to encourage such expeditions – even in school time – and help the children with their expenses, but which nevertheless consider a preliminary visit to the area by the organisers an unnecessary item on the expense sheet. (This visit may be waived where an organiser is very familiar with the area.) If a visit is impossible then the next best thing is a study of large scale maps of the area and a series of letters and telephone calls to gather as much information as possible. It is worthwhile trying to find someone locally who has visited the expedition area recently. Even doing this will leave much of the organisation to be completed when the party arrives on unfamiliar ground. It will probably necessitate an advance party arriving in the area before the main group, and many organisers make this standard procedure – in addition to a preliminary visit.

The preliminary visit has many uses: for example, for assessing the nature of the terrain, walking over as many of the routes as possible, finding out local restrictions on access, and meeting landowners to secure preliminary permission to camp. This should not relieve a junior party of the task of securing permission to camp and thanking the owner on leaving whenever possible, but in practice it is not always easy to contact the landowner or tenant farmer in an area of open country.

Other preliminaries may include: arranging for provisions – or at least locating suitable shops if the supplies are to be bought en route; arranging suitable places to collect mail and other messages; noting the situation and phone number of telephone kiosks en route, finding out details of the local rescue organisation (if any) and noting the telephone number and leader's name; finding out about local hospitals and the address and telephone number of doctors you could contact; arranging suitable contact points for parties and, possibly, fixing the sites for a series of 'sign-in-tins', if this system is to be used. (A person who is self-employed, or likely to be in for the large part of the day like a small shop-keeper, is a potential contact point, but to help in this way is asking a great deal and needs a careful approach.) If 'sign-in-tins' are to be set up they need to be prepared in advance although they may not be placed in position until the day they will be used. In many areas the police will be able to offer valuable advice.

This general reconnaissance provides much of the basis for sound and safe organisation.

Training

Too many expeditions take place with insufficient or no preliminary training. An unaccompanied expedition should contain *only* young people who have had appropriate instruction and practice, for example, in the skills of hill walking, navigation with map and compass, campcraft and basic first aid. An understanding of the problem of exposure and the knowledge of how to deal with it are of particular importance. It is the organiser's responsibility to ensure that the training has been completed satisfactorily although he may not have been in charge of the training programme.

If the chosen area is difficult and new to a party, a number of preliminary training days should be included in the total programme, before the unaccompanied expedition is organised.

Equipment

Another major point is that the party must carry the correct equipment. It is essential to check personal clothing and footwear well before the expedition date. This will allow new boots to be worn-in if they are bought especially for the venture. Before groups leave the expedition base the organisers should particularly check on safety and survival equipment. This includes: waterproof clothing, maps, compasses, (head) torches, whistles, distress flares, spare clothing, emergency food, first aid kits, and emergency instructions. It is recommended that each member of a party going into the hills should carry a 2m × 1m heavy gauge polythene bag or an aluminium foil survival blanket. These are probable life savers in cases of exposure, providing their uses are appreciated. Appropriate quality equipment should be carried for overnight camps.

In making sure that the party is well equipped the organiser must also guard against overloading. Trying to carry too much is one of the many mistakes made by the inexperienced. The use of a high loader rucksack, properly packed, will ensure that essential equipment is transported with maximum ease and comfort.

The Composition of the Party

For junior walking and camping expeditions of short duration, the ideal number in a group is four or six. This allows pairing in the issue of equipment and gives a sufficient number to deal with emergencies. It is generally necessary to ensure that there is some compatability within the group and that there is not too great a range of physical capability. It is good to have strong and competent leadership within a group and, in certain circumstances, a strong group can 'carry' a weaker member. A leader and No. 2 should generally be appointed and the group should accept this leader and his decisions. In every case the organisers should be aware of the strengths and weaknesses of those taking part and in this way try to foresee some of the problems which could arise. Any person ill or injured should not be allowed to take part as this would seriously affect the safety of the whole group. With an expedition of a number of days' duration this means that the chief organiser needs supporting staff, preferably mobile, who can care for and transport someone with a minor illness and perhaps return him to the expedition at a later stage if a rapid recovery is made. If the illness is more serious or lasting it will be necessary to seek medical attention and perhaps send the patient to hospital or home. Again this is best done by staff members of the support group, so that the chief organiser does not lose touch completely with the parties for which he is responsible.

Parental Permission and Insurance

As a teacher organising such activities it is an essential precaution to obtain parental permission for the participation of all young people under the age of 18 years. In addition the organiser needs a list of parents' names, addresses and telephone numbers. This list should be carried with the expedition staff as in an emergency it will facilitate rapid contact with the young people's parents, either directly, or by telephone, or through the police. Conversely, parents should be issued with the expedition itinerary and any suitable addresses and telephone numbers so that the party can be contacted in the case of an emergency at home.

As an additional safeguard it is recommended that the question of insurance cover should be investigated. Local education authorities often have some cover and there are a number of firms which specialise in school journey insurance. In filling in a proposal form it is essential not to disguise the nature of the undertaking and firms may well require increased premiums for unaccompanied expeditions. Cover is generally available for the organisers, for personal accident risks, and for third party claims. Other benefits vary with the cover requested.

Briefing

All parties must be properly briefed. The briefing should deal with all matters concerning the conduct and purpose of the expedition and emergency procedures. It may include, for example, the preparation of route cards in triplicate; at least two for each party and one for the organiser. A bad weather alternative route should also be prepared and 'escape routes', and the conditions under which these should be chosen should be discussed and understood.

Each member of the expedition should carry a written copy of the routes prepared and emergency instructions, including telephone numbers, distress signals, etc., in case he becomes detached from the remainder of his party.

It is useful to obtain an up-to-the-moment weather forecast and discuss this at the briefing. Where there is a Royal Air Force station in the vicinity it should be possible to obtain a really local forecast for the area. In mountainous areas this is very useful as changes can be rapid and include a great variety of weather, particularly when conditions are generally unsettled.

In spring and autumn months the question of weather conditions is of even greater importance and the whole question of whether it is prudent to organise this type of expedition in the major mountain and moorland areas of Great Britain is a very serious consideration. Certainly the risks are far greater. The near arctic conditions which can develop in Britain even as late as Easter-time, require specialised knowledge, techniques and equipment which will not normally be available to young people at this stage in their training.

Normal Procedure for the Expedition Party

Each party should have an appointed leader and splitting of the group either by straggling or over-enthusiastic pace setting must be firmly controlled. The route followed should be that prepared beforehand, checked and left with the organisers, except for very small variations to avoid local difficulties of terrain. It is also important to try to keep to a planned time schedule and this may mean a fairly strict routine, particularly in the mornings, so that late starts are avoided. Sometimes, when young people have spent their first expedition night under canvas, there is a tendency to rise too early and start without a proper breakfast, this again is to be resisted and a regular schedule maintained.

If a rendezvous is arranged with the staff, this must be kept. To avoid long waits by either party this requires sensible planning and good pace judgement by the walkers so that they can time their arrival to within, if possible, a half hour of the agreed time.

Where a 'sign-in-tin' system is used these must be conscientiously sought by the walkers, and full and correct details enclosed. Sometimes parties are late and feel that they must conceal this, so they sign for a time very different from that of their actual arrival. If this happened to be the last contact before an emergency it could obviously lead to difficulty in finding the group.

Occasionally it has been known that other walkers have removed or tampered with 'sign-in-tins', and, if the group is absolutely certain that it has found the correct location, then an alternative message should be left in a prominent position at the correct place.

All messages should be properly dispatched, whether, for example, it is a matter of leaving word at a cottage or telephoning a particular number between certain times during the day. The reason for and importance of all these points must be stressed by the organiser in briefing sessions and due credit should be given for correct compliance at the end of the expedition, especially if assessment is involved.

Normal Procedure for Organisers

As a rule groups should be checked at least twice a day. This may not mean that the party is actually met but that some contact is made. Twenty-four hours is too long a period to retrace when trying to find a group which has gone astray.

Particular points that should be checked are those, for example, where a party crosses a major valley and goes from one country area to another. A number of fruitless searches are made in quite the wrong place when a party has already crossed to a neighbouring region ahead of schedule and without the organisers knowing or being able to check. In practice it is possible to keep a fairly close check on progress by combining a number of methods. Some of the many checking methods which may be used are:

1. Visual checks made by the organisers who may watch from a distance, follow up on the same route, or rendezvous with the party at certain times in the day.
2. Messages left in 'sign-in-tins', or at farms, village shops, etc. These are best written in each case to avoid misunderstandings in passing on information. 'Sign-in-tins' should be fairly easily accessible by road, so that consecutive tins can be checked very quickly (summits are not ideal sites – or any position which requires a major expedition to check one tin).
3. Distinctive signs can be left by the party, made, for example, with stones. These should not deface walls, etc. or make litter. They may be left if 'sign-in-tins' have been tampered with or not located.
4. Telephone messages can be made to a central number. This may have to be limited to certain times in the day when one of the organisers can man the receiving phone.
5. Specific camp sites may be designated where all parties must gather each evening. Even if groups are camping separately, each

should nominate its camping area and this can be visited by one of the staff party. As well as their use for checking, these visits may be useful meetings for provisioning the expedition (if parties are not expected to carry all their food throughout the journey), and recalling or re-routing parties in light of changing conditions. The organisers can continue to get up-to-the-minute weather forecasts after the expeditions have set out.

Emergency Action by the Expedition Party

Action in every case depends on the nature of the emergency, the state of the party and its situation. However, there are certain difficulties which can be foreseen, and ways of avoiding danger and dealing with these situations must be included in training and discussed before the party sets out.

It is less likely that a well trained, well briefed party will become totally lost, although it may get off-course and be delayed. If contact by a certain time is essential, for example, when overnight hostel accommodation is being used and meals are ordered, or on the last day of an expedition where a return bus is booked for a specific time, it may be possible to arrange that the support vehicle cruises along a road bordering the expedition area after an agreed deadline. Most open country areas in Britain, particularly those in England and Wales, are cut up into blocks by roads, and in this case a single bearing retreat of the 'head south' type may take the party to the nearest road, providing such a course would not in itself lead the party into particularly difficult terrain.

If the group is overtaken by darkness or a spell of very bad summer weather it is generally better to make camp before darkness or the storm really sets in. In this case the route can be continued in the morning, or when the weather improves. This may cause the organisers some slight worry but it is the action they should expect a sensible party to take. If the emergency camp is near to a phone which can be reached easily and safely, then the staff can be informed of the change of plan.

In the case of sudden illness or accident, action will depend on the state of the patient. If he is able to move after first aid then the party should act to get him as quickly as possible to a point where outside help can be enlisted, if needed, and the organisers notified. If the injury or illness is serious and will definitely require medical attention, it is useful to send two of the party ahead to arrange for help to be waiting when an accessible point is reached. Again they should also notify the chief organiser.

The question of splitting up an expedition party is always a difficult problem. With a party of more than six it may be possible for at least four to continue while two evacuate the patient if he is a walking case, but in most cases, it is best for the party to stay together and see the ill or injured person safely in the organisers' hands. This may require the whole party's efforts. If the party does split up it is essential that a leader is nominated for the splinter group and a clear plan of action decided on. Splitting up can lead to confusion and it should be avoided as a general rule. Where an accident or illness is so serious that the patient cannot be moved, the party should set up camp at once after rendering first aid. Two or three members of the group of six should be sent to get assistance. These members of the party must be properly equipped with maps, compasses and torches and they should each carry an exact description of the nature of the accident or illness and the position of the patient. Ideally this information should be written down as the messengers themselves may well be suffering from shock and exhaustion and perhaps exposure by the time they reach help.

They should get in touch with the police at once who will then contact the various rescue and medical services available and inform the organisers. If they are sufficiently strong they may be asked to return with the rescuers to speed up the finding of the remainder of the party.

While assistance is being sought those remaining with the patient should attempt to make the injured person as warm and comfortable as possible. Depending on the nature of the accident it may be permissible to give food and hot drinks. The fit members of the party should certainly look after themselves in this way as it may be some hours before help arrives. If possible, the position should be marked so that it is easily seen from a distance and the International Distress Signal kept going. (Six blasts per minute on a whistle, or six flashes per minute with a light.) The use of flares is recommended in such as emergency, making sure some are kept to attract the searchers which the organisers will obviously send out when they do not return.

Emergency Action by the Organisers

Recall

In most cases the organisers can only react to situations as they arise but in the case of recalling parties they may initiate the action, or in the case of bad weather or a worrying weather forecast take the action while the parties are undecided or unaware of the impending change in conditions.

There should be an agreed recall procedure. In the type of organisation outlined here this might involve using the morning or evening contact at camp sites, during the day interception en route, or messages left at various check points, depending on when the recall decision is made. The days of regular use of radio contact may not be too far away.

Overdue Parties

Where contact is lost with a party it is wise to allow one or perhaps two hours before full emergency action is taken. This allows parties time to recover from mistakes in navigation and during this time the organisers can start to check contact points to find the last known location of the party. Where 'an escape route' has been decided this can also be checked, perhaps by a vehicle cruising along a convenient road. If camping equipment is being carried by the party it may be that a decision has been made to camp and continue the next day. If at all possible this assumption should be checked.

If contact is definitely lost and there is cause for concern it is wise to notify the local rescue organisation, even though no immediate action may be required. This ensures that the authorities know that there may be a search in the near future and they may in turn put various helpers on 'stand-by'. It takes time to raise a large search party and the more warning there is the better. The 'stand-by' can always be called off if the missing party turns up.

Accidents

Emergencies in mountainous regions, where the location of the accident is known either from a message or as the result of a search, should generally be dealt with by teams experienced in mountain rescue and having the necessary equipment. Additional accidents and further injury to the patient may result from 'amateur' attempts at rescue. It is a matter of on-the-spot judgement.

The mountain rescue organisation should have been informed direct or via the police if the party has sent a message for help. If this has not been done the organisers must do it at once. During an emergency concerning one party, the organisers must continue to look after the remaining parties and form a support group for the rescue team if this is needed.

In the case of any accident with a school or youth club party it is best to contact the headmaster, local education officer or appropriate adviser as soon as details of the accident are known. These officials can then decide on when and how to inform the parents. If the party is independent, parents can be contacted by telephone or via the police, but it is best to get as clear a picture as possible of the situation before this action is taken.

Accident publicity

The press and other mass media are usually very quick to hear of searches and accidents in open country and it is possible that the organisers will be contacted by reporters and camera men, either in person or by telephone. It is best to co-operate but to give only the barest details. Try not to comment beyond giving the facts. Before any names are given, parents should have been informed. It may be best to prepare a short written statement so that, if details are asked for, it can be read by someone else. This saves the organiser becoming too involved when there are more important tasks to attend to, and it is as well to remember that an accident may be followed by some form of official enquiry.

To Sum Up

Unaccompanied expeditions by young people need very careful organisation to keep the risk levels within acceptable bounds. This essay has deliberately avoided the question of the qualifications of the organisers, taking it for granted on this occasion that the organisers have appropriate experience in depth, technical competence and above all a sense of personal responsibility which extends to care for others.

AUTHOR INDEX

SUBJECT INDEX